The First Four Hundred

MRS. ASTOR'S NEW YORK
IN THE GILDED AGE

The First Four Hundred

MRS. ASTOR'S NEW YORK
IN THE GILDED AGE

Jerry E. Patterson

RIZZOLI
NEW YORK

Front cover: Mr and Mrs. Goodhue Livingston and Mrs. Alfred Gwynne Vanderbilt, photograph from the Library of Congress.

Back cover: Painting of Edith S. Dresser Vanderbilt by Giovanni Boldini. Used with permission from Biltmore Estate, Asheville, North Carolina.

First Published in the Unites States of America in 2000 by Rizzoli International Publications, Inc.
300 Park Avenue South, NY 10010

Copyright ©2000
Rizzoli International Publications, Inc.

ISBN   0-8478-2208-7

LC   99-69788

Designed by Abigail Sturges

Printed and bound in Singapore

Contents

Acknowledgments

My editor at Rizzoli, David Morton, was patient and careful. Jonathon Fairhead at Rizzoli was also most helpful. Abigail Sturges designed the book in a fitting and elegant style. My agent and friend Susan Zeckendorf, who liked the book from the first sketchy idea, was a constant support during the writing. My friends Michele Morgan Mazzola and Anthony T. Mazzola, who have seen me through three books, helped again with this one. Christine Dimino and Thomas F. Lecky patiently steered me through technological shoals. The staff of the New York Society Library, whom I have thanked in many books, were always glad to answer questions.

I am grateful to them all.

Prologue

The *New York Times* was the first of the New York sixteen daily newspapers to run the list in its editions of February 2, 1892: the names, at last, of the Four Hundred. Mr. Ward McAllister, the city's self-appointed social arbiter whose pronouncements were awaited by hundreds of social strivers and thousands of newspaper readers, had finally broken his silence and given a clamorous press the names of the Four Hundred people who, in his well-founded opinion, constituted New York "Society." The occasion for this revelation was the annual ball given by Mrs. Astor, the stately queen of New York; it was unquestionably the most important private entertainment given in the city, where she received "the chosen" as her guests.

Six years before, McAllister had remarked offhandedly that there were only "about four hundred" people in New York Society. Readers naturally demanded names, as Society figures were then followed by the public as avidly as rock stars are now. Readers knew of Astors, Vanderbilts, Livingstons, Whitneys, Goelets, and their curiosity about these remote millionaires and hostesses was insatiable. For a long time McAllister maintained a coy silence. Finally, as he felt his position as man-about-town, organizer of fêtes, and voice of Society weakening, he unveiled the names.

In 1892 "the Gilded Age," as it was dubbed by Mark Twain, was at its height. It was an era in which social behavior was stiff and formal but could also be both ostentatious and careless. Although no one knew it, least of all its central figures, the age was burning itself out. A year later a serious depression set in. When it was over the turn of a new century marked the end of four decades in which many great American fortunes were made and dissipated. McAllister's list caught the Gilded Age in its final days of unparalleled splendor. His Four Hundred were still center stage. The American rich could afford anything: titled sons-in-law, Paris couture, prizewinning paintings from Paris Salons, the occasional European castle and castles in the American landscape, three-hundred-foot-long yachts, and their portraits painted by John Singer Sargent. The rituals, extravagances, and rivalries of this little group fascinated the public and aroused the envy of those who stood on the threshold of Society desperate to enter.

New York Society, which was perceived as the pinnacle of American Society, acknowledged as its leader Mrs. William Backhouse Astor, who preferred to be addressed simply as "Mrs. Astor." Serene and aloof, she was an ambitious woman who, since her marriage in 1853 to one of the richest men in America, had aimed to rule Society—and had reached her goal. She certainly would have been horrified by the notion of having a career—ladies did not work—but in fact she had taken her "social responsibilities" so seriously and worked so hard at them that she was a career woman. She had long ago been placed on a pedestal by her friend Ward McAllister, who basked in the glory of her lofty position. For Mrs. Astor and McAllister, "Society" was to be a select circle of recognizable people who could be counted on to behave conservatively and submit willingly to the guidance, not to say dictation, of their leader and her first chamberlain. Four hundred was deemed by McAllister to be sufficiently limited; it was an orotund number, and when pronounced solemnly by McAllister it assumed an almost mystical significance, which it has retained for the last century.

McAllister, although a lawyer from a dynasty of lawyers and successful at the California bar in his young days, had not an exact mind. He never enumerated four hundred names: there were about 319 on his celebrated list when published. It is necessary to say "about" because several entries are ambiguous as to number: "the Misses Cameron" and "the Misses Chanler," for example. There were only 169 family names. Many listings were mangled either by McAllister or the press; spouses were omitted, the dead resurrected, and kinships muddled. The ambiguities of the list and corrections to it are set forth in the Appendix.

With all its faults, the list of the Four Hundred was essentially what it claimed to be: the names of the core of New York Society in 1892—the people who "counted". The accomplishments of some were confined to the ballroom, but others were distinguished figures in New York politics, business, and culture. Included were a painter, two architects, America's greatest living astronomer, several novelists, Civil War generals, a future Vicereine of India, doctors, philanthropists, and a probation officer. Money, social position, and lineage united the frivolous and the accomplished in a single list, once and for all.

McAllister happened upon an idea that thrives a century later. Magazines like *Forbes*, *New York*, *Avenue*, and *Quest* currently publish new lists of the Four Hundred, based sometimes only on wealth, sometimes on social prominence. About ten percent of those named to today's social lists are either descendants of McAllister's Four Hundred or kin to them. But it all began with the First Four Hundred. Its members, more varied and colorful than might be thought—and in many cases more charming— were at the heart of the Gilded Age. They deserve to be remembered: their backgrounds, daily lives, extravagances, and frolics are the subject of this book.

In 1892 Society was abandoning its long-time strongholds on Fifth Avenue between Washington Square and 34th Street and building much grander houses uptown; north of 50th Street they rose like fortresses along the avenue.

1

Entertaining New York

New Yorkers, since they were New Amsterdamers, have loved a party. The Gilded Age amusements during the reign of Mrs. Astor were rooted in the mid-eighteenth century when the Dutch influence, including that of her own family, the Schermerhorns, was still strong. While the lower classes indulged in crude sports, country dances, and heavy drinking, society mainly entertained itself with balls. Dancing assemblies, which were both clubs and classes, flourished in eighteenth-century Anglo-Dutch New York, and balls, affectionately called "frolics," were given regularly by great families such as the Livingstons and Jays, whose descendants later appeared on the list of the Four Hundred. The party season centered around royal birthdays and holidays.

The New York Dutch, staunchly Calvinist, followed the strictest Protestant traditions regarding holidays and were suspicious of Christmas, which seemed to retain too many pagan elements. But they joyfully celebrated New Year's Day. Dressed in their best, they exchanged visits and hospitality, mostly in the form of hot whiskey punch and other invigorating drinks notorious for their strength. New Year's was not officially a city holiday until 1768, but it was enthusiastically observed for generations before and after. The custom of paying visits on New Year's Day lingered among upper-class New Yorkers, even those not of Dutch descent, until after the Civil War.

On New Year's Day gentlemen walked from house to house; private sleighs or carriages were rare (in 1804 only fifteen citizens of New York kept carriages). Ladies stayed at home and received the callers, offering them wine, punch, and biscuits. Gentlemen competed to see how many ladies they could visit between mid-morning and late evening; naturally the ladies kept score of the number, and quality, of their visitors. To make the round, callers entered, shook hands with the hostess, took a quick drink, and departed; hardly more than five minutes was allotted to each house. Men with a tolerance for liquor made an astounding number of calls: George Templeton Strong hired a carriage on New Year's Day of 1849 and visited eighty houses. A popular lady received upwards of a hundred visitors in the course of the day. In one of her *Old New York* stories Edith Wharton writes of observing "the funny gentlemen who trotted about, their evening ties hardly concealed behind their overcoat collars, darting in and out of chocolate-colored house-fronts on their sacramental round of calls." The New Year's Day ritual ceased by the 1870s: nostalgia for Dutch customs had faded; Christmas, not the New Year, had become the major winter holiday; and in a vastly larger city the neighborhoods where one's acquaintants lived were now too far apart to visit in one day. The behavior of gentlemen who indulged in excessive alcohol consumption alarmed the respectable. The most famous incident involved James Gordon Bennett, Jr., heir to the New York *Herald* newspaper fortune and a notorious toper, who indulged so freely at his fiancée's house that he publicly relieved himself—in either the fireplace (the story varies) or the grand piano. He also relieved himself of his fiancée, whose brother horsewhipped him.

In both European and American Society women presided over social life, and one especially powerful lady decided who was to be included and, more importantly, who was not. In America, Mrs. Astor was acknowledged by all to be the grandest, most respected, and most authoritative of all these ladies.

The grand line of New York Society hostesses begins with Mrs. John Jay, born Sarah Van Brugh Livingston. Her style of entertaining, her intellect, and her personal attractions left a lasting impression. Many great hostesses have been more noted for their conversation than their looks—including Mrs. Astor—but Sarah Jay was acknowledged as one of the most beautiful women of her time; her complexion, "almost translucent," was especially admired. Like Mrs. Astor, Sarah Jay had the necessary social qualifications: she was a daughter of the great Livingston family whose landholdings along the Hudson were baronial. Her father was New Jersey governor William Livingston of Liberty Hall, his great mansion in Elizabeth Town. She married John Jay, descendant of a Huguenot family, in 1774. A contemporary described him as "tall, lean and straight. . . ." Capable and thoughtful, he was an ambitious man, a lawyer who became the first chief justice of New York State at the age of thirty-two. In 1781, the Continental Congress, of which he had been president, sent him to Paris to negotiate the treaty between Britain and the United States that would end the Revolutionary War. He was accompanied by the beautiful Sarah.

Jay's successful mission resulted in the Treaty of Paris. Sarah triumphed socially in the city, charming both royalty and aristocracy. In Europe the Jays moved in the highest circles. When they returned in October 1784 to New York, then the capital of the republic, so that Jay could assume his new post as Secretary for Foreign Affairs of the United States, the town was abuzz with curiosity as to the style in which Mrs. Jay would receive. She hosted elegant dinners and receptions at 133 Broadway, a brick house on the Battery at the very tip of Manhattan. Sea breezes cooled the point during New York's humid summers, and trees and shaded walks attracted strolling citizens, who had no public parks. Unfortunately, the Battery also swarmed with the numerous pigs and cows that roamed the city unchecked. Despite that drawback, to which eighteenth-century New Yorkers were resigned, elegant and important people constantly passed through the doors of number 133.

Sarah Jay entertained so extensively that she made a list of her regular guests, the first known in the history of American Society. Her "Dinner and Supper List for 1787 and 1788," is the ancestor of all lists of socially acceptable people in New York and is the remote ancestor of all American *Social Registers* and *Blue Books*. At the time it made a great impression, and for the next two centuries it was, as *Town & Country* magazine reiterated in 1909, "the surest key extant to the social history of New York City...." Mrs. Jay listed 182 people, counting married couples as two. Since John Jay was responsible for foreign affairs, ambassadors and consuls appeared on the list, as well as members of Congress. Many lawyers were listed, with a few clergymen, many merchants and bankers, several physicians, and a portrait painter. Names still familiar were John Paul Jones, Baron von Steuben, and those famous opponents Alexander Hamilton and Aaron Burr. Mrs. Jay did not neglect her own mighty clan: no fewer than nine Livingstons figure on the list. A century later, Livingstons were holding their own with the most entries on Ward McAllister's list, too. In addition to the Livingstons, the following family names appear on both Mrs. Jay's list and Ward McAllister's: Barclay, Bronson, Cruger, de Peyster, Jay, Kean, Moore, Morris, Rutherfurd, Schuyler, and Van Rensselaer. A number of John and Sarah Jay's own descendants were among the Four Hundred.

Among Mrs. Jay's most conspicuous guests were William Duer, a New York merchant who had become rich from government contracts during the Revolution, and his wife, "Lady" Catherine Alexander. She was Sarah Jay's first cousin and the second daughter of General William Alexander, who claimed the Scottish earldom of Stirling and referred to himself as "Lord Stirling." New Yorkers, even though the Revolution had abolished all ranks, were thrilled to have a titled lady in their midst, and ignored the fact that the British parliament in 1762 had firmly rejected the Alexander claim to the Stirling earldom. Nevertheless, Mrs. Duer called herself "Lady Catherine" and among her intimates was "Lady Kitty." She and her husband lived in grand style supported by his large, but, as it proved, ephemeral fortune. The Duers were said to be the first family in New York to put their servants into livery, which was hardly in keeping with republican simplicity and became the subject of much criticism. The variety of wines served at their table caused comment, too. All this luxury vanished when Duer was imprisoned for debt in 1792.

One of the great hostesses of the 1830s was Madame Charles Bruguière, the wife of a Frenchman who had fled the French Revolution to Santo Domingo and finally settled in New York in 1823, where he became a merchant of French dry goods. Their house was at 30 Broadway at Bowling Green. Madame Bruguière, described as a "queenly woman," entertained grandly. She had the distinction of introducing to Society "Señorita García," the celebrated soprano Maria Malibran, one of the greatest opera singers of the nineteenth century. Madame Bruguière's greatest social accomplishment was giving a "Grand Fancy Ball" on such a scale that she rented the adjoining house on Broadway just for the evening. The invitation cards were perfumed. The stir over preparations for this grand party lasted for weeks. Dressmakers worked night and day to make costumes; some guests were so desperate they raided the wardrobes of New York's theaters. One guest, Charles King, dashing son of Rufus King, former United States Minister to Great Britain, changed his costume three times during the evening; on his third entrance in a new costume the band played *God Save the King*. The handsome Charles married a mercantile heiress, the daughter of Archibald Gracie, and eventually was a respected president of Columbia College.

Wines were of great importance when entertaining. Dominick Lynch was an Irish immigrant who came to New York in 1785. He was a wine merchant with a shop on William Street. Ward McAllister, who knew him well and admired him, called Lynch "the greatest swell that New York had ever known." In 1830, he began to import Château Margaux, of which he was the exclusive distributor. The new French wine caught on immediately; Lynch received about three hundred cases a year, each containing four dozen quart bottles; even the very high price of $75 a case did not deter buyers. Walter Barrett in his *The Old Merchants of New York City* said, "The subscription lists for the three hundred cases contained all the principal people of New York." Lynch was famous for his own entertaining—"the prince of dinner givers," Ward McAllister called him. He was active in civic offices and the acknowledged lay head of New York's tiny Roman Catholic community; he did his best to increase it, too, as he was the father of thirteen children.

In the colonial era the wine most prized by connoisseurs was Madeira, an amber-colored fortified wine with as much mythology surrounding its preservation and serving as port. Ward McAllister called it "the king of wines," and in his memoirs devotes an entire chapter to its praise. On the whole, it was an after-dinner drink, savored slowly by the gentlemen after the ladies withdrew from the table—although a lady might offer a glass of Madeira with a slice of cake to guests making a morning call. Drinkers insisted that the wine benefited by being rocked in the holds of oceangoing vessels; some casks were sent on two- or three-year voyages; Madeiras that had been around Cape Horn twice were especially prized. Each pipe (a pipe was a large cask) was called by the name of its ship and the years of its voyage, which were carefully noted so a host could offer his guests "a glass of my *Aphrodite 1810.*" Ward McAllister said that in his youth the famous Madeiras in New York were, *The Stuyvesant, The Clark,* and *The Eliza.* George William Curtis, a literary man who edited *Harper's Weekly,* remembered four o'clock dinners in old New York, drinking "some of that *Arethusa* Madeira, marvelous for its innumerable circumnavigations of the globe, and for being as dry as the conversation of the host." Frank Gray Griswold of the Four Hundred, whose family was in the shipping business, remembered that when a pipe of Madeira arrived at the firm's offices in lower Manhattan, it was placed in a cradle in a passageway and the clerks were instructed to give it a roll each time they passed. The roll, like the shipping, disturbed the wine to the benefit of its taste. Old Madeira was a favorite for drinking toasts. In 1879 when his son Livingston was born, Stuyvesant Fish wrote his father, "We drank the boy's health and then his Mother's in some of the Madeira which you so providently put away for me when I was about his age."

In the federal period the usual form of entertainment in New York was the dinner party—stately and much simpler than the three-hour-long bacchanalia of the Gilded Age. There were private and public dinners. Americans of the time were addicted to holding public dinners honoring prominent citizens or notable visitors, all-male affairs (women were sometimes permitted to look on from a balcony) that lasted for hours and were the occasion of much oratory which grew florid after a dozen toasts were drunk. Even the good-natured Washington Irving wrote in 1832: "No sooner does a citizen signalize himself in a conspicuous manner in the service of his country, than all the gourmandizers assemble and discharge the natural debt of gratitude, by giving him a dinner." Irving himself had suffered through a number of dinners when he returned from diplomatic assignments in Europe.

In private homes unpretentious folk dined around three or four o'clock in the afternoon, but in mid-century Society began to shift the dinner hour to six and past. While private dinner parties included both men and women, the all-male private dinner party, like public dinners, was far from unknown. A man's wife might greet her husband's friends when they arrived, then gracefully retire when the men sat down to table. Meals were of a length and quantity that would terrify twentieth-century stomachs. Meat, much of it game and seafood, was devoured at every meal, even breakfast, where steaks and chops and grilled fish regularly appeared. On the other hand, when reading the page-long menus it must be remembered that choice among the victuals was offered, and that no one was expected to eat everything offered. That admitted, amazing amounts were still eaten. The consumption of alcohol was prodigious. George S. Bowdoin of the Four Hundred was a member of the "Kitten Club," a circle within the Union Club mainly for the purpose of gourmandizing. Miniature figures of a cat and her kittens were the table centerpieces. At a dinner that Bowdoin offered the club in 1879 the guests had gin cocktails with their oysters, Bass ale with their green turtle soup, Amontillado sherry with their Maryland terrapin, and so on through a dozen courses.

Daily meals were breakfast, dinner, and supper (frequently called "tea"); gradually, as the dinner hour moved forward, people began to eat lunch between breakfast and dinner. Socially speaking, lunch was a feminine meal. Men had a chop and stout or oysters and ale in "chop houses" near their offices downtown. From the 1870s on women entertained each other at all-female lunch parties, or "luncheons," generally conducted in a formal manner, with the ladies wearing their best "morning" dresses (no trains or jewels; you didn't show diamonds before sunset) and keeping their hats on while eating. Elizabeth Drexel Lehr remembered the luncheons taking place in fashionable dimness: "no matter what the season or the weather, daylight was shut out. The more artificial the light, the better, so the window curtains were drawn close and pink shades put around the glass globes and over the candles." The ladies consumed chicken croquettes and ice cream—"ladies' food."

Dinners were becoming much more elaborate: more courses with a greater choice of wines. Mrs. Winthrop Chanler said of New York dinners: "Roman punch was served in the middle of the meal—after soup, fish, entrée, and a first course of meat had satisfied all natural appetite—to stimulate our courage to eat what was coming." Food began to be served rather than just put on the table. Mrs. Daniel Le Roy, a well-connected lady of fashion (sister-in-law of Daniel Webster), was reputed to be the first lady in New York to introduce *service à la russe* at her dinner table. Each dish was offered to the diner by a servant; previously all the victuals had been set out on the table at once (*service à l'américaine*) with the host—or in a surprising number of cases, the hostess—carving and serving each plate. At the head of the table was soup; at the foot, fish. On the sideboard were ham, tongue, and corned beef, flanked by four vegetables. Madeira and sherry were "standing wines," that is, they were placed on the table and diners helped themselves; sauterne and hock (white wine) were handed around. That was just the first course. Later came roast game, lobster, salad, pastry, fruits and nuts ("dessert") with champagne, claret, Bass ale, and porter to accompany them.

Service à l'américaine, although friendly, entailed much passing of plates among the guests, as well as reaching for dishes and the condiments in the center of the table. This cheerful bustle came to seem undesirable and suitable only when the family were eating alone. *Service à la russe*, on the other hand, was not homey; guests no longer gathered around a table loaded with food. Instead, the table was decorated, but bare of food; servants offered dishes at the diner's left side. Freed from the necessity of passing plates, guests could devote more time to conversing with their neighbors, a step forward in sophistication as hosts saw it. *Service à la russe* was also a visible sign of greater wealth, since it required more servants. At first there was an outcry against abandoning the good old American custom of the loaded table, "the groaning board," from which you made your own selection, for a newfangled foreign style in which you could take only what a liveried manservant offered you. Former New York mayor Philip Hone, a great diner-out, was appalled when he was introduced to *service à la russe* in 1838. He confided his irritation to his diary: "The table covered with confectionery and gew-gaws . . . but not an eatable thing. The dishes were all handed around; in my opinion a most unsatisfactory mode of proceeding in relation to this important part of the business of a man's life. One does not know how to choose, because you are ignorant of what is coming next, or whether anything more is coming. Your conversation is interrupted every minute by greasy dishes thrust between your head and that of your next neighbor, and it is more expensive than the old mode of shewing a handsome dinner to your guests and leaving them free to choose." Despite grumblings, mostly from men, *service à la russe* caught on among the style-setters.

Mrs. Le Roy's position in New York Society was so secure she could innovate as she pleased. In addition to introducing a new style of table service, she placed empty silver dishes in a row down the center of her dining table merely for decoration (the 'gew-gaws," Hone mentioned), much to the irritation of her less fashionable—and less rich—relatives, few of whom had so much silver to display. In her youth a trailblazer, in her old age Mrs. Le Roy became quite conservative about social matters: in the 1860s the diarist Maria Daly overheard Mrs. Le Roy and her sister, Mrs. Daniel Webster, lamenting "the degeneracy of modern manners" which, it seems, consisted of "gentlemen driving around with reins and whips [instead of employing a coachman], married ladies supping at Delmonico's without their husbands, and the rompishness of the younger ladies."

Afternoon tea as a simple meal shared with guests became popular only in the late 1870s. Tea had been served along with coffee after dinner, or with a light meal taken late in the evening—really supper. As the dinner hour was pushed forward, the interval between lunch and dinner needed to be broken with a snack. Ladies enjoyed going out to tea because they could appear in bonnets and street dresses and could squeeze several calls into a single afternoon. The only gentlemen at tea parties were young men of leisure and elderly, usually retired, men. Males who worked or were sportsmen looked down on tea parties and were suspicious of men who attended them. Afternoon tea was primarily a feminine ritual in the United States, seldom a family occasion as in Britain, and gradually became the very symbol of elegance and leisure.

Entertaining on Sunday night was a problem. Until the era of World War I even rich people usually left town only during the summer and then for long stays; weekending was virtually unknown. Old New Yorkers were horrified by the idea of going to the country in the winter. As Edith Wharton wrote, "No, thank you—no country winters for the chilblained generation . . . the generation brought up in unwarmed and unlit houses, and shipped off to die in Italy when they proved unequal to the struggle of living in New York!" Everybody was at home on Sunday nights after one or more church services (one morning, one mid-afternoon), with time depressingly heavy on their hands. Even in the second half of the nineteenth century, Puritanism and sabbatarianism (refraining from any worldly activity on Sundays) were observed, either from genuine religiousness or fear of what the neighbors might say if one's house was too brightly lighted on a Sunday. When New York Society still lived downtown around Bond Street before the Civil War, "hot teas" were sometimes served on Sunday evenings. Some hostesses were famous for their waffles, others for tasty innovations with oysters. Later, musicales were attempted by a few hostesses trying to rise above the narrow considerations of sabbatarianism, which forbade music except hymns. New Yorkers, *The Home Journal* sniffed, resented such Sunday entertainments as "a custom which is so obviously continental." Mrs. Astor's solution to the problem was to receive guests "informally" on Sunday afternoons after church had been attended and a substantial lunch eaten. Guests were entertained "only with tea and a little quiet chat." Mrs. Astor's idea of "informality" was probably not everyone's, and although we are told that "conversation touched lightly on the topics of the day," her tea parties sound as formal as her dinners.

In addition to dinner parties, entertainment at well-to-do homes included small musicales, long popular with New York hostesses; in her time Mrs. Bruguière had given musicales. New York was full of music in the second half of the nineteenth century. German immigrants, the largest ethnic group in the city, had created a rich musical life; New York was already one of the musical capitals of the world. Innumerable musicians were eager to perform at private houses, and what could be more elegant than a private orchestra, even if assembled for only an occasional night? The Schermerhorns, Caroline Astor's family, loved music and were leading patrons. Edmond Schermerhorn, Caroline's first cousin, who lived in bachelor comfort in an old Schermerhorn house on Great Jones Street, gave notable musicales. In 1871 George Templeton Strong, devoted to music and active in its patronage in New York, heard chamber music by Beethoven and Hummel at Edmond's house. The following year Schermerhorn presented an entire season of music for an audience of forty or fifty of his friends in his drawing room. Strong was awed: "Edmond has advanced from the quartettes and septets of last year to an orchestra of twenty-five! A most brilliant afternoon!"

Society professed great devotion to the opera. In this, as in so many ways, Mrs. Stuyvesant Fish was an outspoken exception: she frankly hated opera although she had to attend; being seen in one's box was *de rigueur* in society. She complained that she didn't always have the proper expression on her face when listening: "Sometimes when it is just right for listening to 'The Cradle Song' I find that I am listening to 'The Ride of the Valkyries'." She said her favorite instrument was the comb. But most members of Society liked opera, with its courtly origins and its stately ritual in which florid arias were comfortably interspersed with recitatives during which one could survey the house. Until 1886 seasons of opera were given more or less regularly at the Academy of Music on East 14th Street at the northeast corner of Irving Place—a fashionable neighborhood. Opened in 1854, the Academy, even by today's standard, was an enormous hall, seating four thousand people—about the size of today's Metropolitan Opera House. Before closing in 1886, performances by some of the world's outstanding singers were held in the red and gold auditorium, and the production of new operas did not lag far behind Europe. The Academy was superseded by the new Metropolitan Opera House on 39th Street and Broadway in 1883. Monday was the best night at the Metropolitan because there were balls to attend later in the evening—the Patriarchs, the Assembly, the Family Dancing Circle—from January to Lent. Society generally dined in private houses, seldom, if ever, in restaurants, and arrived at the opera at the beginning of the second act.

Of course, the Four Hundred sat in the boxes, which were engaged on an annual basis. The names of the boxholders were published; indeed they were still being published in the 1960s, when the 39th Street house was torn down. Each had a regular night (Mrs. Astor's was Monday). Boxholders paid outrageously inflated prices for the privilege of being seen sitting in grandeur. Extra charges were made on nights when Madame Nordica, the de Reszke brothers, or other international stars were singing. Each box had a little anteroom with divans where entertaining took place during the intermissions and there was much visiting back and forth by gentlemen—women never visited. Mrs. Isaac Jones (Mary Mason, Edith Wharton's aunt, later immortalized as Mrs. Manson Mingott in *The Age of Innocence*), a woman of great style, had her box at the Academy of Music upholstered in blue silk with all the metalwork, such as doorknobs, of silver. However splendid, the boxes were not particularly comfortable: two women sat in front, and four men had to stand behind them, which was not only tiring but gave them a restricted view of the stage, particularly as the ladies were likely to be wearing *aigrettes* (a spray of feathers), tiaras, or other tall ornaments on the head. On the other hand, they had a good view of the bare shoulders of Society beauties.

Despite their proclaimed love of opera, the behavior of Society at the Academy of Music and the Metropolitan left something to be desired. The arrival during the second act by Mrs. Astor and other Society leaders and their guests was bad enough, but even more extraordinary was their departure before the finale, which was usual if the opera ended sadly: "Society does not like death scenes," remarked *Town & Country* complacently. A Society audience was keenly inter-

Regular attendance at the Academy of Music on 14th Street was one of Society's most essential duties. Seeing who was there, how they were dressed, and whom they were with was as important as hearing the music.

ested in showstopping arias by favorite stars but not much else: they listened attentively enough when Christine Nilsson was singing Marguerite's "Jewel Song" in *Faust,* but then they resumed their chatting.

On Monday nights, Ward McAllister was sure to turn up. He visited the boxes like a pastor on his rounds. "He would listen to plans for forthcoming parties with the utmost gravity," wrote one friend, "offer his advice as to whom should be invited [and] restrict the number of guests." The music of Wagner, when it arrived on these shores in the 1880s, divided opera lovers, cutting across the audience. A generalization might be made that Wagnerism was more an upper-middle-class phenomenon than a Society enthusiasm. Society liked arias because they felt free to talk between them; the continuous melody of Wagner provided no comfortable intervals for chatting. Society felt more at ease with the old French and Italian favorites with well-spaced showstoppers like *Faust,* their all-time favorite. The Wagnerians were a belligerent bunch, too, who resented talking during performances and did not hesitate to shush even the boxholders.

Dinners, musicales, and nights at the opera, even at their grandest, entertained relatively small numbers; when you received larger numbers, you gave a ball. Throughout the nineteenth century the ball was the favored form of large party in both Europe and America. There were public balls, generally held in honor of an individual, such as the famous ball for the Prince of Wales at the Academy of Music in 1860, which New York Society never forgot; fifty years later elderly ladies were boasting that they had danced with the Prince of Wales. Any ball was ceremonial and ritualized; everyone knew what he or she was supposed to do—they had been drilled in dancing and deportment almost since infancy—and they proceeded along easy, familiar lines. Women's dresses, coiffures, and jewelry showed to best advantage in candlelit rooms, and hosts were able to display their luxurious domestic arrangements. They certainly occupied the evening: Lucy Morgan Street, who made her debut in 1869, said that her generation usually went to balls between nine and ten o'clock; the latest one stayed was two a.m., but by the end of the century four a.m. was a more usual time for the playing of "Goodnight, ladies," which ended the evening. Contemporary accounts—in private diaries and letters, because only public balls were reported by the press until well after the Civil War—dwelled on the illumination of the rooms. That is why so many balls were described as "brilliant," which referred to the actual lighting rather than to the array of stylish people; only later did the word describe the guests. Expensive wax candles were used—giving a ball was not cheap—until gas lighting was introduced into many private homes in New York in the 1830s. The emphasis on lighting is a reminder of the dimness in which daily life was passed before the electric light came into use.

Since America had no royal courts at which to make presentations, balls were used to introduce young women to Society; along with weddings, they were the principal rituals of Society. Young men were on their own; there was no way to present them to Society except gradually to bring them in as escorts. For a very brief time in the 1880s parties were given to introduce young men to Society in a formal manner. Mrs. John King Van Rensselaer gave a five o'clock tea party "for the purpose of letting people know that her two sons, John and Harold, had reached the age when they were ready to enter Society." Readers were not told what the teenage sons thought of their debut, but it is easy to imagine; there is no record of the experiment being repeated.

The New York Assembly, at which young women made their debuts or "came out" in society, was organized on January 29, 1841. The "managers," all men, were a cross-section of the most prominent names in New York Society:

Abraham Schermerhorn
   (father of the eleven year old Caroline,
    who later became Mrs. Astor)
Edmund Pendleton
James W. Otis
William Douglas
Henry Delafield
Henry W. Hicks
J. Swift Livingston
Jacob R. Le Roy
Thomas W. Ludlow
Charles McEvers, Jr.
William S. Miller
Charles C. King

Some of the managers and many of the guests at the Assembly balls were from families that had attended Mrs. Jay's receptions back in the eighteenth century and would be listed half a century later by Ward McAllister among the Four Hundred.

George Douglas was a Scottish merchant, a hard worker and a very successful businessman, not a man of culture; "His wine cellar was more extensive than his library," said the waspish Moses Yale Beach, editor of the New York *Sun*. He had a socially ambitious wife, Margaret Corné, who was anxious to entertain the best of New York Society at their large house at 55 Broadway. Douglas, who begrudged the expense, used to say grumpily after surveying his wife's guests, "People get too many ideas in their heads. Why don't they work?" Their daughter Harriet Douglas married George Cruger, and after inheriting $400,000 from her father called herself Mrs. Douglas Cruger. Her "palazzo" on West 14th Street was, after her death, the first home of the Metropolitan Museum of Art. She was a scatterbrained heiress who spent years in England and on the Continent forcing herself on literary celebrities, a pursuit then known as "lion-hunting." She called on Sir Walter Scott, who could not bear her pushy way. "She is very plain," he wrote in his journal after her visit, "frightfully red-haired . . . an awful visitation . . . affectation is a painful thing to witness, and this poor woman has the bad taste to make her advances to friendship and intimacy." Wordsworth was more amenable to such tactics, and he actually entered into correspondence with her.

After a ball given by the Douglases, Anne Macmaster, one of the guests, was inspired to list poetically the most prominent members of Society in New York present at the party in a sort of catalogue, like that of the ships in the *Illiad*:

And pray who were there?
Is the question you'll ask
To name the one half would be no easy task.
There were Bayards and Clarksons,
Van Hornes and Le Roys
All famous for making a noise.
There were Livingstons, Lenoxes, Henrys and Hoffmans,
And Crugers and Carys, Barnewalls and Bronsons
Delanceys and Dyckmans and little De Veaux
Gouverneurs and Goelets and Mr. Picot.

Costume balls were popular except when the dancers wore masks. Who knew what assaults on virtue might be attempted under the protection of a domino? Philip Hone spoke for many prominent New Yorkers when he denounced masked balls in his diary with unaccustomed indignation and rejoiced when in 1829 a law forbidding masked balls was passed by the city fathers. Members of the Common Council professed to find them "of immoral and pernicious tendency, subversive of all just and honorable discrimination of character and calculated to encourage the profligate, seduce the youth of both sexes, and promote licentiousness and disorder." "In my judgment," Hone wrote, "it will never answer to allow licentiousness to go abroad in public places with its face concealed." A *bal costumé*, i.e. without masks, was an entirely different matter and catered to upper-class New Yorkers' desire to associate themselves with European traditions. Hone admitted he had a good time selecting his costume (going "in character" it was called), and dressing up. Invitations bore the legend *costume à la rigueur*: no admittance for guests arriving uncostumed. The only gentlemen in conventional evening dress were the managers, who made introductions, checked invitations, and fixed the order of the dances (a waltz, a polka, and a schottishe, then another waltz). At Mrs. Bruguière's fancy ball in 1829, Philip Hone found that "a large proportion of the company went in character. The dresses were generally appropriate, some of them exceedingly splendid, and many of the characters were supported with much spirit." Some of the "characters" were fairly obscure: Hone went as "Cardinal Wolsey" and his son Robert as an easily recognizable "Highlander," but Hone's son-in-law Jones Schermerhorn was dressed as "Gessler," the tyrannous Austrian governor in Meyerbeer's popular opera *William Tell* who forced poor Tell to shoot the apple off his son's head.

The first great costume ball in the social history of New York was that given on February 28, 1840, by Mr. and Mrs. Henry Brevoort, Jr., at their house on

Fifth Avenue and Ninth Street. The Brevoort ball was highly respectable; Philip Hone, who again went as Cardinal Wolsey in a scarlet robe, mingled with the 500 guests and told his diary, "Never before has New York welcomed a fancy-dress ball so splendidly gotten up, in better taste, or more successfully carried through." The ball was notable in more than one respect. New York's numerous newspapers did not cover private social events. No fastidious hostess would allow an impertinent reporter to list her guests or comment on her party; publicity of any kind was in poor taste. The only social occasions regularly reported by the newspapers were receptions and dinners given in honor of public men. Even weddings were only occasionally reported, and then so circumspectly that the bride's given name was not always mentioned; she was merely "the second daughter of Mr. So-and-So." The Brevoorts, however, permitted a reporter from the New York *Herald,* the most irreverent newspaper of its day, to report their costume ball in person. James Gordon Bennett, Sr., owner and publisher of the *Herald*, seems to have persuaded them to commit this breach of convention, possibly intimating that he would print something scandalous if they did not allow his man in. The *Herald* was an outspoken newspaper that shocked the public by using the word "legs" instead of the preferred "limbs" and openly referring to men's "pants." Prostitutes were allowed to advertise their services in its pages. The reporter the *Herald* sent to the Brevoorts' party was named Attree, and he was disguised as a knight in armor. From a concealed notebook he described the costumes and the guests in a full four-page report that appeared the next day in the *Herald*. Guests were listed by first and last initials only. New York Society was small enough at the time that it was easy to fill in the names. The conventional Philip Hone was enraged: "This kind of surveillance is getting to be intolerable, and nothing but the force of public opinion will correct the insolence. . . ."

Press coverage was not the only innovation that set the Brevoort ball apart. Miss Matilda Barclay, daughter of the British consul in New York, attended the ball dressed as Thomas Moore's heroine "Lalla Rookh." A young man from South Carolina—the hostess was a South Carolinian and there were always numerous Southerners at her parties—named T. Pollock Burgwyne (which sounds like a stage name but was apparently genuine) was costumed as Harlequin. The two young people were mutually attracted, and at four a.m., as the ball was ending, they slipped away and eloped—in costume. To the consternation of friends and family, they managed to find a minister to marry them. That is the deliciously scandalous way the story has been told, but it seems likely that there was some pre-party arrangement, and the elopement not quite as spontaneous as it appeared. Still, the impression made on nervous parents, who blamed the ball, was so great that it was some time before any other host dared to give a costume ball. The prejudice was part of American prudery that lasted throughout the century. As late as 1889, when a winter costume ball was held at the Academy of Design on Fourth Avenue and East 23rd Street, Mrs. Stephen Van Rensselaer Cruger of the Four Hundred caused some comment when she came dressed as Queen Louise of Prussia; her gown was looped up on one side, giving an undoubted glimpse of her leg. "New York did not look away," wrote one observer, "but stared hard and criticized." Society looked slightly askance at Mrs. Cruger, anyway, as she wrote novels.

Prudery was strong but not always well-informed. In 1857 a ball was given by Mrs. William Colford Schermerhorn (married to Caroline Astor's cousin) in her house on the corner of Great Jones Street and Lafayette Place, the very epicenter of social New York, in the style of Louis XV of France; the house was even redecorated to befit that time. Ward McAllister wrote that "the ball was meant to be the greatest *affaire de-luxe* New Yorkers had ever seen. The men as well as the women vied with each other in getting up as handsome costumes as ever were worn." Apparently it never occurred to the ball-goers that some of the characters they imitated might not be up to the moral standards of nineteenth-century New York. Were they not aware that Diane de Poitiers had been the mistress of Henri II of France? Quite possibly they were not. George Templeton Strong and his wife were present. Strong attributed the success of this ball to the uniformity of style; he preferred the host to choose a theme instead of permitting guests to dress as their fancy dictated. "The chaos of nuns and devils, Ivanhoe and Harlequin . . . cavalier and Swiss peasant . . .," he wrote in his diary, "is so incoherent and insane that a thoughtful spectator would certainly be qualified for the Bloomingdale [Insane] Asylum."

Dancing at balls was stately except when a "country dance," more or less a square dance, was called. The introduction of the waltz with its sweeping steps changed that. The waltz caught on slowly, being regarded in the English-speaking world as slightly scandalous because it required the couple to embrace. Once accepted, it became the most popular dance. The liveliest dance seen in New York ballrooms was the polka, introduced to America by a Hungarian army officer named Korponay in 1844. Hungarian bands were popular with American hostesses for a century. They were still strumming at debutante balls in the 1930s. The musicians dressed in gratifyingly bright Magyar costumes with scarlet and gold coats and tight black breeches, colorful male plumage among the monotonous black evening suits of the guests. The polka, like the waltz, involved an embrace, was fast, and had high steps when a forbidden female ankle might be glimpsed. For a long time it was regarded by the conservative as "low" and even shocking. John Gordon Bennett, Sr. who had opinions on all subjects that he was not reluctant to share with the public, excoriated the polka: "We must say that the indecency of the polka . . . stands out in bold relief from anything we have ever witnessed among the refined and cultivated *ton* of European cities. It even outstrips the most disgraceful exhibition of the lowest haunts of Paris and London."

A "grand march" opened balls with the dancers in couples circling the ballroom in slow procession. There was an order of precedence that gave rise to disputes and hurt feelings. Quite early in her career, Mrs. Astor took first place in these marches, her partner sometimes being Ward McAllister. The dancing of one or more quadrilles, usually about halfway through the evening, was a fixture at balls from the Civil War until the nineteenth century's end. The quadrille was a sort of square dance for four couples who executed five or six different movements called "figures." Quadrilles were named: "The Star," "The Hobbyhorse," and "The Opera Bouffe" were typical. They required special dresses and other accoutrements, and were planned long in advance. They had to be practiced; young people, at a time when "dating" was unknown and private meetings between the sexes difficult to arrange, gave small afternoon or evening parties to practice a quadrille. These informal sessions were chaperoned, of course, but a certain amount of levity was permitted.

After the quadrille, supper was served. The menu, although the meal came so soon after dinner, often comprised a full meal but of lighter foods such as cold ham, chicken, ices. The evening climaxed with the performance of a cotillion, sometimes called "the German," a series of maneuvers on the dance floor so complicated they were almost a playlet and required someone to direct the performance. The director, invariably a man, was "the cotillion leader," respectfully mentioned in all accounts of nineteenth-century balls. The leader needed great tact and a wide knowledge of society; it would never do, for example, to couple an heiress with a penniless fortune-hunter. The leader had from six to twelve couples under his control. They waltzed and then each chose a new partner and danced figures with names, such as "The Windmill" or "The Mirror." The latter was an especially elaborate figure. The young lady sat on a chair in the middle of the room with a looking glass in her hand. The cotillion leader brought a prospective partner up behind the chair, his reflection showing in the lady's mirror. If she did not want to dance with him, she shook her head.

Mrs. Astor's squadron of men who danced and led cotillions at her larger parties included Peter Marié, a bachelor of means who lived engulfed by bibelots at 6 East 37th Street.

Prospective partners were rejected, one by one, until the girl approved of one young man. Men hated this ritual but women, particularly those much admired, reveled in it. Cotillion leaders were, generally, men who had few more solid claims to fame, but hostesses who wanted a decorous ballroom needed their specialized services and flattered men who excelled in this arcane skill. Caroline Astor had her favorites: Elisha Dyer, Jr., James V. Parker, Worthington Whitehouse, Peter Marié, and, late in her life, Harry Lehr. Accounts of her parties listed these men and a few others year after year; some grew gray leading her cotillions.

Peter Marié, a stockbroker by profession, a partygoer by inclination, and as one historian wrote, "New York's most famous diner-out," attended a "calico and chintz" costume ball at Delmonico's restaurant on Easter Monday of 1875. He had the prettiest ladies present—imagine the competition—professionally photographed. Artists then painted miniature portraits on ivory from the photographs, having received careful directions from Marié as to the color of eyes and hair and complexion. The completion of these was the excuse to give a party at which they were exhibited. Marié pursued this hobby for years at other balls and parties: he finally had no fewer than 284 portraits of ladies in New York Society, nearly all of which were hung on the walls of his cluttered house on East 37th Street. He bequeathed the whole collection to the Metropolitan Museum of Art, but that institution did not consider them worthy as works of art and declined the gift. His estate then gave them to the New-York Historical Society, where they remain.

Marié was a fixture in New York Society from the Civil War to his death in 1903. He never married, but was a great flirt, constantly smirking at young women and squeezing their hands when opportunity offered. The term for flirting then was "making love," which in no way implied sexual intercourse. Marié was always making love and proposing marriage; one assumes that he would have been devastated had any woman taken up his offer. He finally became tiresome to women with his perennial pawing and arch remarks. Daisy Harriman (Florence Jaffray Hurst) remembered his whispering to her at a ball while conducting her into supper, "Shall I introduce you as my fiancée or my daughter?" When she promptly answered "daughter, of course," he was much annoyed. Anna de Koven remembered a dinner at which Marié and James V. Parker, another perennial bachelor, vied in flirting with her and teased each other as "an old fool." "They alternately left the table," wrote Mrs. de Koven, "to kneel at my feet, giving me an example of other times." Maud Howe, strongminded daughter of the strongminded Julia Ward Howe, did not tolerate this senile nonsense. At Newport, she wrote, Marié was "the perennial beau, said to have proposed to every beautiful debutante" for years. In 1883, of a party at Newport, she reported, "foolish old Peter Marié made wild love to me, whenever I was not dancing." He was still following Cupid's path in 1894, when, unusually, he visited Saratoga Springs (he was a Newport man). "[He] was as gallant to reigning belles," wrote Hugh Bradley, historian of Saratoga, "as he had been to their grandmothers."

"Elisha Dyer, Jr. led the cotillion": for decades, paragraphs in the press ended with that. Dyer, tall, slim, black-haired, was the son and grandson of governors of Rhode Island. Ostensibly a stockbroker, he lived on inherited income and had ample time to conduct a vigorous social life in New York and, especially, in Newport—Dyer country, so to speak. In addition to leading cotillions, he excelled in the refined art of selecting favors to be distributed among the dancers. Married to a Maryland widow, Sidney (Turner) Swan, the always immaculate Dyer was considered the best-dressed man in Newport. Daringly, he wore purple neckties, then regarded as decadent. He was patrician in manner, not to say haughty: a contemporary chronicler said of him, approvingly, "He steered clear of the spectacular and democratic." Daisy Harriman said of him and his fellow cotillion leader Worthington Whitehouse, "Those two were magnificent at inventing figures. . . ." She admired their tact in the distribution of favors "to those they wished particularly to distinguish without making the rest of the company anything but happy."

James Vanderburg Parker, a bachelor of ample private means, quadrilled and cotillioned his way through half a century of Mrs. Astor's dances and three generations of ladies. "Dignified grandmammas tell their debutante grand-daughters" remarked *Town & Country*, "that they did not consider themselves properly introduced unless asked by Mr. Parker as a partner in the German." During the Newport season he lived in a cottage on Merton Road famous for the red rambler roses that covered it. When autumn came, he resumed his duties in New York. As he grew older, he was a living recollection of things past. Mrs. de Koven wrote that he "will always be remembered for his whimsical face, with his white hair modishly cut over his dark eyes, another survivor of the old New York when it really was an aristocracy."

At the end of the cotillion favors were distributed to the dancers, little gifts that might be anything from a bouquet of paper flowers to real jewels. Nothing better demonstrates the increasing wealth and extravagance of New York Society from the Civil War to the Spanish-American War than the evolution of ball favors from nosegays to sapphires. Originally, favors were simple and light-hearted, bonbons, for example, tissue paper caps, and little horns. At her early parties Mrs. Astor distributed paper butterflies perching on the end of a wand. Daisy Harriman remembered and disapproved that simple souvenirs had evolved into gold pencils and jeweled pins. And Constance Cary Harrison lamented that, "Each hostess strove to outdo the other in sensational display. The giving of costly gifts to invited guests was begun and overdone." They were laid on a table at the end of the room—jeweled stickpins, cigarette cases, watches that pinned to the shoulder. There was a shop in Newport that specialized in supplying clever favors, and hostesses sought out new and striking gifts on trips to Europe and brought them back by the trunkful to dazzle their guests.

Private theatricals were do-it-yourself entertainment for Society, extremely popular in New York during almost the entire nineteenth century. Society loved to dress up—the popularity of costume balls demonstrated that—and appearing in theatricals gratified a suppressed desire to perform in public. Otherwise, it was impossible to appear on the stage and retain social position. Robert Cutting proved that when he married the actress Minnie Seligman, became an actor himself, and was immediately cast adrift from the Cutting family and its large funds. Designing costumes and fitting them, memorizing lines, and rehearsing a play absorbed whole days and were taken with the greatest seriousness by amateur casts—busywork for those who had few duties. Rehearsing plays, like rehearsing quadrilles, was an acceptable way for young people to meet in informal, if well-chaperoned surroundings. The scene at an amateur rehearsal in New York must have been much like the rehearsal in Jane Austen's *Mansfield Park*. Since the performers were mostly rich, the stage dresses and scenery were often astonishingly lavish. Typical was the performance in 1862 of a play by Jules Sandeau, *Mlle de la Seiglière*, translated by William Colford Schermerhorn, performed by members of the Schermerhorn family and William Bayard ("Willy") Cutting. Some Society actors were genuinely talented and developed a reputation among their peers. Evert Jansen Wendell, member of an old New York family related to the Astors, was one of those known for his acting ability. He had other interests: he liked to "work with boys" in settlement houses. During the 1970s a frank private diary was found that disclosed that some of his work with boys was more personal than the settlement house authorities might have approved.

Besides acting in full-evening plays, members of Society performed at so-called "concerts" where various members of Society did little "turns" on stage, one-act plays, songs, dances, or recitations. Preparation for these briefer appearances was not taken lightly. William K. ("Willie K.") Vanderbilt, exuberant grandson of Commodore Vanderbilt, became a fixture in the audience of a popular Broadway revue called *Pousse Café*, studying the comedy team of Weber & Fields so he could imitate their routines with his partner Russell Sage at a Society concert. Sometimes Willie K. got a little carried away at the show, standing up in his box and conducting the orchestra in *The Star-Spangled Banner* by waving his handkerchief as a baton. The Breese brothers were famous for their clog-dancing, performed to great applause at various Society concerts. Clog-dancing, a low-life entertainment popular in Bowery dance-halls, was an Irish jig performed wearing heavy shoes that made a great deal of noise.

Ambitious members of Society not only performed but wrote original playlets or operettas for others to perform. Doris Francklyn, daughter of C. G. Francklyn of the Four Hundred, wrote an operetta entitled *Flora-Florizel*, in which "the Queen of the Fairies forsakes her throne for a mortal man." Debutantes attended its performance in droves and enthusiastically applauded, led by Gladys

From the heart of the Four Hundred, who loved amateur theatricals, came Ruth Draper, who broke ranks to become a professional actress, world-famous for the monologues she wrote herself.

Vanderbilt, "who was also the first to pelt Miss Doris with her violets when the young girl stepped out on the stage," noted a Society journal. Constance Cary Harrison also wrote a play for amateur production. The audiences at the private performances were so enthusiastic that it was transferred to the public stage and given at the Madison Square Theater in the 1880s for nearly a hundred nights. The monologist Ruth Draper, granddaughter of Charles A. Dana, editor of the New York *Sun*, and niece of Paul Dana of the Four Hundred, was the most accomplished performer to come out of the milieu of Society theatricals. She wrote and delivered with incomparable style on the public stage sketches in which she played a number of characters such as the "German governess" or "the debutante in the conversatory [sic]." Her nephew Paul Draper carried the family theatrical talent into another generation as an innovative tap dancer.

Then and now, weddings were the principal ritual of Society. The French visitor François de Barbé-Marbois , who had a place in Sarah Jay's "supper list," writing of his visit to New York, said that during the first week of married life, a bride and groom, surrounded still by their bridesmaids and ushers, received guests, men in one room, ladies in another. In a variant the couple stayed in their own families' houses and received. "Time passes in an infinitely agreeable way," wrote the much-impressed Barbé-Marbois, "in drinking tea, punch, wine, and other liquors with the crowd of friends with which the house of the newly married man never ceases to be filled throughout the week." By the time of McAllister's list, weddings, like most Society events, had become extremely elaborate, preceded by long engagements, trousseaux to last a lifetime, endless prenuptial parties, and general nervous exhaustion. Weddings were among the earliest Society events mentioned in newspapers, humble beginnings of the "Society page" of twentieth-century newspapers. When Henry O. Havemeyer, the vastly rich sugar refiner, married Mary Louise Elder, another sugar heir, at the South Reformed Church on Fifth Avenue in 1870, *The Home Journal* complained that "the four ushers created several blunders and considerable confusion by their want of tact and composure. Ladies were hurried up the aisle in the most unceremonious manner, gentlemen were rudely addressed, and, altogether, the inefficiency of the ushers marred the enjoyment of the occasion." The organist didn't "give satisfaction" either: "He performed the most doleful and inappropriate selection of music it has ever been our duty to listen to."

Weddings were the special province of Isaac Hull Brown. All self-conscious societies require a master of ceremonies and in New York Society for decades the major-domo was Brown, sexton of Grace Episcopal Church from 1845 to his death in 1880.

Never as many Americans attended church as nostalgia would have us believe, but the people who counted and left records did: the middle and upper classes regarded regular church-going as a badge and obligation of respectability. New York Society's churches were Episcopal or Presbyterian, occasionally Dutch Reformed or Congregational, seldom Methodist or Baptist, and almost never Roman Catholic; only a handful of Catholic families had entered Society (less than half a dozen in the Four Hundred), and they were more or less on sufferance—"the only Catholics in the house are in the kitchen," the saying went. Even among Episcopalians and Presbyterians, further distinctions were drawn. Grace Church on Broadway, for example, counted numerous prominent families among its parishioners, as did the First Presbyterian Church on Fifth Avenue. Protestant churches generally leased their pews for a specified number of years. Prices were determined at an annual auction. Grace Church pews were among the most expensive in the city, a sure indication of its social prominence. In 1846, when Grace Church's new sanctuary was completed, pews sold for prices considered extravagant, $1,200 or $1,400 with an additional annual rent of eight percent. Philip Hone remarked, "that the word of God as it came down to us from fishermen and mechanics will cost the quality who worship in this splendid temple about three dollars every Sunday." On reflection, he decided the high prices might be a good thing: many of the parishioners, "though rich, know how to calculate, and if they do not go regularly to church they will not get the worth of their money."

Over this "splendid temple" Isaac Hull Brown presided, ranking after the minister and the vestry. William Rhinelander Stewart, vestryman of Grace church, local historian, and one of the Four Hundred, knew Brown well for many years. "He was nearly six feet tall," Stewart recalled, "had a ruddy complexion, was always clean-shaven [sign of an ecclesiastical position], and had a considerable paunch of which he seemed to be proud. When on duty in Grace Church, he always wore a swallow-tail coat and low-cut waistcoat showing an expanse of shirt front and a black bow-tie and moved like a younger and lighter man." Brown created himself a kingdom at Grace Church, more of earth than heaven. As sexton, his primary duty was to conduct funerals, but he took it upon himself to supervise weddings and christenings too. Weighing more than 300 pounds, he was an imposing figure patrolling the aisles, ushering members into their expensive pews and placing unknowns in drafts. Grace Church prided itself on the singing of its choir, small but highly trained, which stood in the gallery. In most Protestant churches the congregation joined in singing the hymns, but at Grace Church the choir went it alone. Brown was known to tap the shoulders of worshippers unaware of this practice who were singing and tell them severely, "We hire the choir to do the singing in this church." He also took it upon himself to advise visiting preachers, regardless of their ecclesiastical dignity, that they shouldn't preach for more than twenty minutes.

He stood in front of the church before services greeting congregants he knew. He summoned the carriages of the favored; Ward McAllister said that Brown "knew always everyone's address" and his son-in-law and successor as sexton added, "He was the connecting link between Society and the curb stone." Having one's carriage summoned by one's name was an important status symbol. Having one's own carriage anyway marked one as rich: private carriages were rare, expensive to set up and maintain; middle-class people hired carriages by the hour, the poor took horsecars or (mainly) walked. Sometimes when calling car-

A social hierarchy existed among New York churches, based on the prominence of their congregations. Grace (Episcopal) Church on Broadway at 10th Stsreet ranked first in the opinion of many; both Mrs. Astor and Ward McAllister were among its communicants.

riages Brown bawled out references known only to himself. Stuyvesant Fish recalled Brown shouting for his sisters' carriage to pull up at the church entrance: "Call the seven wise virgins," which, as Fish testily pointed out was neither biblical (it's *five* virgins in the Bible) nor the correct number of his sisters.

Brown also summoned the carriages at private parties and weddings, as well as doing the catering; his services were available for a fee. According to William Rhinelander Stewart, "He was an undertaker by day, a caterer and major domo who supplied the supper and summoned the carriages at private parties or weddings at night. . . . He was a most proficient man at each of these callings." He was one of the established figures in New York, constantly mentioned in the press: "For years, no Society wedding or funeral meant either marriage or death unless conducted personally by Brown," said *The Home Journal*. Sometimes he even offered a toast at the wedding breakfast. At the wedding of Phoebe Lord, daughter of the lawyer Daniel Lord, to another lawyer, Henry Day (thus founding the famous law firm of Lord & Day), Brown toasted the bridegroom, "This is the Lord's Day."

Anyone aspiring to a role in Society at any level needs a good memory for names and faces; Brown's was unparalleled. Ward McAllister wrote "His memory was something remarkable. He knew all and everything about everybody. . . ." *The Home Journal* called Brown the "perfect walking, talking American edition of *Burke's Peerage*, adapted to New York." Of the Four Hundred of his day (he died before McAllister's list was published), the magazine claimed "he could narrate the histories of, say, three hundred and ninety-nine. . . ." In 1849 William Allen Butler, a lawyer who was poet-laureate for upper-class New York (he wrote "Nothing to Wear," the classic comic poem about a young lady in Madison Square in that predicament) also wrote a poem about Isaac Brown which ran:

> Oh, glorious Brown, thou medley strange
> Of churchyard, ballroom, saint and sinner
> Flying by morn through fashion's range
> And burying mortals after dinner
> Walking one day with invitations
> Passing the next at consecrations
> Tossing the sod at eve on coffins
> With one hand drying tears of orphans
> And one unclasping ballroom carriage
> Or cutting plumcake up for marriage
> Dusting by day the pew and missal

Sounding by night the ballroom whistle
Admitted free from fashion's wicket
And skilled at psalms, at punch and cricket.

Brown, who claimed to be descended from an ancient Huguenot family named De Bruyn, a claim no one took very seriously, revered New York Society, at least old New York Society. He didn't care for newcomers, "shoddies," he and others called them because they were generically suspected of having made their fortunes by selling inferior cloth ("shoddy") to the United States government for uniforms during the Civil War. Once, when standing in front of Grace Church summoning carriages after a wedding, he told a bystander that the crowd was first class: "No shoddies here." When Brown was hired by hosts for entertainments, he supervised all arrangements, delivering invitations ("cards") by hand, laying a red carpet across the front sidewalk to the street, arranging flowers, hiring musicians, and catering the victuals. A commanding presence, he imposed decorum. His specialized knowledge, acquired from years of experience, of who was in Society, and exactly at what level, was invaluable to nervous hosts. If he knew you, you were acceptable, fit "to be received," as the expression was. Brown's demeanor on these occasions was jovial—again, if he knew you. Ward McAllister said Brown "was good nature itself, and cracked his jokes and had a word for everyone who passed into the ballroom." To others, shoddies perhaps, he was aloof. He was particular as to which parties he managed, concentrating on the aristocratic purlieus of the city which, when he began his career, were below 14th Street. The social center kept moving north, but he remained faithful to the old-fashioned neighborhoods; when millionaires began to build their mansions on upper Fifth Avenue he declared firmly, "I cannot undertake to run Society above 50th Street."

Brown sometimes supplied guests, as well as food and drink and an orchestra for balls. Young men who danced were the hunted hares of American Society, and there were never enough of them. Brown kept lists of this desirable game. They were known generically as "extra men" since it was assumed that you had to have more young men at a party than young women, a convention that remains part of American social life. Brown enrolled about a hundred extra men he could send to parties—a large number considering the small size of New York Society in those days. They were known as "Brown's 100" or "Brown's Brigade." They needed, according to their master, "commanding figures, fashionable tailoring, and an ample supply of small talk at their tongue's end." Handsome young men of modest background enlisted in the hope of snagging an heiress. Rumor had it that strivers offered Brown as much as $500 to get on his list. He claimed to turn away these offers; Society was to suffer no dilution during his reign. For large balls Brown hired one or more policemen. Even in a New York relatively free of crime there might be drunken or unruly guests and gatecrashers to be ejected. It was a convincing gatecrasher who could get by Brown, who claimed he knew the face of everyone in Society in New York, but some tried. When the refreshments were served, Brown supervised the household's own servants and the extra help in passing the wine and in arranging the seating at supper, that all-important interval in an evening when pairing-off of young men and young women was even more important than partnering during the cotillion.

The sexton was soon indispensable: the *Home Journal* remarked in 1857 that Brown "seems to have become a necessity of fashionable entertainments, and where he has the supervision, the machinery is always well combined and managed." His opinions on social life were treated with respect by the press and by Society itself. During a financial panic in 1854, when parties suddenly became few and the festivities at weddings noticeably diminished, George Templeton Strong held a conversation with the sexton about the diminished frivolity: "Brown of Grace Church admits the deficiency," Strong wrote in his diary, "but says he'll do his best to make the funerals as pleasant as possible."

At a reception in 1857 at the home of Dr. and Mrs. Isaac Townsend, it was reported, "Mr. Brown, supported by policemen, stood near the entrance, to protect, direct, and suggest." The evening was a typical *soiree* of the time. Townsend was the inventor of a patent medicine called "sarsaparilla," a cure-all panacea for several generations, later a popular soft drink. The Townsends lived on the northwest corner of Fifth Avenue and 34th Street in a large, pretentious, and remarkably ugly house. The main entertainment that evening was the exhibition of a "panorama" entitled "A Tour Along the Hudson." Panoramas were enormous oil paintings on rolled canvas depicting scenery or an historical event—the Mississippi River, say, or the Battle of Trenton. The canvas unrolled slowly before the audience, sometimes with a spoken narration; panoramas were very remote ancestors of motion pictures. Often praised as "the Rhine of America," the Hudson River was thought "sublime" or "awe-inspiring," perhaps under the influence of its major chronicler, Washington Irving. After the unrolling of the panorama, Mrs. Townsend's guests amused themselves at billiard tables and a bowling alley in the basement of the house. Then Brown and his well-drilled troops took over, and supper, always sit-down, was served.

The high point of Brown's career as social impresario came in 1860, when he supervised arrangements for a reception and ball honoring Edward Prince of

Wales at the Academy of Music on East 14th Street. Social New York had gone mad for the prince; the Irish and other recent immigrants were not so enthusiastic. Invitations were sought like passports to paradise, and the most august families did not hesitate to beg and bribe for them. The night of the ball Brown and his cohorts admitted the chosen, carefully checking cards of invitation. There was nearly a tragedy when the dancing started: an insufficiently braced section of the floor collapsed, leaving a huge, gaping hole. Brown sprang into action and directed quick repairs. George Templeton Srong, who was present, remembered "Brown, peering down into the oblong hole, looked as if engaged in his ordinary sextonical duties at an internment. . . ." Dancing and supper proceeded as planned.

In 1863, three years later, came an event at Grace Church which contravened Brown's standards: the wedding of Charles Stratton and Lavinia Warren. Stratton was a midget better known as "General Tom Thumb." Just thirty-three inches tall when fully grown, Stratton was one of the most popular performers in P. T. Barnum's "Museum," where for years he enchanted the crowds with his conversation, singing, and dancing. In 1843, when he was eleven years old, Philip Hone found him a "handsome, well-formed, and well-proportioned little gentleman," and throughout his life his manners were much admired. He traveled in Europe, where he appeared before royalty and attracted huge crowds. At the age of twenty-five he met and fell in love with another midget, Lavinia Warren, who at twenty-four inches in height, was even smaller than he. She was not in show business and had been a schoolteacher. Their engagement aroused national excitement, and not just among sensation-seekers. New York Society was much interested: Mrs. August Belmont (Caroline Slidell Perry), one of the city's most prominent hostesses, gave a children's party at which Lavinia entertained and showed her engagement ring and the diamonds that the General had given her. (Tom Thumb's love of rare and expensive jewels later got the couple into serious financial difficulties).

P. T. Barnum, manager of Tom Thumb's career and more aware than anyone of the public's taste, planned the wedding as still another publicity triumph. Only fashionable Grace Church would do for the service. The rector, Dr. Thomas H. Taylor, wary of Barnum's publicity machine and afraid of vulgar spectacle, was inclined to refuse the use of his church, but Barnum persuaded his superior, Horatio Potter, Bishop of New York, of a Four Hundred family, to permit the wedding. Indignant parishioners circulated the story that Barnum had made a substantial contribution to the church to help along the permission. Among the most indignant was Isaac Brown, so affronted by what he considered the coarse sensationalism of the event that he refused to perform his usual nuptial services. Maria Lydig Daly told her diary with some satisfaction (she was a Roman Catholic and loved to report scandals in Protestant churches) that "poor Isaac Brown, the sexton, was so disgusted that he would not be present, and the police took his place" directing traffic. A platform was erected before the altar on which the bridal couple stood so that the congregation could see them. Crowds gathered outside the church and cheered when the wedding party emerged. Isaac Brown sulked. He soon returned to his duties at Grace Church, however, and continued to the end of his life to help Society entertain itself and to bury its members when the time came. His long career even secured him a place in American literature: he appears under his own name and profession at his own church in the wedding scene in Edith Wharton's *The Age of Innocence.*

Also not a servant but indispensable to New York Society in the Gilded Age was a South American lady named Maria de Barril. She was the daughter of a minor South American diplomat. As she advanced in life her antecedents grew in rank; she finally claimed to descend from the Incas. A rich uncle, according to her account, came to New York from Peru to add to his fortune and to be "received" in Society, but promptly lost all his money, and his niece, who had had expectations of inheritance, had to go to work. She had a distinctive and elegant handwriting, the copperplate so loved by the nineteenth century. Ward McAllister arranged for her to address invitation cards on piecemeal pay—she charged two cents an envelope. McAllister introduced her to Mrs. Astor, who liked her handwriting and her ladylike manner, and relied on her for years. Her work for society's queen of course brought her other work. She was short, stout, and dumpy but attempted to be stately and dignified, as befitted a descendant of the Incas. Her gowns were trimmed in "bugles" (glass beads), and she was draped with brooches, chains, amulets, and other tinkly ornaments. When Society emigrated to Newport she went along, taking a room in the same boardinghouse every year. She had a little parlor with a lace-covered table laden with heart-shaped objects in silver, wood, porcelain, and glass. Her hobby was collecting hearts, and her clients responded with frequent gifts. Because Miss de Barril was responsible for the invitations, she knew the dates of parties well in advance. Hostesses got into the habit of asking her what dates were free; she was a sort of social daybook. Reporters checked with her to confirm social events and soon she was not only ordering the engraved cards, and addressing and sending them out, but helping to arrange the entertainment.

Entertaining during the Gilded Age progressed, or at least changed, from relative simplicity to ostentation. Hostesses were richer, their parties grander. Dining tables were longer, dinners slower, food more varied and more elaborately prepared. Dance favors were more gilded and bejeweled, and, of course, more expensive. Footmen wore knee breeches. Plenty of Old New Yorkers lamented the changes. Conservatives like Constance Cary Harrison were scandalized: "What would have been thought in that [earlier] epoch of New York," she wrote, "of a table stretched to the limit of the dining room, with chairs so pushed together as to prevent free movement with spoon and fork, where forty or more guests, corralled to eat insidious messes served by caterers are shepherded by strange waiters on tiptoe thrusting between them fish, flesh and fowl with their attendant cates [delicacies] and condiments, at quarters so close the alarmed diner must shrink back in order to avoid contact with the offered dish!" Mrs. Harrison sadly concluded that "Magnificence in entertainments had come to stay. New families, new houses, flunkies in plush breeches, gold services at dinner, the importation of priceless pictures, tapestries, wall panelings, doors, ceilings and furniture from Old World places, the building of sumptuous dwellings, rose to the front and remained there. . . . People of the old order, of moderate means and hospitable impulses, found their invitations superseded by those of the beneficent plutocrats of the new."

By the nineties fashionable people were no longer so reluctant to have their names and their parties appear in public print. Henry Collins Brown wrote: "Zealous reporters infested the back stairs and bribed the servants' hall for the tittle-tattle of the great. All the big functions were covered and the costumes described in detail for the delectation of those remaining millions who were not there to see." New York Society had once been proudly reticent; now it had succumbed to the power of the press. A faint attempt was made at pretending that hostesses never cooperated with the press in giving lists of their guests, but in fact much information was to be found in daily newspaper reports that could only have come from the mistress of the household. Mrs. Astor certainly never gave interviews or assisted the press. She apparently was not reluctant to have Ward McAllister do that for her, however. For years he extolled to the press her place in Society and her style of entertaining.

E. A. Carolus-Duran was a French Salon painter who rarely offended his sitters. His portrait of Caroline Webster (Schermerhorn) Astor, who hated to be drawn or photographed, depicts her at her grandest — the way she received her guests..

2

The Mystic Rose

❧

She will always be known as "Mrs. Astor." The vast wealth of her husband's family, "New York City's landlords," and the glamour of their name in America and England have long since overwhelmed her own origins. In her mind and in the minds of her contemporaries, her own family name, was every bit as "good" as the Astors. In fact, many old New Yorkers would have said that she "married down." She was born Caroline Webster Schermerhorn, daughter of a Knickerbocker dynasty beside whom the Astors were upstarts. She belonged to the seventh generation of Schermerhorns born in New York State, the fourth generation born in the city. Her first ancestor in this country, Jan Jansen Schermerhorn, came from Holland to settle in Albany in 1643. He was a trader, exchanging European goods with the Indian tribes along the Hudson for their beaver skins and other furs. Like many settlers in New Netherland he fell foul of the high-handed Governor Peter Stuyvesant, who scorned him as "a peddler" and accused him of selling guns to the Mohawks, which was against the law. The governor went so far as to banish Schermerhorn from the colony on this charge and even muttered threats about the death penalty, but noisy public indignation forced him to back down. Schermerhorn survived and when he moved to New Amsterdam he prospered as a merchant, held the office of magistrate and belonged to the consistory (governing body) of the Dutch Reformed Church. He was the forefather of a shrewd and industrious line that rose in wealth and influence as the colony grew.

The Schermerhorns were never landed gentry like the Van Rensselaers or the Livingstons, lords of vast domains along the Hudson River. They were city people, engaged in business; warehouses and docks were their real estate. As was common in the Dutch dynasties, property used for business in colonial times became immensely valuable in the nineteenth century. Knickerbocker families like the Schermerhorns, the de Peysters, the Van Cortlandts, and Rhinelanders were "in trade." Socially it was preferable to be a Hudson River landowner, but being "in trade" was perfectly acceptable in New York, where successful businessmen were always looked up to. Later, after the Schermerhorns and other clans became very rich, they looked down on "trade." That attitude didn't stop the city merchants and the landed gentry from blending: intermarriage began almost immediately after the families settled in New Netherland.

About 1810 Peter Schermerhorn, Caroline's grandfather, established himself as a "ship's chandler," supplying marine equipment and provisions for the many vessels sailing from New York's great harbor. He also began the Schermerhorn family's great Manhattan real estate fortune by purchasing "water lots" along Fulton Street. Although investing in lots lying under water was a hoary joke elsewhere, in New York water lots were the source of some notable fortunes. Since slow transportation was making expansion up the island difficult and expensive, entrepreneurs widened Manhattan below Canal Street, where most people lived and worked, by buying from the city submerged acreage along the shoreline, filling it in, and, as business expanded, selling the new ground at immense profit. Favored buyers got water lots at bargain prices without competitive bidding. The system reeked of special favors and bribery and the corruption of city officials; it was a sort of permanent municipal scandal. Peter Schermerhorn filled his water lots with rocks and soil to a point 600 feet from the original shoreline and built a row of brick warehouses in the federal style called "Schermerhorn Row" on Fulton Street. They still stand. After a steam-powered ferry began running to Brooklyn in 1814, Fulton Street became one of the busiest sections of the city, and the Schermerhorn property exploded in value in the 1830s and '40s.

The Schermerhorns were by then very rich indeed and one of the prominent families of New York. While some members devoted themselves to real estate, which had turned out to be much more profitable than ship chandlery, others lived off family trusts and patronized the arts, especially music; all, workers and drones alike, served on boards of great New York institutions, presided over clubs, and, if they were ladies, entertained with great dignity and considerable splendor. Trade was behind them. All were members, as Edith Wharton wrote, of "a prosperous, prudent and yet lavish society." They had coats-of-arms and liveries, and even an inner-circle pronunciation of their name: "Skairmorn." Schermerhorn doings were chronicled by both of New York's great nineteenth-century diarists, Philip Hone and George Templeton Strong. Hone's favorite daughter, Mary, married Jones Schermerhorn, and Hone, a tireless diner-out, loved to attend the dinners that Abraham Schermerhorn, Caroline's father, gave in honor of visiting politicians. Strong was friendly with many Schermerhorns, served with them on various boards, including Columbia College, the Church Music Society, and Trinity Church (like other Knickerbockers, the Schermerhorns had quietly switched from the Dutch Reformed to the Episcopal Church). A particular friend of Strong's was Caroline's cousin, William Colford Schermerhorn, of whom the historian Allan Nevins later wrote, "An admirable representative of the best of old New York, he devoted a long life to the family estate, to music and the church and to quiet public service and benevolence." He was a trustee of Columbia for forty-three years and a major building on the Morningside campus, still in use, bears his name.

Strong and his wife went to parties at various Schermerhorn houses and entertained Schermerhorns in their own home on Gramercy Park (Isaac Brown was in charge of the catering and summoning the carriages). As a lawyer, Strong drew wills for the family and was unwillingly involved in disputes among them about trusts. To his diary he confided sarcastic remarks about various Schermerhorns, their wealth, and their tender concern for it. Strong lived beyond his means for most of his life, and although he was a lawyer with an established practice, money was always his weak point. In 1852 he noted that "Peter Schermerhorn [Caroline's uncle] is said to be failing rapidly, his constitution undermined by a chronic disease—an enlargement of the bank account—which has shattered his nervous system by sleepless nights and hypochondriacal anxiety," and when Schermerhorn died, added rather unkindly, "Peter Schermerhorn was reduced to destitution, deprived of all his property and estate real and personal. . . . He must be sadly bored in a world where there are no rents to collect and no investments to be made. . . ." Strong drew the will of Caroline's brother Archibald (called "Bruce"). In 1862 Bruce died unmarried and left his estate, which was considerable, to his little sister Caroline. Their sisters, Mrs. Walter Suydam and Mrs. John Treat Irving, were, as Strong put it, "wrathful" at being left out. Ten years later Strong found the Schermerhorns again at odds, this time about one of the family trusts, and was shocked at their greed: "Strange how these millionaire families quarrel among themselves about money—brother alienated from brother, sister at daggers drawn with sister—and all about property, of which every one of them has more than enough!"

Caroline's father, Abraham Schermerhorn, was in the ship's chandlery with his father and his brother Peter in the first quarter of the nineteenth century. He married a rich wife, Helen White, who owned among other properties inherited from her mother, a Van Cortlandt, 9 and 11 Broadway, later the site of the Atlantic Garden, an outdoor pleasure resort. When he died in 1850, George Templeton Strong remarked maliciously "Abraham Schermerhorn died yesterday, in spite of his half million." Between 1816 and 1839, the Abraham Schermerhorns lived at 1 Greenwich Street; Caroline, the youngest of their nine children, was born there on September 22, 1830. They later moved "uptown," as did many patrician families when it became unacceptable to live in a mercantile neighborhood. The Schermerhorns settled at 36 Bond Street, the grandest residential street in New York, where they had as neighbors Lorillards, Wards, de Forests, and Jays. The Wards were relations of Ward McAllister, who in the future would be indissolubly linked socially with Caroline Astor.

The Schermerhorn summer residence was Jones Wood, a house on a slight bluff overlooking the East River between what are now East 64th and 68th Streets, the site of Rockefeller University. Other Schermerhorns lived on what is now East 84th Street, looking out toward the Hell-Gate and the East River islands. "The family owned at one time considerable real estate in this section," wrote John Flavel Mines ["Felix Oldboy"] in his *A Tour Around New York*, "and several houses were built by and for the younger members where they lived surrounded by New York's first families—Joneses, Winthrops, and Kings."

She was given the name Caroline Webster in honor of Mrs. Daniel Webster (Caroline Le Roy). Webster himself was greatly admired by Abraham Schermerhorn, who feasted the great orator whenever he visited New York. Like most women of her class Caroline (called "Lina" by her family) received a primary education that included only deportment, dancing, penmanship, and needlework at a school conducted by Mrs. Bensee, a Frenchwoman. She was then sent to school in France. She spoke fluent French all her life and was at home in Paris, where she maintained an apartment at 146 Avenue des Champs-Élysées, where she spent four or five months annually, entertaining much as she did in New York and Newport. Her guests were members of the *gratin*, as the leading families of French society were, and are, known, and visiting members of her American circle. Often rich Americans of her time idealized the life led by the English gentry and nobility and emulated it as best they could with their stately homes and pursuit of foxes. Not Caroline. Like her great rivals the Vanderbilts and some other families of the Four Hundred, she looked to Paris; she hardly ever visited Britain. In a rare public remark she said her ideal in entertaining was the French *salon*. In 1885, to give an example of her continuing fondness for France, she gave a tea at which poems of Victor Hugo were recited "with the true accent of the Théâtre Français." Her large

The Schermerhorns lived for two centuries at the tip of Manhattan close to the warehouses and docks where their fortune was made. In Caroline's childhood they followed other well-to-do families to Bond Street, "far uptown."

collection of paintings were mostly from the contemporary French School. Her clothes were made by Worth. She was a true Francophile.

The women of Caroline's family provided for their little girl examples of the New York Society leader at her most polished; many Schermerhorn ladies and even more from the White and Van Cortlandt families, her maternal relations, were notable New York hostesses. Her great-grandmother, Mrs. Henry White, born Anne Van Cortlandt, lived at 11 Broadway, one of the finest houses in New York, inherited from her father. "A lady of great wealth," as the historian Martha Lamb called her, she had been married to Henry White, a prominent New Yorker who had been a Loyalist during the American Revolution. That was not regarded as any great failing in New York, which had been "the capital of Tory America" with one third of its population accompanying the British forces when they evacuated the city at the end of the Revolution. The Whites were among those refugees, and Henry White died in London in 1786. His widow returned to New York to introduce her daughters, "conspicuous belles," to New York Society and was famous as a hostess. Although great-grandmother White died at the extraordinary age of ninety-eight in 1836, when Caroline was only six years old, the tradition of an expansive social life and active entertaining was entrenched among the Schermerhorns. Caroline was to bring the tradition to full flower.

On September 20, 1853, two days before her twenty-third birthday, she married William Backhouse Astor, Jr., second son of William Astor, head of the family and the richest man in America. A year older than Caroline, William, Jr. was almost literally the boy next door since the Astors lived near the Schermerhorns in a red-brick Georgian-style house on Lafayette Street. The young people had known each other all their lives; they were, in fact, remotely related through the Beekman family. The couple were so suitable for each other that the match was probably an arranged one. The Astors were a lot richer than the Schermerhorns—the Astors were richer than *anybody*—but the Schermerhorns and their circle were not unduly impressed. For one thing, William was not the eldest son, and since the Astor family inclined toward primogeniture, could expect to inherit far less money than his older brother, John Jacob.

Caroline's husband was the grandson of John Jacob Astor, the founder of a still-existing (in both England and America) dynasty and in his time the richest American who had ever lived. He was born in the German village of Walldorf (the Astors later adopted the name as a Christian one but dropped an "l") near Heidelberg in 1763, the son of a butcher. He and his three brothers were adventurous: George went to London, where he joined an uncle who was a maker of musical instruments; Johann Melchior became a steward on a German nobleman's estate; Henry went to New York, where he became a butcher like his father. He sent for John Jacob, the youngest brother, who arrived in New York in March 1784. He found employment with the prominent Quaker merchant Robert Bowne, who dealt in fur skins, mostly beaver trapped by the upstate Indians. John Jacob started in a humble way but immediately became absorbed in the fur trade, a good occupation for an eager young man since pelts were among New York's major exports. His contemporaries noticed that John Jacob "absolutely loved a fine skin," and even after he was successful he would hang a superior fur on the wall in his counting room as though it were a tapestry. He

Numerous members of the Astor family lived in houses given to them by the patriarch John Jacob Astor I. He also built 425 Lafayette Street, which became the Astor Library and today is the Public Theater.

liked to caress the skin and extol its quality and value, remarking perhaps that he could get $500 for it in the Chinese market. In two years he set himself up in the fur business on his own. The first (1790) New York City directory listed him as "Astor, J. J., Fur trader, 40 Little Dock [now Water] Street." He bought, beat, cured, and packed the skins himself with the help of his wife, Sarah Todd. It was

The dynasty founded by John Jacob Astor in the eighteenth century had become New York Society's first family by the middle of the nineteenth century. Their supremacy was unchallenged until the rise of the Vanderbilts in the 1880s.

dirty, smelly work, but he loved it. In 1800 about six million furs—from a variety of animals but mostly beaver—were sold in the United States. Prices ranged between fifteen cents and five hundred dollars a pelt. In London, a good beaver skin sold for about twenty-five shillings, ten times what it fetched in western New York State. But it was in China that the vastest profits could be made. The cold northern parts of China were an immense market for American furs, where they were a badge of rank as well as comfort among the Mandarins. John Jacob was one of the first Americans to trade with China. A single voyage by one of his ships produced profits of $30,000; sometimes he made as much as $70,000. He also imported musical instruments and made a trip to London with a load of

The fur trade, shipping, and New York City real estate gave John Jacob Astor his fortune. Son of a small-town German butcher, he began his career in America selling pianos for his brother in London. When he died in 1849, leaving $20 million, he was the richest American.

skins during which he made an arrangement with Astor [his brother George] & Broadwood, piano-makers, to represent them in New York. The sign on his shop at 71 Liberty Street now read "Furs and Pianos." After he had made a substantial fortune in those businesses, John Jacob began to buy real estate, especially corner lots, in Manhattan. He soon felt as passionately about real estate as he did about furs and constantly bought and sold (but mainly retained) lots and tracts all over the growing city. As he often said, he would have liked to own all Manhattan; he made a good stab, buying so much property and building so many tenements on it that he and his descendants became known as "New York's landlords." No other family has ever owned so much of the city or kept it so long.

John Jacob and Sarah Todd Astor lived for years at 223 Broadway in a modest house at the time when the Schermerhorns were living grandly in the aristocratic lower end of Broadway. He later built the Astor House, New York's most important hotel, on that site, the first foray of the Astors into the hotel business, where they would be active for a century, and moved several times before settling "uptown" on Lafayette Street, then a swank new neighborhood. Even in a larger house, he retained the simple tastes of his German background: drinking beer, playing a game of checkers, taking a ride on horseback, and going to the theater. He had a great respect for literary men; Washington Irving was a friend and an executor of his will. And John Jacob's only benefaction to a city where he made a fortune was the foundation of a quasi-public library (the public was admitted under stringent conditions) on Lafayette Street. But his mind was never far from business, and he earned a reputation for hardness that, next to his fortune, was his most lasting legacy: "In all transactions he kept in view the simple object of giving the least and getting the most," admitted even a largely sympathetic biographer, James Parton. "To get all that he could, and to keep nearly all that he got— those were the laws of his being. He had a vast genius for making money, and that was all that he had." His comment on the War of 1812 and its trade embargo, which cut into his profits, was typically self-centered: "But for that war, I should have been the richest man that ever lived." As it was, he was the richest American when he died in 1848 at the age of eighty-four: his estate, difficult to calculate because so much of it consisted of undeveloped lots, was over $20 million and quite probably as much as $30 million, by far the largest fortune any American had ever accumulated. Along with this stupendous amount of money he left his descendants a legacy of self-absorption combined in many of them with a sort of melancholia and lack of pleasure in the good things they had been given. Always prominent because of their astonishing wealth, the Astors were neither much admired nor much liked.

John Jacob declared in his will that he was a member of the German Reformed Church, but he was buried in a vault at St. Thomas Episcopal Church on Broadway with a service conducted by no fewer than six doctors of divinity—although it is difficult to imagine why he merited so much ecclesiastical attention. If the clergy hoped their churches would be remembered in his will, they were to be sadly disappointed. The body was later transferred uptown to Trinity Cemetery at 155th Street in Manhattan, where he lies surrounded by numerous descendants. Although he was escorted to his grave by plenty of preachers public sentiment was hostile. Out of his vast fortune he made only one

During the lifetime of William Backhouse Astor, John Jacob's son, the Astor fortune doubled. The explosion of New York's population and commerce benefited no one more than the Astor family, "New York's landlords."

charitable contribution of any size, $400,000 for his library. The outspoken New York *Herald* called it "a poor, mean and beggarly result!" and thought that at least half of his property ought to have gone to the people of New York. That was the beginning of a general unpopularity of the Astors with the mass of New Yorkers, not dissipated until the late twentieth century.

The eldest Astor child, Magdalen, a notorious shrew, married Adrian Bentzon, governor of the then-Danish Virgin Islands; her second husband, John Bristed, an Anglican minister, fled her yoke in 1821. Her cousin Henry Brevoort sympathized with the husband: "He is literally wasted to the bone by the severity of her discipline. Their fracas have furnished the town with scandal these six months. She is certainly a maniac." Another daughter, Dorothea, eloped with a soldier, the handsome Colonel Walter Langdon, who was poor but described as "dashing"; her father, angered at first, forgave the couple, and in his will richly endowed them and their four boys and four girls with Manhattan real estate that assured their comfort for generations. Their descendants were numerously represented in the Four Hundred.

There were two Astor sons. The elder, John Jacob II, was mentally defective, so it happened that the second, William Backhouse, became his father's principal heir, receiving the bulk of the fortune. That didn't sit well with the press, or the public either, who saw in the legacy a European leaning toward primogeniture and the endowment of a dynasty. William was a dull dog, at his father's beck and call until he was nearly sixty years old. He learned a lot from the old man about managing real estate and devoted his life to the Astor Estate, as the family holding company was called, preserving its properties, spending the least money he could on repairs, and collecting rents mercilessly. No office job was too routine or too uninspiring for him: he was essentially a bookkeeper. He doubled the fortune he had inherited, but the vast expansion in value of the Astor properties was due more to the growth of the city than it was to any shrewd investing on his part. Harvey Sutherland, a writer generally friendly to the rich, wrote in the exasperated tone that New Yorkers often used when discussing the Astors: "The Astors buy land and they keep it. I do not think they even promise to make rents cheaper. If they do not get the price they think they ought to from a piece of property, they let it lie idle rather than scale the rent. Or they let you pull the house down and build on a twenty-one year lease . . . . At the end of twenty-one years, the Astor Estate has all the ground rent of the house you have built. . . ." In 1875 the Astors owned lots on eleven of Manhattan's avenues, on fifty-nine of the numbered streets between Third Street and 185th, and on forty-five of the named streets. These last, all lying between the Battery and 14th Street, were the heart of the Astor empire.

William was a notorious tightwad, always turning the gas light low when he stepped out of a room and carefully buying his winter coal supply in June. He was timid to a fault and never shook the tree: during his prime the Tweed Ring was robbing the city of New York of millions; as New York City's largest taxpayer he might have been expected to protest, but he did not, on the contrary issuing a statement of confidence in the city government. The disgrace of the Astors' properties and at the same time the principal source of their income were the

Samuel Ward, Ward McAllister's uncle, was married to an Astor and provided a tenuous family link between McAllister and Caroline Astor. The most successful lobbyist of his time, he was celebrated for his knowledge of food and wine. At his table the young McAllister mastered the tenets of gourmandizing.

acres of tenements the estate owned on the Lower East Side of the city. Their crowded and unhealthy state was well known and they were the targets of endless governmental and private investigations and of ceaseless complaints by reformers and social workers. By most calculations the Lower East Side tenements were the most overcrowded human habitations in the world, more packed with humanity than the slums of Calcutta or Shanghai.

These tenements made William the richest man in the United States, but he spent little on himself and adhered to the Old New York style of "living handsomely but not lavishly." He "married up," to a young lady who had no money

William Backhouse Astor, Jr., was profoundly unimpressed by his wife's leadership of Society. For most of their forty-year marriage he and Caroline led separate lives, she entertaining on Fifth Avenue, he sailing on his mammoth yacht.

but aristocratic lineage. His bride in 1818 was Margaret Rebecca Armstrong, daughter of General John Armstrong and Alida Livingston, who brought the Astors into the charmed circle of the Knickerbockers. The career of Margaret's father, at least on paper, was impressive: delegate to the Continental Congress, general in the Revolutionary War, United States Senator, Minister to France, and Secretary of War, but as one authority wrote bluntly, "He distinguished himself in none of these offices" and notes that his service as head of the War Department during the War of 1812 "was particularly unfortunate." His wife, Alida Livingston, was considered "fascinating"; legend holds that during her sojourn in France as the American minister's lady, Napoleon told her that she spoke French like a Parisian. Her greatest social victory was marrying her daughter to the son of the richest man in America. Margaret (Armstrong) Astor was aristocratic and aloof and not particularly popular in Society, although the wife of the head of the house of Astor could never be ignored. She was not beautiful, but her "peach-bloom" complexion was admired; her husband—but no one else—called her "Peachy." Although no social climber, old John Jacob Astor was proud when William married into the Hudson River aristocracy, but, characteristically, he insisted that Miss Armstrong surrender her dower rights in the Astor fortune in a prenuptial agreement.

The fifth of their six children who lived to adulthood was William B. Astor, Jr. Born in 1829, he was a year older than his bride Caroline Schermerhorn, well educated (first in his class at Columbia College), well traveled, and the most cultivated and attractive of the Astors. That wasn't saying much since the Astors were notorious for their lack of good looks. He was slightly jollier than most members of his somber family. Although extremely rich, as the younger son he inherited only about a third of the immense Astor estate. His older brother, John Jacob, whom he detested (although their wives got on well), got the lion's share and carefully excluded William from management. Still, the young Astor-Schermerhorn couple were among the richest in the city: George Templeton Strong liked them both, but he wrote sarcastically in his diary, "I hope the young couple will be able to live on their little incomes." They settled on East 22nd Street, near Broadway in, of course, an Astor-owned house. Caroline immediately began a family: Emily was born in 1854, Helen Schermerhorn in 1855, Charlotte Augusta (named by Caroline for her sister-in-law, Mrs. John Jacob Astor), Caroline Schermerhorn in 1861, and, finally, the heir, John Jacob Astor IV, in 1864. Contemporaries agreed that Caroline was a good mother; her children were devoted to her.

After ten years of childbearing, she began to take her social position seriously and to attend to what were called the "social responsibilities" of women of her class, which did not mean working in soup kitchens but upholding one's proper place in Society. "Duties" were attending weddings, balls, dinners, private (seldom public) receptions, and paying calls. In America of the Gilded Age these were serious duties and, if well-performed, a matter of congratulation. Mrs. O. H. P. Belmont (not Mrs. Astor's favorite person in Society—she had been divorced) said, "I know of no profession, art, or trade that women are working in today as taxing on mental resources as being a leader of Society."

At 350 Fifth Avenue Mrs. Astor gave balls in the art gallery of her house, the famous room supposed to hold only four hundred guests, a number assigned to Society by Ward McAllister. On the walls hung her collection of contemporary French paintings.

Caroline had four daughters who were "coming out," and although she was secure in her family's social position, it was just as well to remind everyone of it. "Subscription dances" highlighted the winter social season in New York: The Family Circle Dancing Class, The Assemblies, The Patriarchs, The First Cotillion (with four hundred subscribers, an early use of that magical number), and her own Mrs. William Astor's Dancing Class were schools of conduct, marriage markets, and courts that solemnly decided who was in Society and, more importantly, who was not. Taking her place as a matron in her mid-thirties, she was not altogether pleased by what, or rather who, she found in Society, and took it upon herself to assume without any fanfare that position in New York Society to which her family and wealth entitled her: in a word, the top. Caroline received the call to rule

Society in the late 1860s. As she and others, including Ward McAllister, saw it, New York was swarming with "new people" (the "shoddies") who had made fortunes in the Civil War and were outrageously arming to invade "good Society."

It was in connection with the Family Dancing Class that she became friends with Ward McAllister, also beginning a career in Society. McAllister was truly awed by Caroline Astor and remained impressed by her until his dying day. "I then for the first time," he wrote, "was brought in contact with this grand dame and at once recognized her ability, and felt that she would become Society's leader, and that she was admirably qualified for the position." Her qualifications included, he enumerated, "good judgement and a great power of analysis of men and women, a thorough knowledge of all their surroundings, a just appreciation of the rights of others. . . ." From then on they often danced together in cotillions and McAllister and his wife were frequent guests at Astor parties. There was no romance involved nor even a close friendship; McAllister acted as her herald, her chronicler, and, generally, her publicist. She never acknowledged publicly his role in proclaiming her monarchy, but she is not known to have discouraged it either.

She began her campaign by modifying her name: she persuaded her husband to drop "Backhouse" with its vulgar euphony, then to drop the "Junior," and finally to abandon his own given name. Her calling cards were engraved simply "Mrs. Astor," and she insisted that her mail be addressed that way. This maneuver was in direct contradiction to the rules she professed to abide by: the simple style "Mrs. Astor" was reserved for the wife of the eldest son of the family, in this case her sister-in-law, Mrs. John Jacob Astor. That Mrs. Astor was Charlotte Augusta Gibbes, an aristocratic and easygoing South Carolinian, active in charities (unusually so for an Astor) and quite indifferent to petty distinctions. John Jacob was not happy with Caroline's aggressiveness, but it was in the next generation that her claim to the semi-royal title brought an open quarrel within the family. John Jacob and Charlotte Augusta's only child, William Waldorf Astor, an irascible and haughty man, claimed, rightly, that his wife was "Mrs. Astor." He and his Aunt Lina went head-to-head on this subject: Caroline won and was "Mrs. Astor" then and now, but the dispute with her nephew-in-law simmered. There is no record that William Backhouse Astor paid any attention to these quarrels or even to the changes in his name; he and his wife were seldom under the same roof and he was quite indifferent to her social campaign.

Caroline then decided that 22nd Street was out of fashion, "a dullish backwater," Edith Wharton once wrote of the neighborhood, where she herself was born, "between Aristocracy to the south and Money to the North." Lafayette

Street, where numerous Astors had clustered, was also becoming common—too close to the Astor Place Playhouse, which attracted rowdy audiences, and middle-class Vauxhall Gardens, a place of public resort—so in 1859 she and William built a new house at 350 Fifth Avenue on the southwest corner of 34th Street where the Empire State Building now stands. They were surrounded by relations. Her brother-in-law John Jacob Astor followed, building an almost identical house on the corner of Fifth Avenue and 33rd Street, the two establishments separated by a garden. Father William B. Astor, Sr., had moved to Fifth Avenue near 35th Street after his wife's death; two of his daughters were at Madison Avenue and 34th; the hated Waldorf Astor was on 33rd Street; and two of Caroline's daughters lived nearby on Fifth Avenue after they married. The reason was not so much familial affection as the fact that these were all Astor properties where the heirs lived at no cost.

The house at 350 Fifth Avenue, scene of Caroline's greatest triumphs and in which the Astors were living when Ward McAllister issued his list, was a four-story brownstone, quite nondescript in appearance when viewed from the street. It was conservative and solid but not splendid, a monument to the old Knickerbocker adage about "living handsomely but not lavishly." Once seen, the interiors would always be familiar to any guest: nothing was ever changed except the upholstery when it wore out; it was then replaced with exactly the same fabric. Elizabeth (Drexel) Lehr wrote: "At Mrs. Astor's you would have recognized . . . the drawing-room or the ballroom after years of absence; the curtains and carpets and chairs would all have looked the same even though they had been changed [re-upholstered] several times."

Once settled in 350 Fifth Avenue, Caroline began the relentless entertaining that would continue for the next forty years. Mrs. Astor's emergence did not go unnoticed. "At this period," intoned Ward McAllister, "a great personage (representing a silent power) that had always been recognized and felt in this community so long as I remember by not only fashionable people but by the solid old quiet element as well, had daughters to introduce into society, which brought her prominently forward and caused her at once to take a leading position." By 1872 Caroline's campaign for social supremacy was in full swing. *The Home Journal* carefully described for its readers her yearly schedule: "Mrs. Astor is most methodical as to her movements. . . . Each winter [she] gives a series of dinners and one large evening reception. . . . She always sails for Europe the last week in February. . . . In Paris, Mrs. Astor has a beautiful apartment in the Avenue Champs-Élysées, where in the early spring she gives a few dinners and perhaps a musicale. . . . [She] returns

William Astor, Jr. had built for him the Nourmahal, the first family yacht of that name. Caroline claimed that sailing made her so seasick that she never ventured to board the vessel. William and his seafaring cronies, however, had other feminine companionship.

the first week in July, when she goes to Newport. She opens her town house in November." Although like most hostesses she was more comfortable in her own home than other people's, when she did go out to dinner she was always seated at the host's right hand. She relished that. Mrs. Winthrop Chanler, who was impressed by very few people, said that Caroline "had pleasant cordial manners and unaffectedly enjoyed her undisputed position."

William Astor seldom attended these festivities. When he did, he was likely to be disagreeable, on occasion bluntly telling guests to leave. Despite his solid education and extensive travel in Europe, his manners were rough—the revenge, no doubt, of an intelligent but disappointed man on a family that refused him any responsibility. But, apparently, he never begrudged the cost, which was enormous, of his wife's entertainments, the apartment in Paris, the house in Newport, her clothes and jewels. His income was said to be around $5 million a year, and Caroline had money of her own. Without any real occupation he spent his time at "Ferncliff," the country place he built at Rhinebeck on the Hudson. There were five hundred acres with a carriage road from the main entrance that was nearly a mile long. When he bought his first farm and began to assemble the land for an estate, it was mainly devastated forest land. In twenty years William had transformed the acreage into a showplace. Very occasionally, Caroline visited Ferncliff, the purpose of the visits being, it seemed, to assure the world that despite appearances the Astors were still a couple. She was certainly no lover of country pursuits.

William took up yachting. In 1884 he launched a great steel-framed steam yacht that he called the *Nourmahal*. He and his cronies spent much of their time sailing along the East Coast of the United States. Gossip had it that the guests included agreeable females. Caroline never appeared: she used to say she suffered from seasickness so badly that she was prevented from ever making even a single trip on her husband's yacht; of course no one was rude enough to point out that she often crossed the Atlantic in midwinter. The marriage was effectively over. William was an early visitor to the fleshpots of Florida, which he reached by yacht. This was long before the heyday of Palm Beach, which only became a resort after 1900, and Florida was regarded by New Yorkers as the haunt of snakes and alligators. Desperately ill people sometimes went to St. Augustine for their health; otherwise one did not visit Florida, which was socially off the map. William's headquarters were at Jacksonville, where he made investments and, being an Astor, bought considerable real estate. He entered into the life of the town, even becoming a member of the Masonic Solomon's Lodge there in 1877.

Caroline wended her own way toward social supremacy, overcoming such handicaps as an ill-tempered and largely absent husband and her own lack of physical attractions. She was not a regal figure. Although tall, she was stout, with heavy jowls. She was dark in an age when blondes were especially admired. Frank Crowninshield, editor of *Vanity Fair* magazine, who knew her well in his youth as man-about-town in New York, described her as "tall, a little on the heavy style, dark, with a slight, but not disfiguring, cast in her eye." Her hair apparently began to thin early in life, and for most of her social career she wore a jet-black wig, instantly identifiable as such and quite familiar in New York social circles. She was usually heavily veiled when she went out during the daytime and, surprisingly, at night as well. Concealing her face was a guard against photographers: she hated being pho-

"She entered the room like a meteor." Caroline Astor was fond of jewels and owed it to her position as queen of Society to blaze at parties. Her blue sapphire and old-mine diamond ornament, mounted in platinum and yellow gold, was worn in the hair, but the 248 round diamonds were detachable and could be worn as brooches and pins.

tographed, and very few photographs of her exist. She preferred to be known by the famous and so-often-reproduced portrait of her by Emile Carolus-Duran. All commentators agree that she had great dignity, which, as Ward McAllister said, enabled her to exert "a great restraining influence on the more frivolously inclined in her own set. . . ." She was serene, a quality then especially admired in women. She had the stiff posture of Old New Yorkers and moved in the slow and stately manner cultivated by her Dutch ancestresses after they rose above doing their own housework. "Her manner is almost old-fashioned," wrote one magazine, "in its mingling of simplicity with stateliness." She was not the bustling hostess of the twentieth century, air-kissing arrivals, making introductions, and generally jollying her guests into having a good time. From Mrs. Astor you got a firm handshake, a cordial but reserved greeting, and then you were on your own.

Many people considered her a simple, earnest person without affectations: she did not, for example, use the English broad "a," which many American Society women then affected. She was good-natured, never showing resentment, or vexation, although she was quite capable of sending anyone who violated her standards off to a social Elba, from whence only she could recall the now humbled offender. A newspaper wrote that, "She is the most simple and unaffected of all the women of note in American Society." Reserve was her key characteristic: she kept everyone at a distance. It was often remarked that she had many friends, but no intimates. "Mrs. Astor," wrote Elizabeth Lehr, "never confided, was naturally sincere and gracious, and her friendship once given was not lightly withdrawn." But being a friend had well-understood limits: "She gave friendship, but never intimacy," wrote Lehr. "No one ever knew what thoughts passed behind the calm repose of her face." What she did not want to see, she saw not, nor did she listen to words she did not want to hear.

She was a devout Episcopalian and rented pews at four of the city's churches, Grace Church being her favorite. She was charitable, a trait of the Schermerhorns although not of the Astors. In 1873, for example, George Templeton Strong, treasurer of Trinity Church, received Mrs. Astor's check for $300, a very considerable sum, "to give the poor children of Trinity Church a picnic or rural holiday of some kind."

Frank Crowninshield, inclined to flatter the rich, is the only observer who maintained that "anything resembling fun appealed to her so irresistibly." He fails to give any examples of this amiable trait, nor did anyone else detect it. Entertainments she gave were so stately and orderly they were like minuets. One never reads of any sparkling wit at her table, and high jinks of any sort would not have been tolerated. Choosing partners for the cotillion was about the most amusing thing that happened.

Parties on the grandest scale required the finest clothes and jewels. Caroline stinted on neither, and her appearance was unforgettable. She was a strange mix of the reserved Old New York, which abhorred display, and the overdressed world of the late nineteenth-century city, where unrestrained ostentation was admired. On each trip to Paris she bought six or eight gowns from Worth. She seemed to think that Worth was the only dressmaker in the world; she was not alone in this as he had an immense clientele, European and American. During Caroline's career, he was at the height of his fame. He had succeeded at a time when there had been no designers of women's clothes, only dressmakers, who were always women. As early as 1868 *The Home Journal*, describing his unusual success but not knowing what to call his new profession, referred to him as "the celebrated male *modiste* of Paris" and added, "He is the absolute monarch in the kingdom of fashion. Everything from him is accepted, and everything he invents is copied by all."

From Worth, Caroline often ordered gowns of royal purple or deep green, her favorite colors, in heavy fabrics often adorned with rare laces.

Her jewels demanded notice. She certainly had no need to call attention to herself, but she habitually wore jewelry of such value and showiness that it nearly blinded observers. "She entered the room like a meteor," one commentator said. To a small dance she wore a Worth gown of pale French gray satin brocaded with long sheaves of wheat, with a diamond and pearl tiara, a matching necklace, and a large bowknot of diamonds supposed to have been once part of the French crown jewels. As if that were not enough, she also wore diamond bracelets, diamond pins and pendants, and solitaire diamond earrings of enormous size. She had the strange habit of wearing two necklaces at once, one on her bosom, the other rippling down her back. At her January, 1878 ball she appeared in a rose-colored velvet overdress covered with lace and looped with pale blue velvet and clusters of diamonds. "The corsage was literally blazing with diamonds," wrote a Society reporter. Among her jewels was a so-called "Egyptian snake ring" constructed of flexible gold wire in which a huge ruby was set. When the ring finger was moved, the wires quivered and seemed to go round the finger with "a weird, serpentine movement," wrote the hypnotized reporter. This fairground ornament, however valuable, would never have been worn by a Van Cortlandt. The same year, when her daughter Helen Schermerhorn Astor married James Roosevelt at Grace Church, Mrs. Astor wore her hair in puffs, each adorned with diamond rosebuds. Her shoulders and bosom were covered ("literally armored" wrote an excited reporter) with diamond pins and pendants; she wore a row of diamond bracelets on each arm and the solitaire diamond earrings. All these effects, though she would not have admitted it, were playing to the gallery: as Queen of New York she had to live up to the title.

By 1892 Caroline Astor had reigned over Society for twenty years. She inspired awe; many, if not most, of her guests were, quite frankly, afraid of her. Wags said that her manner was "Astorperious." If anyone broke her rules—if, for example, another woman tried to rival her—it was enough for Mrs. Astor to omit her name from one or two parties; the offender soon came to heel, humble and anxious to please. This awful solemnity had its origin in her unlimited belief in herself and her mission to be dictatress of society, a mission in which she fully succeeded. "A debutante who does not interest Mrs. Astor," it was said, "is not a debutante."

Ward McAllister named her "The Mystic Rose," revealing a surprising knowledge of the classics. The Mystic Rose in Dante's *Paradise* is the heavenly figure around whom all other figures in Paradise revolve. That is the way he saw

Caroline, and apparently that is the way she saw herself, although she never put the notion into words; that was not her style and ladies did not talk about their emotions. She thought it was her duty to uphold the old standards of decorum and the formalities and dignities of her youth, the Van Cortlandt and Schermerhorn traditions. To do that she surrounded herself with her relations and William Astor's and with New Yorkers of similar background. Social life was seen by her and Ward McAllister as a stately minuet in which everyone performed his assigned part with elegance and dignity. Social life was conducted the way it had been a hundred years ago by her great-grandmother Anne Van Cortlandt, despite the fact that New Yorkers of her class were now much richer and had many more opportunities for ostentation. Frank Crowninshield wrote, "She was essentially a conservative; a Tory of the first order. Throughout her life she had little use for novelties or newcomers. Her taste was always for old families, old ways, old servants, old operas, old lace, and old friends."

She never commented on her friendship with Ward McAllister: that would have been completely out of character. He, on the other hand, frequently told the world of his admiration for her, always in the most respectful, if florid, words. He said once of Caroline: "She had a just appreciation of the rights of others and, coming from an old colonial family, a good appreciation of the value of ancestry; always keeping it near her, and bringing it in, in all social matters, but also understanding the importance and power of the new element; recognizing it, and fairly and generously awarding it a prominent place."

The glory of Caroline's year was the great annual ball she gave the last week in January or the first of February. Other parties with dancing that she gave were merely dances; the mid-winter event was a ball. The date was roughly the beginning of Lent, though that was little observed except by the highest Episcopalians. *Town & Country* said of the ball, "It is a function representing the perfection of conventional entertaining, and in these days when hostesses strive for the bizarre and the original, the conventional approaches the novel." The magazine remarked in 1908, after her death, "Mrs. Astor's ball was an annual event that will someday be considered of historic significance, for the character of social life in New York, the rise and fall of certain contingents, has its basis in matters better understood by the sociologist than by the society butterfly. Nothing has taken the place of her ball."

Scheduling was inflexible. Most guests went to the opera first, since the balls were invariably held on Mondays, the most fashionable evening at the Metropolitan. None arrived at Mrs. Astor's before eleven o'clock. At the ball of January

31, 1900, the hostess, dressed in black velvet trimmed with jet and lace and wearing a stomacher, a necklace, and a tiara of diamonds, received in the entrance hall. There was informal dancing until supper, which began at midnight. At 1:30 or 2 a.m., the cotillion began. One set was led by Elisha Dyer, Jr. partnering Carrie (Astor) Wilson, the other led by Harry Lehr partnering Ruth (Livingston) Mills. The cotillion favors were *directoire* wands, Dutch tiles made of *papier mâché*, and *japonaiserie*, little fans and other trinkets that were all the rage.

Caroline's guest list was conservative but not fossilized; despite legends that the list never changed and that it was impossible to enter the charmed circle, newcomers *were* admitted, provided, of course, that they met her standards of background and conduct. Astonishingly enough in light of a later reputation as an inflexible snob, she was regarded by her contemporaries as somewhat more liberal in the matter of invitations than some other notable hostesses. Mrs. Frederick Thurston Mason, the Semiramis of Philadelphia, ruled Society in that city by sheer terror, deciding single-handedly who counted. And it was ancestry alone, together with obedience to Mrs. Mason's dictates, that made you admissible. By such tough standards, Mrs. Astor was kind-hearted. "If the applicant's past has been credible, she is not hypercritical as to pedigree," *Town & Country* commented favorably in 1905, when comparing the two hostesses, while Mrs. Mason insisted on "both past and pedigree in considering the qualifications of a new-comer." Against this liberal image must be placed evidence of Mrs. Astor's "persistence at times in remembering the shortcomings of families [divorce for example] 'unto the second and third generations,' and refusing positively an introduction." The distribution of invitations resulted in both social exultation and chagrin, "many going," *Town & Country* explained, "to old families who live quietly, to men whose ability in art and literature have commended them, while many of the much longed-for cards pass by the social climbers whose energy and ambition exceed their charm and tact." The Mystic Rose was Argus-eyed, and although she never gossiped herself, she made it her business to keep abreast of the latest Society scandals (who was divorcing, who was "carrying on" with another's spouse, whose child was making an unsuitable marriage). One slip might not be irretrievable; Caroline Astor could forgive. When she invited a social transgressor to her annual ball it signified forgiveness of social sins, and such was her authority, other hostesses followed with their invitations. Even after the publication of the Four Hundred's names the press remained curious about the Astor guest list. "This list makes revelation as to whom new favors have fallen upon, whom disapproval has descended upon, and who has been reinstated, by the decision of this 'first lady' of New York, for Mrs. Astor's leadership remains unquestioned, and will, until she herself relinquishes her reign."

There was the problem of young people. Mrs. Astor said, "I invite young people to my balls. I like to have them come, but they must look after themselves." She was as good as her word: on the list of the Four Hundred are in fact quite a few young people. The average age was between thirty and forty. Her court was mainly composed of men. Ward McAllister said, "She had the power that all women should strive to obtain, the power of attaching men to her, and keeping them attached, calling forth a loyalty of devotion such as one yields to a sovereign whose subjects are only too happy to be subjects." In the 1880s her entourage included such figures as De Lancy Kane, James Otis, Thomas Cushing, Peter Marié, James Parker, Frank Sturgis, and her sons-in-law Coleman Drayton, Orme Wilson and James Roosevelt Roosevelt. In the 1890s she added a younger guard. Five of those led her cotillions—Elisha Dyer, Worthington Whitehouse, Henry Bull, Craig Wadsworth, and Harry Lehr.

Entertaining on her scale required extreme efficiency, and Caroline Astor was businesslike in an understated way. She never discussed her arrangements—that would have been common—but entertaining and feeding hundreds of guests a year in three houses was obviously almost an industrial operation; under Caroline's direction it proceeded smoothly. She had the assistance of her famous butler, Thomas Hade (addressed as Thomas, rather than the customary Hade), who became her confidant and almost a friend as well as a longtime employee. Resourceful and good-natured, he kept a vast staff running smoothly. He was at her bedside when she died. She was extremely observant, not only in her own house, but in other people's. When she traveled, one reporter said, she was quick "to criticize any defect of lighting or ornamentation, or arrangement [and] she was not backward in chiding the management for it. . . ." She had the rather endearing liking for a hot dinner. Dinners were served promptly; woe betide a tardy guest. "Anyone who waits more than ten minutes for a later-comer at dinner," she said sternly, "commits an outrage on all her other guests."

Her rooms were bedecked with flowers. American Beauty roses were known as "Mrs. Astor's flowers." The American Beauty was the most distinctive and the most expensive of flowers, and synonymous with luxury; Caroline Astor, with her lavish use of the rose, was partly responsible for its reputation. At her balls the mantels and console tables along the walls were hidden by American Beauties and a huge rose tree in full flower stood in the center of the ballroom; the stairs and balustrades of the house were outlined with the roses; a dazed guest said that "everything seemed lighted with a rosy tint." Like so much decoration in the Gilded Age the use of American Beauties trespassed what would later be considered the boundaries of good taste. The public was amazed: American Beauties cost two dollars each, an astounding price when most cut flowers cost a few cents. At the January ball she had the house decorated with poinsettias, the marble hallways and stairs carpeted in matching crimson. Bunches of pink roses were tied with pink ribbons to the newel posts of the grand staircase. Hothouse Easter lilies and the inevitable American Beauties were arranged in tall Japanese porcelain vases in the entrance hall and violets and other fragrant flowers scattered throughout the reception rooms. Fleischman, a fashionable florist, decorated the house and was also responsible for floral favors at the cotillions. The floors, if too slippery from varnish, were sprinkled with pumice stone; if too sluggish, the surface was coated with oatmeal. Mrs. Astor, majestic in her Worth gown and blazing with jewels, sat on a large divan raised on a dais at one end of the ballroom. She invited favored ladies to sit beside her at intervals to watch the dancing. An invitation to join her was regarded as a royal command and was the subject of congratulations and envy.

Caroline, in fact, had it all down pat. For contrast she should be compared to a contemporary hostess, Mrs. Cornelius Vanderbilt II (Alice Gwynne). Her husband's family was every bit as rich as the Astors and, like Caroline Schermerhorn, she had colonial ancestry, too, although she was not a New Yorker. She was a small woman, plain, with tight lips and "piercingly cold gray eyes," as her grandson wrote. "She herself lacked all facility and finesse as a hostess. She was not especially gay or amusing; her demeanor, glacial and forbidding, failed utterly to attract and to keep a following of attractive and attentive men, without which it was impossible to give a successful party. . . ." She was not reluctant to spend money: when her daughter Gertrude had her debut ball in 1895 the favors of gold cigarette cases and fans alone cost $10,000. People dutifully went to Mrs. Vanderbilt's parties, but they did not enjoy themselves. In contrast, despite her legendary dignity and remoteness, Mrs. Astor was popular and her guests happy. Success in Society, wrote Elizabeth Lehr, "meant incalculable triumph and power—incalculable because it was so vague and because there were such indefinite limits to the use of power." She continued, "Mrs. Astor was the only woman living who had the power to maintain a semblance of real exclusiveness. . . . Her power has not been disputed. One journalist summed it up: "To tread her marble floors was to know social success."

Peter Stuyvesant, who governed New Amsterdam in the name of the Dutch West India Company, landed in the little city in 1647. He was to remain there for the rest of his life. His descendants retained their wealth and social position for generations and many were listed in the Four Hundred.

3

Mr. Make-A-Lister

When he electrified the press and its readers in 1892 by naming the Four Hundred people who constituted New York Society, Samuel Ward McAllister was a short, plump, sixty-five year old with a bald head and a wagging goatee. His manner was patronizing and pompous, and he was an authority when cotillions, calling cards, and proper sauces and wines were under discussion. "He would spend ten minutes discussing the wording of an invitation," a friend said, "[and] the color of a sheet of note paper." He was more than happy to instruct in these arcane subjects ("keep your claret in the cellar and your Madeira in the attic"), and eager to make pronouncements on New York Society and the relative positions of its members. By 1892 he had been manning the social barricades in New York for thirty years.

He was a Georgian, born in Savannah in 1827. A faint Georgia accent was detectable under the nobby British speech mannerisms ("Don'tcherknow" and "Howjedo") that he affected. He was no parvenu: his family, although not plantation rich, were Southern gentry with some superior connections in the Northern states and spent summers in Newport. A great-uncle was Francis Marion, hero of the American Revolutionary War battles in the South, known as "the Swamp Fox" for his cunning in evading his British pursuers.

McAllister's father, Matthew Hall McAllister, "a grave man with fine manners," his niece Maude Elliott remembered, was a lawyer, a judge, twice mayor of Savannah, and a member of the Georgia State Legislature. Ward's mother, Louisa Charlotte Cutler, "a splendid looking woman, tall, very straight, with side ringlets and a small waist," Elliott remembered, was a Newport girl and the aunt of Julia Ward Howe, author of *The Battle Hymn of the Republic*, of "Uncle Sam" Ward, a very successful lobbyist in Washington, D.C., and their sister Louisa, wife first of Thomas Crawford, the accomplished American sculptor who spent most of his life in Italy, and, second, of the expatriate American painter Luther Terry. Francis Marion Crawford, a best-selling novelist in his time, was her son. Ward McAllister deferred to the Astors, but by any contemporary standard he was better-born than they were. Unlike most Southerners of his day and class, however, McAllister preferred discussing the pedigrees of New York millionaires to talking about his own. He was the white sheep of his distinguished family. In the myriad letters of Julia Ward Howe, F. Marion Crawford, and Laura Howe Richards the children's writer, all kin, they mention McAllister very little, probably because as intellectuals and achievers they looked down on what they considered the frivolous New York Society where he spent his life. His cousin Maude Howe Elliott once wrote with somewhat muted praise, "He was a man of social gift and charm who did much to preserve the more elegant traditions of an earlier day." His uncle Sam Ward was the only one among them who cared about Society and moved in fashionable circles: his first wife was Emily Astor, William Astor's daughter; this marriage constituted the tenuous link between McAllister and the Astor family. McAllister felt some affinity for Sam, a man who loved good living and was very conscious of his social position ("Sam Ward could strut even when sitting down"), but he seldom referred to his more intellectual relations. He never talked or wrote much about Georgia, either, where he grew up, or California, where he had some success as a lawyer. From mid-century, when he settled in New York, until his death forty years later, New York and Newport bounded his horizons. He never considered "going South" during the Civil War; his only battles were in the social wars.

As a young man on his first trip to New York, McAllister visited a rich relative (he does not mention her name in his memoirs but it was undoubtedly one of his Ward relations), a spinster from whom he hoped to inherit a fortune, or from whom he "had expectations" as he expressed it. Despite his cousinly attentions, she left him nothing. When another relation did leave him $1,000, a substantial sum, he spent the entire legacy on a costume for a fancy-dress ball given by a patroness he had found, Mrs. John C. Stevens, the well-connected (she was a Livingston from the Hudson River aristocracy) wife of the Commodore of the New York Yacht Club. Known as "Mrs. Commodore Stevens," she was an eccentric who alternately dressed in the most expensive new fashions or looked like an old clothes woman, shocking New York Society by walking her dog, "led on a string," down Broadway. Ladies did not walk dogs in public; that was servants'

Like many cartoonists, Thomas Nast, famous for his political caricatures in Harper's Weekly, *found the pompous Ward McAllister with his Olympian dictates about Society a fitting subject for his pen.*

work. When she gave a party, it was a dazzling masquerade. Even as a young man, McAllister did not have the figure for doublet and tights, and he seems to have passed unnoticed in the crowd. He went to parties indefatigably, however. By day, he worked as a book-keeper. He regarded this employment and this period in his life as the nadir of his fortunes. Weary of the struggle to impress New York Society, he returned to Savannah to "read law" with his father. But the recently discovered California gold soon affected his life.

Brother Hall McAllister was the first member of the family to go to California. After being admitted to the Georgia bar, he set off on a trip around the world, during which he heard of the discovery of gold in California. He broke off his trip at San Francisco, not going to the fields, however, but building up a law practice in claims, a much more lucrative profession as it turned out. He persuaded his father, Matthew McAllister, and Ward to join him there in the practice of law by the effective method of sending them one of his fees, a bag of gold dust worth $4,000. They went, although both at first thought they were foolish to forfeit assured, though not very remunerative, positions in Savannah for chancy California. Matthew retired after two years, during which he had made a fortune, and went to live in Europe. After a few years, he returned to California and remained there for the rest of his life, a model citizen and civic leader in San Francisco and eventually a federal judge. McAllister Street, one of San Francisco's principal streets, is named for him. Brother Hall also became an important California judge. Their memorable legal careers and municipal endeavors and the respect they gained on the West Coast form a strange contrast to Ward McAllister's life of Society maneuvering and tutoring on the East Coast. For Ward, with his taste for elegance and ritual, Gold Rush California was clearly not the place to settle; it was not noted for its gentility and had little call for a social arbiter. Already it was McAllister's ambition to be more than a member of New York Society—through his mother's family he was born to that—he wanted to lead it.

In 1852 he returned to the East with a modest fortune; California, like Georgia, was forgotten for the rest of his life. In Washington, D. C., he used the political connections of his cousin Sam Ward not to obtain office, but to advance socially. He managed, for example, to be named to the committee of the inaugural ball for President Franklin Pierce. It was a start. Another step in his progress was marrying in 1853 a lady named Sarah Taintor Gibbons, who had money (she was described as "a Georgia heiress") and a personality so mild and unobtrusive that, unlike her husband, she was hardly ever noticed by anyone. They had two sons and a daughter and lived most of their lives in a house on East 19th Street.

The McAllisters went to Europe in 1857, apparently on a delayed honeymoon. They spent two years there, with Paris as headquarters, passing the winters in the town of Pau in the Pyrenees, and summers at Baden-Baden, the great German spa. McAllister used the trip to prime himself for social authority: he studied protocol and food and wine. In his autobiography, published in 1891 under the title *Society As I Have Known It*, he recounted his conferences with experts on these essential matters in his usual condescending manner. He gave dinners of which he boasts at length in his book, but he does not appear to have made many distinguished acquaintances. He did meet some young sprigs of the English nobility whom he entertained when they visited New York later, but it was easy to get titled English people to entertain in the New World; some of them openly boasted of the way they took advantage of American generosity. Americans loved titles: even the cynical George Templeton Strong confided to his diary his pride in entertaining some young lord or the other. In the town of Windsor, McAllister met one of Queen Victoria's chefs and heard about the palace menus. In Germany, he dined at a restaurant "within one or two tables" of the Prince of Prussia (afterwards Kaiser Wilhelm I) and noted what the royal party ordered (he was disappointed, the meal was very simple). He blandly related these encounters in his book, apparently undisturbed that he had only skirted the fringe of high life. He and his wife were not presented at any court, although scores of Americans, after being vouched for by the local American ambassador, were then making their bows before various sovereigns.

In 1858 the McAllisters turned up in Newport, then a modest little resort on unpretentious and unprosperous Aquidneck Island, far from the summer showplace of the Gilded Age it later became. McAllister, who had known the place since childhood, called it "the most enjoyable and luxurious little island in America." Cousin Julia Ward Howe was already there, beginning an annual summer residence that lasted until her death in 1910, when she was the grand old lady of both American letters and America's premier American summer resort. McAllister bought "Bayside Farm." It wasn't really a farm, of course—the sandy soil was hardly suitable for growing anything but social aspirations—but a good setting for outdoor, or *plein air*, as McAllister would say, entertaining. He rented a flock of Southdown sheep and several cows to lend a little rustic verisimilitude. At Bayside Farm, he and the shrinking Sarah gave a series of picnics, which he preferred to call *fêtes champêtres*; his guests drank champagne and danced on the grass after reaching the McAllister place in beribboned farm wagons. He often served what he called "Saratoga Lake dinners," referring to the upstate New York resort rapidly losing out to Newport as the place to be seen: Spanish mackerel, Saratoga (potato) chips, soft-shell crab, woodcock, chicken partridges, and lettuce salad. The dinners and dancing were much enjoyed, and the air was filled with coy allusions to Marie Antoinette and her courtiers frolicking at her royal play farm. Newport loved the picnics. McAllister had brought some vivacity into a resort then noted for its simplicity and propriety. "Life, for him to enjoy it," wrote Mrs. John King Van Rensselaer, who knew him well and was a keen observer of the social scene, "had to be gilt-edged and multi-colored."

His Newport success boosted McAllister's stock in New York, where he spent the winters. He joined the Union Club and was a regular member of the committees that received distinguished persons visiting the city. Reception committees were very important in New York and other large American cities for most of the nineteenth century; no important visitor escaped being "waited on by a committee of gentlemen" anxious to do him honor, to invite him to their houses, and to ask him as many questions as possible, most of which foreign visitors such as Dickens and Thackeray found impertinent. When the Prince of Wales visited New York in 1860, a high point of the city's social history in the nineteenth century, he was said to have behaved in a most friendly manner to McAllister, one of the committee to receive him and a guest at the famous ball in honor of the prince. In fact, McAllister was supposed, not least by himself, to resemble the prince physically. Years later, the satiric *Life* magazine proposed that McAllister and "Albert E. Wettin" (Wettin was the royal family's name) should run on a ticket for president and vice-president of the United States. The resemblance ended with their being short and square; the Prince of Wales (later Edward VII) was fourteen years younger and all his life sleekly groomed and a clothes horse, while McAllister was aggressively indifferent to his appearance.

At the time, New York was in what McAllister considered a state of social innocence. Big spending on lavish living had only just begun; it was, after all, only five years after the conclusion of the Civil War and new millionaires were feeling their way. McAllister wrote: "At this time there were not more than one or two men in New York who spent in living and entertaining over $60,000 a year. There were not half a dozen chefs in private families in this city." He took it upon himself to show the way. He could gas on for hours about the proper way to *frappé* (he would never use a simple word like chill). The wine ought to be placed in a tub of ice for exactly twenty-five minutes, after which, according to McAllister, a few flakes of ice would appear in the neck of the bottle when the wine was poured. "This is a real *frappé*," he declared triumphantly. When it came to dinners, he was rather conservative in his choices of dishes, and his dinners, although he boasted of them, were not very innovative. On October 9, 1880, for example, he gave a dinner at the Union Club which began with green turtle soup and oysters and proceeded through turkey, lamb chops, veal chops, lettuce salad, and ice cream. Perhaps the only thing on the menu that was a little unusual was a boiled sheep's head with Hollandaise sauce.

McAllister's rise in New York was not meteoric; before he achieved a position leading Society, or at least making the public believe he led it, he patiently served a long and somewhat bumpy apprenticeship attending dinners and balls and serving on committees. But he was steadily working toward a more solid position—and at the same time as Mrs. Astor. Their stars were bound to cross. His first move was a series of "cotillion suppers" that he organized in 1866–1867. These acquainted him with some of the social leaders of the time, mainly ladies. In the season 1870-1871, he arranged small subscription balls in "the blue rooms" at Delmonico's restaurant. There were three hundred subscribers. In 1872 he organized "The Patriarchs," twenty-five socially elect men who gave three sub-scription balls a year. "Subscription" meant you had to take the whole series. The name "The Patriarchs "was feebly humorous, as the members were actually for the most part quite young. McAllister liked to refer to the Patriarchs as "an American Almack's," and he made the doubtful claim that the comparison caught on in New York. Almack's, the nineteenth-century ballroom in London run by lady patronesses that set social standards and was a sort of supreme court that ruled who should be received and who banned, appears in innumerable Victorian letters and memoirs. In a rare egalitarian mood McAllister asserted that the Patri-archs was actually a democratic organization, "thoroughly representative," in which met New Yorkers of colonial descent, "our adopted citizens [he meant people from other American cities, not immigrants]," and "men whose ability and integrity had won the esteem of the community, and who formed an important element in Society," in other words, the new rich. He assured the Old Guard that the new rich would be subdued: "We wanted the money power," he said, "but not in any way to be controlled by it."

The twenty-five original Patriarchs were as follows, bold-face indicating a gentleman who twenty years later would be one of the first Four Hundred. The order of names on the list is McAllister's:

John Jacob Astor	Edwin A. Post
William Astor	A. Gracie King
De Lancey Kane	**Lewis M. Rutherfurd**
Ward McAllister	Robert G. Remsen
George Henry Warren	William C. Schermerhorn
Eugene A. Livingston	Francis R. Rives
William Butler Duncan	**Maturin Livingston**
E. Templeton Snelling	**Alexander Van Rensselaer**
Lewis Colford Jones	Walter Langdon
John W. Hamersley	F. G. D'Hauteville
Benjamin S. Welles	C. G. Goodhue
Frederick Sheldon	William R. Travers
Royal Phelps	

A member was entitled to invite four ladies and five gentlemen to each ball. McAllister managed the festivities and took his responsibility very gravely. "Man-aging" meant ordering food and drink and musicians, determining the order of the dances, and arranging the quadrilles, an indispensable feature of any ball, and composing the guest list. The last was the weightiest duty, and the one that McAllister felt most important. From the beginning, he fretted that "nobodies" without proper credentials would creep in and mar the perfect social symmetry of the evening. Each Patriarch was plainly told he was responsible for the acceptability of his guests. "If any objectionable element was introduced," McAllister wrote in almost constitutional terms (he was a lawyer, after all), "it was the Management's duty to at once let it be known by whom such objectionable party was invited, and to notify the Patriarch so offending that he had done us an injury and pray him to be circumspect. He then stood before the community as a sponsor of his guest, and all Society, knowing the offense he had committed, would so upbraid him that he would go and sin no more."

As an assistant, McAllister hired a factotum called "Johnson" (called by his last name as Isaac Brown was called "Brown" to indicate he had some position and was not an ordinary servant; in that case he would have been merely "Isaac" or "John"). Johnson vetted invitation cards at the door. He took his duty with deadly seriousness and became as autocratic as his employer. At one of the balls of the 1888–1889 season a row broke out when Johnson stopped Miss Elsie de Wolfe (many years later the famous interior decorator) because her invitation was "irregular." The matter was straightened out and Miss de Wolfe admitted, but the snub hurt, since the de Wolfe family's social position was at best precarious and the incident called attention to that sad fact.

The Patriarchal decree was the earliest manifestation of McAllister's ambition: the direction of New York Society. Although no one had asked him, he assumed the mantle of authority, deciding who was in Society and who was not, issuing his decisions with Old Testament firmness. His rules were odd and not entirely consistent: sometimes one member of a family was accepted while others were ignored. McAllister was more than usually pontifical on the subject: "Fashion selects its own votaries. You will see certain members of a family born to it, as it were, others of the same family with none of its attributes. You can give no explanation of this; 'One is taken, the other left.' Such and such a man or woman is cited as having always been fashionable. The talent of and for Society develops itself as does a talent for art." Many are called, in other words, but few are chosen, and those by McAllister. He divided Society into the "Nobs" and the "Swells." Nobs were the older families and were admitted without any application, unless they had committed some grievous social solecism. The Swells might be admitted, but they had to prove themselves first by the proper clothes, a dignified style of entertaining, conduct, and acquaintances. McAllister said coolly, "You can never be absolutely certain whether people are in Society or not until you see them at four or five of the best houses. Then you can make advances to them without the danger of making a mistake." He liked to talk as though acceptance into New York Society was a lengthy procedure, like progress from a knighthood to the peerage. Actually, this being America, advance could be quite rapid: it used to be said that two successful seasons in Newport could insure acceptance in New York. It is amazing that anyone paid any attention to McAllister's twaddle, but thousands did. He had a vision of Society although he was never able to articulate it clearly; he was a terrible writer and not much better as a speaker. In his book *Society as I Have Found It*, he fumbled for a reason for his career, but sputtered in futile pomposities. Mrs. Winthrop Chanler's explanation of his list of the Four Hundred was: "He mentioned them all by name and made a sort of diagram of the hierarchy, not unlike Dante's description of Paradise with the greater and lesser saints in their appointed places around the Mystic Rose."

The historical figure on whom Ward McAllister seemed to model himself and to whom he liked to be compared, was Richard Nash, called "Beau Nash." That eighteenth-century gentleman was the social arbiter of Bath, the English spa town. Nash was elevated on his own initiative to the post of master of ceremonies of the Bath Assembly Rooms, where he passed on the social credentials of visitors, introduced guests to one another, arranged dancing partners, and maintained the decorum of each dance. He was responsible in large part for the emergence of Bath as a social center of England in the eighteenth century. McAllister saw himself as the social director of New York, presiding over an orderly scene where only the "right" people were admitted, and once admitted performed a stately pageant with requisite dignity. He was obsessed with "fixed position" in Society; in his numerous statements to the press he always harked back to that expression. He relished comparing European society, of which he actually knew little, with American, always to the latter's disadvantage: in London, he lamented, "everyone has a fixed position, but in New York they have not," adding, "The present is an era of multi-millionaires, who aim at keeping out as many of their kind as possible from the inner circle which they have formed." McAllister may have fantasized, but he was certainly sincere. When he told the press that "There is no power like the social power; it makes and unmakes," he meant it, and his lifework was supporting this dubious proposition.

It was in connection with the founding of the Patriarchs in 1872 that he became friends with Mrs. William Astor, whom he made "special adviser" to the group, to help him in assessing credentials. She was forty-two, he was forty-five. Both were marching steadily toward the top positions in New York Society, Mrs.

Astor slowly and diligently, supported by her husband's colossal wealth, her own considerable fortune, and her Knickerbocker ancestry; he with good connections, some financial means, and ample leisure to meditate on precedence and protocol. Caroline Astor and Ward McAllister viewed Society in America as urgently in need of guidance. "Profiteers, boors, boorish people, people with only money," said McAllister, must be kept out. Those admitted must have what McAllister called "the three B's": birth, background, and breeding. Together, they proposed rules of society as rigid as the Code Napoléon.

Once the Patriarchs flourished, McAllister organized another group that met regularly, the Family Circle Dancing Class. This was not exactly what the name indicates: the subscribers were not children; they were young men and women chosen more for the prominence of their families than any desire to practice cotillions. McAllister passed on all applications. Unkind people said that he arranged the classes so that his ugly daughter might meet eligible young men. Six private houses were selected for the rendezvous of the Family Circle Dancing Class: William Butler Duncan's, William Astor's, De Lancey Kane's, George Henry Warren's, Lewis Colford Jones's, and Ward McAllister's. The evenings began with general dancing, then at eleven o'clock there was a quadrille of sixteen couples. Each of these had a theme with costumes: "Mother Goose," "Pinafore" with music from the hit Gilbert & Sullivan operetta and men wearing sailors' uniforms with straw hats and flying ribbons, and the "Hunting Quadrille" with the men wearing the traditional pink coats. According to McAllister, the Family Circle Dancing Class involved him in unaccustomed labor, much of it of a delicate nature. "My mornings were given up to being interviewed of and about [the classes]; mothers would call at my house, entirely unknown to me, the sole words of introduction being, "Kind sir, I have a daughter."

In 1880 *The Home Journal* called McAllister "the prime factor of social gayeties [sic] in New York." By 1890, he was so famous that his name featured in an advertisement: a druggist named "Dr." Campbell, who had invented "arsenic complexion wafers for men's youthfulness" and sold them at his shop at 220 Sixth Avenue, took out a newspaper advertisement saluting McAllister as "principal ancestor of the fourteen hundred assembled at the Metropolitan Opera House on the occasion of the late New Year's ball. . . . The McAllister ball in point of elegance, economy and completeness knocked the Centennial ball into a 'cocked hat.' Long live Ward McAllister!" (Arsenic may seem an odd product to have attached to your name but for most of the nineteenth century both men and women were convinced that the ingestion of arsenic was highly beneficial to the skin, and they did not hesitate to take the dangerous drug in various forms, not always with the desired result.) This much-admired ball was given on New Year's Eve at the Academy of Music. Three hundred servants in livery waited on 1,400 guests. Fourteen hundred is hardly an exclusive group so people asked: what of McAllister's rigid limiting of Society? McAllister defensively explained that for such a large assemblage "we go outside the exclusive fashionable set, and invite professional men, doctors, lawyers, editors, artists and the like," whom he apparently was kindly prepared to treat as though they were real people.

Years of such labors had paid off: by 1892 McAllister had enjoyed a decade of social authority. After a ball in 1884 an anonymous lady wrote to him the following lines which he reprinted gleefully in his memoirs:

> He does not reign in Russia cold,
> Nor yet in far Cathay
> But o'er this town he's come to hold an undisputed sway
> When in their might the ladies rose,
> "To put the Despot down,"
> As blandly as Ah Sin, he goes
> His way without a frown.
> Alas! Though he's but one alone,
> He's one too many still—
> He's fought the fight, he's held his own,
> And to the end he will.

McAllister had developed his philosophy and rationale for society in numerous statements to the press and in his memoirs. His thoughts had a rather apologetic air, and he felt it wise to justify them: "The elegancies of fashionable life nourish and benefit art and [the] arts," McAllister declared. The spending of money was a good thing as it distributed the wealth. Society brightened and enlivened life and its performances "really prevent our people and country from settling down into a humdrum rut and becoming merely a money-making and money-saving people. . . ." Contradicting himself about the values of the past, McAllister declared that, "Progress is fashion's watchword; it never stands still; it always advances, it values and appreciates beauty in woman and talent and genius in man." Along with his philosophy, McAllister dispensed advice to aspirants to Society. His golden rule was, "If you want to be fashionable, be always in the company of fashionable people."

A happy date in McAllister's life should have been the great Centennial Ball held at the Metropolitan Opera House in 1889, a major New York occasion since

George Washington had been inaugurated as first president of the United States in downtown New York on April 30, 1789. McAllister assumed he was to manage the ball, but the committee, consisting of Hamilton and Stuyvesant Fish, Elbridge T. Gerry, and Colonel William Jay, the very gentlemen whose birth and manners McAllister most admired, did not recommend him, Stuyvesant Fish saying unkindly to the press, "McAllister is a discharged servant. That is all." In revenge, McAllister referred to the party as a "Fishball" and poked heavy-handed fun at guests he found unworthy. But the slur was a serious setback in his career. Dr. Campbell's advertisement, which sneered at the Centennial Ball that McAllister did not manage and praised the New Year's Ball that McAllister *did* manage, may well have been a plant. He was actually an excellent and justly admired manager of festivities. In 1894 it was estimated that giving a private dinner party for a dozen guests in New York involved the host in an expense of $200 to $300. Bradley Martin of the Four Hundred, a lawyer from Albany married to an heiress, gave a dinner and ball for four hundred guests—that magic number—in the early 1890s that cost $10,000. Yet the three balls given each season by the Patriarchs under McAllister's management cost them a mere $6,250 total. Ever-curious reporters asked McAllister how he kept costs so comparatively low? He blandly replied that "my influence among florists and caterers, together with contacts of twenty years' standing" were the reasons.

McAllister did not always abide by his own supposedly inflexible rules of admission to Society; he played favorites. Talk as he might about "birth, background, and breeding," when he chose, McAllister overlooked these supposed inflexible requirements. The list of the Four Hundred was studded with names that could not possibly have met his stated requirements. Take, for example, Mary Victoria Leiter, a great favorite of his, who was not a New Yorker, had no connections among the Knickerbocracy, and was the daughter of a tradesman—a very successful one, but without doubt, a tradesman. Her father, Levi Ziegler Leiter, was a Pennsylvania German who had been the original partner of Marshall Field in his Chicago department store. Living with her parents at Dupont Circle in Washington, D.C., Mary Victoria came to New York for a Patriarchs' Ball, where she met McAllister, who immediately asked her to lead the grand march and later listed her among his Four Hundred.

In 1888 McAllister began to refer to "The Four Hundred" when speaking of New York Society, the way one refers to an unseen but awesome power. He was deliberately mysterious about the group, only specific enough to state that Mrs. Astor's ballroom held that number comfortably. More importantly, he

*Mary Victoria Leiter
was introduced to
New York Society by
Ward McAllister.
He would have been
gratified to know that
she later married the
British statesman
Lord Curzon and
became Vicereine
of India.*

thought there were only about four hundred people in New York who would feel comfortable there. "If you go outside that number," he said, "you strike those who are either not at ease in a ballroom or else make other people not at ease." That is the generally accepted story about the origin of the famous phrase. There is another version, told much later by Frank Crowninshield. According to this version, a reporter asked McAllister how many guests he expected at the next Patriarchs' Ball. "Well," said McAllister, "I suppose about as many as the ballroom at Delmonico's will hold." When asked to be more specific, he consulted his wife, who said, "About four hundred." (This is the only recorded remark by Sarah Gibbons McAllister). The next day the newspapers declared in excited language that

Ward McAllister had said there were only four hundred people in Society in New York.

The press immediately adopted the phrase "The Four Hundred," which satisfied the public's desire for an exact, if cryptic, figure and the journalists' need for a convenient shorthand. Next, they demanded a list of names. McAllister was in the proud position of having invented a phrase that inspired an obvious question—who *are* the Four Hundred?—that only he could answer. He relished the position, but he couldn't hold off the press indefinitely. By 1892 he must have seen that he couldn't keep up the suspense forever and had to answer the question. He chose the occasion of Mrs. Astor's annual ball to give the press the names of the Four Hundred. Typically, he had not thought out his answer: he could only come up with 319 names, and those represented just 169 families. The press was satisfied, and the list was published immediately in most of the city's sixteen daily newspapers and reprinted in a pamphlet. The curiosity was enormous; one can imagine readers who only knew Society from afar by poring over the list and playing the exciting game of discovering who was "in," and, much more exciting, who was "out." Some of the omissions were puzzling, and equally some of the inclusions.

In 1924, a generation after the list of the Four Hundred was published, Mrs. John King Van Rensselaer, born into the Old Guard and also married into it, wrote that, "Social distinction in America, at present, is a citadel set upon an eminence which can be scaled by any one of three routes—birth, wealth, or, less frequently, achievement. A half century ago a single trail led to that envied height . . . the sanctioned pathway of birth and breeding. A patrician lineage was then the prime requisite for recognition by Society. Social circles of that time were composed entirely of the established aristocracy." Despite the dreamy reveries of Mrs. Van Rensselaer, it was never true that high birth was the sole entryway into Society; American Society has always been more open. McAllister treated the Astors like royalty, but William Astor was the grandson of a German immigrant who never lost his accent, tanned hides for a living, and had primitive table manners. On McAllister's list were true American aristocrats of colonial lineage whose families had lengthy distinction as statesmen, judges, and clergy, but there were also: Richard Wilson, a poor boy from Tennessee who made a vast fortune in southern railroads; Luther Kountze, who started a bank in his hometown of Omaha, Nebraska; Anna Lusk, daughter of a successful gynecologist; and Mary Victoria Leiter. New York was not so particular about social credentials as other American cities: a list drawn up at the same time in Boston or Philadelphia would have been shorter and narrower, and not just because of the smaller size of the cities.

McAllister never apologized for his Four Hundred selections, but under a barrage of questioning he sometimes attempted to explain them. In general, the explanations were not very flattering to the chosen, and, in fact, for a man who prided himself on his social suavity, his remarks were frequently tactless and even wounding. He professed, for example, to be embarrassed that the first name on his list was Frederick H. Allen, and told the press dismissively, "It leads off, don't you see, with a little boy from Boston—Fred Allen. It puts him ahead of the Astors dontcherknow. Of course, that's an alphabetical accident . . . the Astors are at the very front of Society. . . ." (McAllister never failed to honor his Mystic Rose). Actually, Fred Allen came from a distinguished New England family with rather an exotic background: his father, originally American consul in the Hawaiian Islands, served the Hawaiian monarchy in various capacities and was eventually chief justice of the kingdom. Fred himself was partner in an important law firm and president of Pelham Manor, an aristocratic community at Pelham, north of New York. A few months later, in June 1892, he married Adele Livingston Stevens, the granddaughter of the Mrs. Commodore Stevens, who had invited McAllister to his first costume ball forty years before. Again, when the name of Heber Bishop was queried, McAllister said offhandedly, "[He] works for it, dontcherknow. He's an old man [he was fifty-two!], but he will work away dancing all night." This picture of senile dissipation hardly jibes with reality: Bishop was a man of substance, having made a fortune in Cuban sugar before he was twenty-one years old; he was a trustee of many institutions, including the Metropolitan Museum of Art, to which he bequeathed the famous collection of oriental jade that he had displayed in the handsome house he built at 881 Fifth Avenue. McAllister was quite without any sense of irony. He used to say, "Brains before Beauty and Mind before Money," when it was obvious from his own list that intelligence was not required for a place in Society if one had the blood of the Van Cortlandts or the money of the Astors. And certain members of Society could do no wrong: when Edward Neufville Tailer was criticized for wearing green suits in town at a time when men wore colors only in the country, McAllister said, "When you are a Tailer, married to a Suffern, you can wear what you please."

Society folk customarily professed a great horror of the press. J. P. Morgan once told young Cornelius Vanderbilt, Jr., who was aspiring to newspaper work, "That's awful! A journalist usually winds up by either becoming a chronic drunkard or by remaining a journalist. I do not know which is worse." But a large audience of readers developed in the 1880s who would never themselves attend the best parties and were therefore fascinated by them. As Marcel Proust was to write a little later, "parties have no reality until the next day, when they fix the attention of those who were not invited."

The Home Journal, a weekly much read by Society, began carrying its "Social Intelligencer" column in 1867. By the 1880s Society news was being printed regularly by many newspapers. Once the press got in, it was impossible to control. From respectful reports of balls and receptions that merely gave the names of guests and a description of the floral decorations (but seldom the food), the press moved on to comment, not always respectfully. Society news soon became Society gossip. Hostesses learned that if they wanted flattering reports of their entertaining, they had better be gracious to the press and supply guest lists.

Mrs. Astor made no comment on the list and never acknowledged its existence. She never gave interviews to the press and was serenely unaware of its ravenous interest in her and her entertaining. She notoriously disliked gossip, and the list of the Four Hundred could be classified as gossip. Her real attitude is shown by her personal address book, which still exists, and by the names of guests at her parties printed in the newspapers. They were almost invariably drawn from the Four Hundred, proving that despite its omissions and inaccuracies, it was indeed the queen's almanac. McAllister, on the other hand, as her chamberlain, gave no sign of being annoyed by questions about the Four Hundred. In any event, he was impervious to criticism, believing, it seems, that with the strong support of Society women, he could make what pronouncements he pleased. The men of Society hardly more than tolerated him, but he ruled the kingdom of the Amazons. The separation between the sexes was extremely marked in America. Foreigners were always amazed at the power of women in America, nowhere more than in Society. Men, for the most part, left Society to their wives and daughters, and they left McAllister to them, too. He was neither sportsman nor businessman; his profession of social arbiter was not in the businessmen's ken. Caricaturists found him hilarious and could be quite cruel. Perhaps McAllister felt it was better to be scorned than ignored. As to the possibility he knew he was absurd and played to the gallery, that does not seem likely: his memoirs and his numerous statements to the press ring with good faith and lack of self-consciousness. Most of the ladies who knew him well treated him kindly when they came to write their memoirs. Mrs. Reginald de Koven, wife of the well-connected composer ("Oh, Promise Me") called him "the solemnly devoted social arbiter, who firmly believed that his mission was to allot the proper places to everyone in the social heaven." She thought his list was on the whole accurate and commendable, which was generous of her because her name did not appear. "The Four Hundred," she said, " whose limited scope really did include what was best in New York in those days, was his enumeration if not his creation." The sharper, or more disillusioned, Elizabeth Drexel Lehr said, however, that Ward McAllister arrived on the scene "with the idea that he was born to keep Society up to a standard which—he never seemed to realize—it had attained without his help."

To the press he was "the greatest snob that ever lived," "the Guardian of the Gates," and "The Lord High Separator of the Sheep from the Goats." After the list of the Four Hundred was finally released, he was known as "Mr. Make-a-Lister." He and his life work particularly amused and annoyed Charles Dana Gibson, who began his work as caricaturist of the Gilded Age in 1885, most of his work appearing in the comic *Life* magazine (not the present-day *Life* magazine). He himself came from an old family, once well-to-do, who lived in Flushing during his childhood. (The saying was that decayed families "lived in the Oranges, if they had lost some of their money; in Morristown, if they had lost most of their money; and in Flushing if they had lost all their money"). Generally speaking, when satirizing "high Society," which he did in hundreds of drawings, Gibson never used real names in the captions. McAllister was the exception; Gibson regarded him as fair game. The cartoons were pointed and clever: one showed McAllister riding on a hobbyhorse leading a parade of the Four Hundred. "Each marcher appeared with tabards and banners emblazoned with his escutcheon," wrote Gibson's biographer. "Fur pelts, lumber, groceries, and money bags were among the designs on these coats-of-arms." Another time he was shown by Gibson as an old woman ladling out "Society slush" to pedigreed poultry. Yet again, McAllister was a goose girl herding a flock of the elite. How ironic that in 1893 Gibson met Irene Langhorne, his future bride, at a Patriarchs' Ball where McAllister had just asked her to lead the grand march with him.

Later in 1892, after the list had given him nationwide fame, McAllister was scheduled to attend, with a group of New York Society figures, the opening of a tony new health resort, the Four Seasons Hotel, at Land Gap, Tennessee. His visit was announced in the local newspapers and even in those remote parts elicited excitement, or to be more exact, curiosity: mountain folk flocked to see "the greatest dude in the world." As it turned out, McAllister wasn't able to attend but, according to Constance Cary, one of the New York party, James Brown Potter was jestingly pointed out to the locals as McAllister. One "butternut-garbed horseman in cowhide boots," wrote Cary, "gazed his fill at this unfamiliar figure and said, 'Waal, I've rid fifteen miles a-purpus to see that dude McAllister, an' I don't begrutch it, not a mite."

The Van Rensselaers were at the core of the Knickerbocracy along with the Livingstons, Beekmans, de Peysters, and Van Cortlandts. Alexander Van Rensselaer, in later life a notable yachtsman, was painted at the age of twenty-three by the Society portraitist G. P. A. Healy.

4

The Knickerbocracy

With the air of imparting a state secret, Ward McAllister once wrote: "Behind what I call 'the smart set' in Society, there always stood the old, solid, substantial, and respected people. Families who held great social power as far back as the birth of this country, who were looked up to by Society, and who always could, when they so wished, come forward and exercise their power." As usual, he overstated the case, but it is true that anyone in New York with social ambitions, or even an interest in the workings of Society, looked up to the one group that was, unquestionably, at the pinnacle. The "Knickerbockers" were the old, genealogically secure, and rich families of colonial Dutch descent—Van Rensselaers, Van Cortlandts, de Peysters, Schuylers, Suydams, Beekmans, Rhinelanders, Schermerhorns. They were Caroline Astor's tribe: she was born a Schermerhorn, her grandmother was a Van Cortlandt, and her husband was descended from the Schuylers and the Beekmans. Throughout her career she surrounded herself with Knickerbockers; they were the core of the Four Hundred, though she never restricted her guest list only to the old families. There weren't enough of them for one thing: by 1892 they were not producing enough young people, the indispensable dancers, to fill her ballroom. Some Knickerbockers, including various members of her own family (due to disputes over inheritances) were out of her favor. Others were boring, indifferent to society, or too eccentric to be presentable. Like all great hostesses, too, she knew you couldn't congeal Society; fresh blood, properly vetted, of course, had to be introduced occasionally. Nevertheless, like the Princesse de Parme in Proust's novel who was willing to overlook failings in royalty she would never forgive in commoners, Caroline Astor always gave extra points to Knickerbockers when making out her guest lists. She didn't use that name, however. They never called themselves Knickerbockers. The term invented by Washington Irving, as we shall see, was satirical and slangy and distasteful to the aristocrats. They preferred "Old New York" when speaking of these families. Edith Wharton, whose mother was a Rhinelander and who knew well the society she described, called her great collection of short stories *Old New York*.

In nearly four hundred years of New York's history, the Dutch ruled for only forty years. Officials of the Dutch West India Company were the first to recognize the potential of the great harbor and "the long, skinny island between the North and East Rivers" and settled the first colonists on its shores. Dutch traders and homesteaders had already reached Albany, and the company granted vast patroonships in the wilderness on either side of the river. In New Amsterdam, the principal port of the colony, was laid from 1624 to 1664 the foundations of a world capital. Despite its brevity, the Dutch presence was stamped on the memory of later New Yorkers. The recollection, not very accurate, was of clean Dutch towns with industrious and genial inhabitants. The slovenliness of New Amsterdam and the notorious quarrelsomeness of its citizens were forgotten. Nostalgia for Dutch New York remained strong throughout the nineteenth century. Dutch-speaking villages, famously drowsy, thrived along the Hudson all the way to Albany: this was the land of Rip Van Winkle that Washington Irving knew so well and transformed into literature. New Amsterdam was never drowsy, or even orderly, but it was pleasant for New Yorkers of the late nineteenth century, enmeshed as they were in municipal corruption and crowded by unintelligible immigrants, to reminisce on what they convinced themselves had been better days.

The Knickerbockers of 1892 were more than two centuries removed from their New Amsterdam ancestors, but, as Ward McAllister noted, they were still an identifiable group. Dignified, ponderous, and clannish, they tended to isolate themselves and to marry within a fairly restricted circle of other colonial families, mainly Dutch, English, and German. Newcomers were not quickly accepted by the Knickerbockers. Edith Wharton found Dutch traditions still strong in her childhood, and despised them. What the nostalgic viewed as dignified, she thought stodgy; what they admired as thrift, she regarded as stinginess; what they thought of as cautiousness, she thought of as timidity. It is true that the conservatism of the Knickerbockers had in many cases solidified into inactivity. Novelists and visitors to New York who were fascinated by the

Washington Irving, son of Scottish immigrants, wounded the feelings of many Old New Yorkers when he poked fun at their stodgy Dutch ancestors in the rollicking History of New York *that he published under the unforgettable name Diedrich Knickerbocker.*

Knickerbockers probably exaggerated their aloofness. While many of the men did not hold regular jobs, they were shrewd and quite capable of looking after the investments that supported their comfortable lifestyle. And the Knicker-bockers were, after all, New Yorkers, who could not live apart from their fellow citizens in this narrow and overcrowded city. They were involved in municipal affairs, not so much political life as charitable and cultural activities, prominently seated on the boards of libraries and schools, large donors to charities and sup-porters of churches.

Their strongest tradition was religious: the New York Dutch were staunch Protestants. Some of their ancestors had taken refuge in the Netherlands dur-

Washington Irving spent more than half of his adult life in Europe, but he was devoted to his native city: "There is a charm," he wrote of New York, "about that little spot on earth . . . that has a perfect spell over my imagination."

ing the religious wars of the sixteenth century, fleeing persecution by Roman Catholics before coming to America. The Reformed Church was the most important denomination in the colony. Services were very formal: the minister wore vestments and was escorted to the pulpit by the beadle, who carried a great bible on a cushion before him. A drift of congregations into the Anglican communion, the denomination of the ruling class in the colony, slowly followed English rule. The Reformed Church made some effort to accommodate: it was a major change when in 1763 the Middle Dutch Church on Nassau Street hired a minister who could preach in the English language as well as the traditional Dutch. New York was always a religiously diverse town; when Governor Peter Stuyvesant tried to prevent Jews, Quakers, and Lutherans from settling in the colony because he wanted it to be purely Calvinistic in faith, he was reprimanded by the citizens in the great Flushing Remonstrance of 1657, which appealed to the States General of Holland to confirm freedom of conscience. Nevertheless, there was among upper-class New Yorkers, who remembered the persecution of their ancestors, a persistent dislike of Roman Catholicism. When the Hamilton Fish family (descendants of Governor Stuyvesant) were touring Europe in the 1850s, Stuyvesant Fish, Jr., recalled, "Whenever the family spent Sunday in a Catholic town, they scrupulously recited the Episcopal service in their room." Fewer than half a dozen Roman Catholics appeared on McAllister's list.

Trinity and Grace were popular Episcopal churches with "Old New York," although *Town & Country* magazine claimed in 1900, that, "The old Knickerbocker families have adopted Calvary Church as their place of worship." Calvary, on Fourth Avenue (now Park Avenue South) and 21st Street was—and is— the church of Gramercy Park, the neighborhood where the Fish, Rutherfurd, Stuyvesant, and other Knickerbocker families lived. It was designed by a Knickerbocker, too, James Renwick, Jr., also the architect of Grace Church and St. Patrick's Cathedral.

Other strong traditions among the Knickerbockers were dignity, deference to rank, and solidity of possessions. Sobriety was never especially emphasized as a virtue, but a well-stocked table was admired: long, heavy meals were inevitable in Knickerbocker entertaining, and hostesses like Mrs. Astor kept their guests at table for two hours. The Dutch were not notable collectors of paintings, except the stiff portraits of their ancestors, or books, but their everyday possessions, especially silver, were weighty and solid and of fine workmanship.

The first use of the term "Knickerbocker" is precisely dated. Washington Irving, a twenty-six-year-old newspaper and magazine writer, fathered the term, using the pen name "Diedrich Knickerbocker" to author a burlesque narrative about New Amsterdam called *A History of New York from the Beginning of the World to the End of the Dutch Dynasty*, published in 1809. Knickerbakker ("marble baker") was the family name of a friend, John Knickerbakker; Irving thought the name hilarious and asked his friend if he could use it, with a few letters changed, for his satire. He also used the names of many Dutch families with living descendants, among them Van Rensselaer, Van Cortlandt, Beekman, and others.

Irving, the son of Scottish immigrants with no family connections whatever to Old New York, could not resist poking good-natured fun at the citizens

Gulian Crommelin Verplanck, a lawyer, theologian, and politician of Dutch descent, was pained by Irving's "vulgar" depiction of New Amsterdam and its hard-drinking Dutchmen in the Knickerbocker History *and publicly denounced it. The amiable Irving toned down some of the indiscretions in later editions.*

of New Amsterdam with names like Wouter van Twiller—what comic writer could? His book, really a collection of sketches, was immensely popular from the first with the general public. The English-descended inhabitants of New York and those of other origins liked seeing the haughty Dutch satirized. They roared over *Knickerbocker's History*, in which the Dutch colonists were depicted as none too bright and hopelessly befuddled by strong drink and the rasping tobacco they smoked in their long pipes. The descendants of Irving's characters, who became known against their will as Knickerbockers, did not at all care for the disrespectful treatment of their ancestors. Irving's irreverence toward the "van" families upset them greatly. In addition to being irreverent, the book was found "vulgar" and "coarse." While not exactly bawdy, *Knickerbocker's History* had an eighteenth-century frankness that was becoming unacceptable in the arriving Victorian age. Walt Whitman—of all people—and Ralph Waldo Emerson, among others, were distressed by the book's "coarseness."

In 1818, nine years after the *History* was published, Gulian C. Verplanck, himself a Knickerbocker, as might be guessed from his name, solemnly commented to the New-York Historical Society that, "It is painful to see a mind [Irving's] . . . wasting the riches of its fancy on an ungrateful theme, and its exuberant humour in a coarse caricature." Verplanck presented himself as a sober defender of old Dutch virtues, but he, too, had been a satirist: a few years earlier he had rioted with his classmates at the Columbia College commencement in 1811, been fined by Mayor De Witt Clinton, and thereafter published pamphlets brutally ridiculing Clinton and his political allies. Irving, a mild-mannered sort, took no offense, only remarking, "I offended many good families by bringing their names into [*The History*] in ludicrous points of view and several persons never forgave me for it." However, when a new edition of the work was demanded, he purged it of the gamier references to ancestors of living Knickerbockers. The Knickerbockers were not appeased and never got over their pique. Fifty years later members of old Dutch families still deplored Irving's picture of their ancestors. But literature triumphed over history and hurt feelings: Washington Irving won the day when his New Amsterdam became the accepted and enduring image. In his operetta town, Governor Peter Stuyvesant, actually intolerant and spiteful, is a lovable old coot, and the other local officials topers and bumblers. "Knickerbocker" was soon a word everyone knew, and it has had a long life, attached to beer, sports teams, and gossip columnists among other things. The term "Knickerbocracy" for these old Dutch families as a group was coined by Nathaniel Parker Willis, a lightweight essayist of the 1840s.

In 1835, probably to make further amends, Irving said coyly at a public dinner, "There did not exist such a thing as a society of old New Yorkers, some of whom I have written about sometime since." This peace-offering led to the formation of the St. Nicholas Society, the stated objective of which was the preservation of the early history of New York. According to the rules of admission a member (males only) had to be descended from a man, not necessarily Dutch, who had settled in New York before the year 1785. The name St. Nicholas, the patron saint of Holland, clearly emphasized the Dutch element. The date was of course that of the end of the American Revolution, but it permitted the membership of Irving himself; his parents had arrived in New York in 1763. There was certainly some hatchet-burying: Peter Gerard Stuyvesant was the first president of the society, and when Gulian Verplanck succeeded him, Washington Irving was first vice-president.

It took half a century for the true Knickerbockers to respond—they were not a fast-moving race—but in 1885 they organized the Holland Society, with much narrower requirements than the St. Nicholas, restricting membership to descendants in the male line of Dutch who had settled in New York prior to 1675, or descendants of families that had taken refuge in the Low Countries before coming to America. Both the St. Nicholas and Holland Societies are still active. The Knickerbocker Club, founded in 1871 as an offshoot of the Union Club, merely took a well-known New York expression as its name and never had any genealogical requirements.

Among the best known Knickerbocker families were the Van Cortlandts, who arrived in New Amsterdam in 1637; the Schermerhorns (Mrs. Astor's family), who came in 1643; the Kips, also arriving in 1643; the Stuyvesants, descendants of Governor Peter Stuyvesant, who came to govern New Amsterdam in 1647; the Beekmans, who came with Stuyvesant; the Schuylers (1650); and the Van Rensselaers (1658). Added to them were families that were actually French but had been living as Protestant refugees in the Netherlands before they came to America, such as the de Peysters (1649), Goelets (1667), and Lispenards (1670). Any list of the Knickerbocracy abounded in social subtleties. The Vanderbilt family, for example, was rarely included although their ancestor Jan Aertson van der Bilt had settled in Flatbush in 1650. The Vanderbilts had not flourished during the colonial period, remaining poor farmers until Cornelius Vanderbilt, "the Commodore," began his rise to wealth early in the nineteenth century. It was seldom admitted, but social standing among the Knickerbockers depended on wealth as well as ancestry. It was not until the Commodore's descendants had become rich that their colonial ancestry was remembered and Cornelius Vanderbilt II became president of the St. Nicholas Society and numerous Vanderbilts figured among the Four Hundred.

While some of these families came to the tiny Dutch settlements on the edge of civilization to better themselves, others did not fit the image of the bedraggled and desperate immigrant. Kiliaen Van Rensselaer, whose descendants still pepper the pages of the *Social Register*, belonged to a family prominent in the Gelderland province of The Netherlands. A jeweler in Amsterdam, he was rich enough to be a shareholder and a founding member of the Dutch

Stephen Van Rensselaer,
ancestor or kinsman of
many members of the Four
Hundred, was the "Last
Patroon" of his family's vast
land holdings around
Albany. He was president
of the Erie Canal
Company and founded
Rensselaer Polytechnic
Institute. In his old age
he was painted by
Chester Harding.

West India Company, sponsor of the colony of New Netherland. His nephew, Wouter van Twiller, was at one time governor of the colony, a remarkably inept one. In 1629, just twenty years after Henry Hudson's discovery of the river that bears his name, Kiliaen Van Rensselaer's agents were buying land along the Hudson in what are now Albany, Rensselaer, and Columbia counties from the Indian tribes. By the time they had finished, Van Rensselaer was the owner of no fewer than 700,000 acres and was called "the Patroon," a title of great respect among the colonists. Kiliaen died in Amsterdam in 1643 without ever seeing his New World principality, but his nephew, Jeremias Van

Rensselaer, came out to New Netherland in 1658 and established the family in the colony. His descendants were patroons for generations. The last to preside over the family's vast inheritance was Stephen Van Rensselaer called, even during his lifetime, "the last patroon." His estate was disturbed by a series of violent disputes with his tenant farmers (there were 2,000 of them!) known as the "anti-rent wars." The New York State Legislature, responding to complaints about "feudal" practices on the great Hudson River estates, passed laws that effectively broke them up. After that, few Van Rensselaers were truly rich, but they were still prominent in Society: three Van Rensselaers were listed by McAllister and at least a dozen more members of the Four Hundred had Van Rensselaer blood.

Oloff Stevense Van Cortlandt, an ancestor of Caroline Astor and her many relatives among the Four Hundred, on the other hand, had no great connections at home in the Netherlands; he was merely a quick-witted soldier in the fort at New Amsterdam who saw the possibilities of commerce in the town and, retiring from the military, became a successful merchant. His son, Stephanus Van Cortlandt, in 1677 became the first native-born mayor of New York. The Van Cortlandts mostly lived in lower Manhattan, but from 1691 to 1889 they owned a thousand-acre estate in northwestern Bronx that they gave to New York City in 1889. Part of the acreage became the first municipal golf course in the United States, the remainder one of New York's largest parks.

The hero of Dutch New York and the only figure of seventeenth-century Manhattan permanently impressed on the American mind was Petrus (or Peter, as the English called him) Stuyvesant, ancestor of many nineteenth-century Knickerbockers. Washington Irving's image of him as a short-fused but essentially good-natured figure, far though it was from reality, has been preserved in painting, in fiction, and in Kurt Weill's musical comedy *Knickerbocker Holiday*. The reality was quite different: the Governor was opinionated, bad-tempered, and constantly at odds with his colonists and officials. "Peg-leg Pete," who had lost his right leg fighting the Portuguese in the West Indies, where he had previously been governor of the island of Curaçao, arrived in New Amsterdam in 1647 at the age of thirty-seven and stayed until his death twenty-five years later in 1672. After surrendering the city to the English in 1664 and seeing its name changed from New Amsterdam to New York, he retired from public life but remained in Manhattan. After a lifetime spent in the service of the Dutch West India Company in the Caribbean and New Netherland he would have been a stranger in his native Holland.

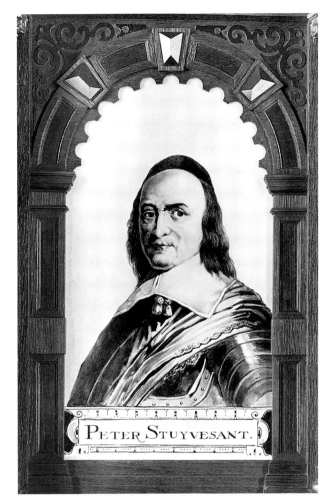

As the centuries passed Peter Stuyvesant's belligerence and attempts at tyranny were forgotten and he emerged as a kindly old Knickerbocker. In 1906 the Holland America Steamship line commissed this portrait for its ship SS New Amsterdam and had it photographed by the famous New York photographer Joseph Byron.

He had bought a *bouwerie* (Dutch for plantation) from the Company in 1651, 550 acres lying between present-day East Fifth and 23rd Streets from the East River to Fourth Avenue. Stuyvesant's country manor, surrounded by an orchard, stood approximately where present-day East 10th Street intersects Stuyvesant Street, just west of Second Avenue. The house was destroyed by fire in 1778. After his death the land was divided among his descendants, who continued to live thereabouts for generations, known in society as the "Second Avenue set." Although respected for their lineage and their wealth, they were usually regarded as back-numbers in the life of the city, self-absorbed and reclu-

St. Mark's-in-the-Bouwerie (Protestant Episcopal) church on East 10th Street stands on the site of Governor Peter Stuyvesant's private Dutch Reformed chapel and was attended by his descendants, many of whom lived nearby, for generations.

sive. In one of her society novels Mrs. Burton Harrison (Constance Cary) dismisses "the Second Avenue set" as "people who have bad throats and don't go out much at night." But in their old neighborhood the name "Stuyvesant" is commemorated in numerous sites today, including Stuyvesant Square and the vast housing project named Stuyvesant Town.

In 1660 the former governor, a devout Calvinist and son of a minister, put some of the forty black slaves he owned to building a Reformed chapel for himself and his family. In 1799 St. Mark's-in-the-Bouwerie, an Episcopal Church, was built on the site where, after various reconstructions, it remains, with the Stuyvesant family vault, in which the governor is buried, on the grounds. Descendants were married and buried in the church for generations. In 1910 Elizabeth Winthrop Stevens, eighth in descent from Peter Stuyvesant, married

John de Koven Bowen before the altar "where Peter Stuyvesant in a stained-glass window portrait and many other old Knickerbockers look down on the congregation," newspapers reported. Although the Stuyvesants lost political power in 1664, they retained vast social prestige and great wealth which increased as the city extended northward into Stuyvesant property. In the nineteenth century several of the governor's descendants, notably the Fish family, regained some political power as well.

The governor's great-great-grandson, Peter Gerard Stuyvesant, head of the dynasty in the 1830s and '40s, was one of the leading citizens of New York. Seeing the city rapidly expanding onto his hereditary landholdings, he began developing the estate, transforming it from rural retreat to urban real estate. The houses of the Stuyvesant descendants were lost in the transition, to their great monetary advantage, it must be said. Hamilton Fish, Sr., Peter Gerard's nephew, "got his love for country life," according to his grandson, "by living in Stuyvesant Street which, before his death, was to be surrounded by the slums of a great city." Peter Gerard Stuyvesant did his best to hold off the encroachment

Generations of the Hamilton Fish family have been the most politically active descendants of Governor Stuyvesant, representing New York throughout the twentieth century. The still-existing 1804 Federal house at 21 Stuyvesant Street was given to Nicholas Fish when he married a Stuyvesant.

Descendants of Governor Stuyvesant proliferated in the eighteenth and nineteenth centuries, among them Edith Stuyvesant Dresser, portrayed here by Giovanni Boldini. She married George Washington Vanderbilt and was chatelaine of their vast (125,000 acres) North Carolina estate, Biltmore.

of slums, profitable though they might be to landlords—to the Astors, for example. In 1836, he donated to the public Stuyvesant Square, approximately in the center of what used to be Stuyvesant's *bouwerie*, as a haven of green and calm, divided into two parts by Second Avenue. St. George's Episcopal Church, J. P. Morgan's church and a favorite with Society, overlooked the square. The square was the center of a neighborhood still thick with Stuyvesant descendants: Fishes, Rutherfurds, and Winthrops. Stuyvesant Fish, Jr., said that when he was growing up near the square ". . . more than twenty of our first cousins . . . used to play in the Park." Peter Gerard died in 1847, shortly after hosting a dinner to commemorate the 200th anniversary of Governor Stuyvesant's arrival in New Amsterdam. The obituaries were respectful: "He was a man closely concerned with the best social life of New York," wrote one journal, "the representative of an enduring Knickerbocker family, and the possessor of a great colonial estate." A century later (1936) a statue of Governor Stuyvesant by Gertrude Vanderbilt Whitney was placed in the center of Stuyvesant Square.

The living symbol of the Stuyvesant dynasty's long inhabitation of this district was Governor Stuyvesant's celebrated pear tree growing on the corner of Second Avenue and 13th Street. Thought to have been brought to New Amsterdam by the governor when he arrived, by the nineteenth century it was the sole remaining tree of the orchard he had planted on his *bouwerie*. Two centuries old, it was an object of veneration: a number of essays narrating its history and poems extolling its antiquity were published. Philip Hone, dining with Peter Gerard Stuyvesant in 1838, was delighted to hear the history of the pear tree from the lips of the direct descendant of its planter. Ten years later, when he was dining at Hamilton Fish's surrounded by Stuyvesants, Fishes, and Winthrops, he was still expressing his admiration of the relic. The family had some blossoms gathered and sent to the diarist, "which I intend to preserve," he wrote, "as a specimen of long-lived vegetation, and a floral reminiscence of the Stuyvesant dynasty." The cult of the Stuyvesant pear tree came to a dramatic end on February 27, 1867, when it was run down by a wagon.

Peter Gerard Stuyvesant was not only the patriarch of the Stuyvesant descendants but the family's mainstay in practical terms. Hamilton Fish (Columbia College, 1827), and his partner Peter Augustus Jay, admitted that most of their business came through Uncle Peter Gerard, who had no children. To keep the Stuyvesant name going he left a large inheritance to his great-grandnephew Stuyvesant Rutherfurd but only if the boy, then five years old, would reverse his name and become Rutherfurd Stuyvesant. He was the eldest son of the great astronomer Lewis Morris Rutherfurd and his wife Margaret Chanler, a Stuyvesant descendant, members of the Four Hundred, and he already bore a name that was Old New York and honored. Nevertheless, the legacy was so large (and Old New York was very alert when it came to money) that his parents complied with Peter Gerard's wishes; it took an act of the New York State Legislature in 1847 to reverse his names, but the child received an immense and ever-mounting estate.

Hamilton Fish was a grandnephew who received a substantial legacy from Peter Gerard Stuyvesant that enabled him to build a new house on Stuyvesant Street, not only gracious but comfortable, with the admirable new luxury of a bathroom—"considered quite a piece of 'swank' in its day," as Fish's grandson wrote. The house is still standing, property now of New York University. The legacy also enabled the Fish couple to educate their sons in Europe. Hamilton, Jr., and his brother Nicholas were put in a Swiss school in 1857, when they were only eleven and eight years old. Their little brother Stuyvesant was sent to the same school later; according to family legend he traveled, aged six, from Paris to Geneva by himself.

The de Peyster family arrived in New Amsterdam in 1649. They emigrated for religious reasons: they were French Protestants (Huguenots) who had sought refuge in Holland from the persecutions of King Charles IX of France and later decided to settle in New Netherland. They were not poor: Johannes de Peyster, the emigrant, was said to own the first carriage in the colony. And they prospered as merchants in the New World: Abraham de Peyster, born in the colony in 1657, was sent by his parents to the Netherlands to work in the family office. He returned to take a major role in the city government and also increased the trading fortune that his father had begun until he was one of the colony's richest men. When he built his splendid three-story brick house on Pearl Street in 1695, it was furnished with mahogany chairs, oil paintings, and fine silver, much of which has survived among his descendants. A painter called "the de Peyster Limner" (his real name is unknown) portrayed members of the family, works that are now major icons of American colonial art. When he died in 1728, he had not only made a fortune as a merchant, he had held most of the important offices of the city and colony, including that of mayor of New York in 1691 (his father had declined the office in 1677 because he did not speak English). A century later his descendants figured on Mrs. John Jay's "dinner and supper list for 1787 and 1788," then two centuries later Ward McAllister's list, and three centuries later are still numerous in the *Social Register*.

The de Peysters, like the Schermerhorns, Goelets, and other Knickerbock-

New Yorkers were awed by the ancestry, wealth and social authority of Frederic J. de Peyster. From his barely furnished family home on Union Square he directed the affairs of the New-York Historical Society and numerous other aristocratic organizations.

ers were not landed gentry; they were city merchants and proud of it. Frederic de Peyster, an eighteenth-century descendant of Abraham, sold glassware, hair brushes, flour, and gin in "pipes" (large casks). Gin was mother's milk for the Dutch; the distilling and selling of it was a good foundation for a fortune. Even by the early nineteenth century this trade and other commerce, and of course the great increase in the value of the de Peyster city property, enabled most of the family to live without working. Frederic de Peyster of the Four Hundred, senior member of the family in 1892, lived most of his life in the family house on University Place near Union Square, then a highly desirable neighborhood.

The de Peyster family was proud of its ancestor Abraham de Peyster, mayor of New Amsterdam in 1691 and one of the town's richest citizens. In 1896, the family honored him with a statue by George E. Bissel which once stood on Bowling Green and now ornaments Hanover Square.

When the de Peysters moved there they had an uninterrupted view of both New York's rivers from the house; when Frederic died fifty years later neither could be seen on account of thickly crowding new buildings. The neighborhood had become mostly commercial, and the de Peyster house was the only residence in its block. Frederic de Peyster was president of the New-York Historical Society, then near his house in a building on Second Avenue and East 11th Street; it was a haunt of Knickerbockers, who were its major benefactors and loved to attend lectures there. Mabel Osgood Wright, who grew up not far away, said of the Society that, "It was one of the few places where history and art both received impetus, and it held an important niche in the bygone days when a good lecture was classed as an amusement." Other de Peysters were major benefactors to the Society: when Miss Catherine Augusta de Peyster, Frederic's cousin, died, she left the bulk of her large estate to it along with the "de Peyster Limner" portraits and her share of the family silver.

Frederic de Peyster had the characteristic Knickerbocker solemnity. He was eccentric in appearance. Mabel Wright called de Peyster "The Owl" because "he was well-feathered by whiskers, two horns of hair were brought from the sides to conceal baldness, and his full eyelids drooped and blinked, closing his eyes in sections in a perfectly owlish manner." Although he owned much of the massive de Peyster family silver from the colonial era, including urns, coffee pots, salvers, and tea caddies, his house was notorious for its scanty furnishings; perhaps he practiced Dutch austerity and economy. He was regarded by newcomers to Society as a moss-covered survivor of ancient times hardly worth cultivating. What must have been their annoyance when President and Mrs. Rutherford B. Hayes visited New York, and the only private house where they were entertained was Mr. and Mrs. Frederic de Peyster's.

Mrs. de Peyster was born Augusta McEvers Morris and was the descendant of a great colonial landed family, Morris of "Morrisania," an estate north of Manhattan. She was noted for her efforts on behalf of New York's numerous slum-dwellers. Before ready-to-wear clothing was cheap and easily available, sewing "classes" at which well-to-do women made clothes for distribution to the poor, especially poor children, were a fixture in American charitable endeavors. They were not really classes as these women, even the most patrician, certainly knew how to sew: needlework was part of every girl's education, regardless of her background. Sewing classes, or "circles," were of varying efficiency and seriousness: many were social and did not admit just anyone who was handy with her needle; chat was likely to be as important as the stitchery. One former member of

Solid merchants, rather then the colonial aristocracy, built the first houses along Washington Square North in the 1830s. The austere facades reflected the comfortable but unextravagant life that was their ideal. In the Gilded Age their children were richer and had begun a new life "uptown," where ostentation was not avoided.

The Monday Sewing Club said of her fellow seamstresses, "They lunched and hemmed diapers for the Children's Aid Society—at least they sewed a few stitches and paid someone to finish them all." Mrs. de Peyster, on the other hand, led a businesslike class in which "tea and gossip" were firmly kept to a minimum. "The Infant Orphan Asylum, one of the oldest institutions in New York," wrote *The Home Journal*, "where the babies enjoy the personal acquaintance of the society people who protect them, will profit by the work of this class." The de Peysters, unlike some of the other Knickerbockers, were not absolutely standoffish. In 1867 *The Home Journal* took obvious pleasure in describing a de Peyster party "in which the Second Avenue mixed charmingly with the Fifth Avenue" and concluded that "the Rip Van Winkleism of New York is gradually fading away under the influence of lovely women and fast men."

Another de Peyster listed among the Four Hundred, Major-General John Watts de Peyster, Frederic's first cousin, was the seventh generation of his name in New York and the sixth generation born in the first ward (the aristocratic) electoral district of the city. The middle name came from his ancestor John Watts, one of the richest men in the English province of New York; in the 1880s the general and his fortunate guests were still drinking wine from the famous Watts cellar. General de Peyster married into another famous colonial family: his wife was Estelle Livingston. Although he fought in the Civil War along with his three sons, his title of general, used for the rest of his life, was actually only a brevet rank granted by the New York State Militia. General de Peyster was one of the most prominent Knickerbockers of his time—one almost might say a professional Knickerbocker, who loved to talk and write about New Amsterdam. He was a genealogist and a great preserver of traditions, responsible for erecting the monumental statue of his ancestor Abraham de Peyster, handsomely bewigged, standing today in Hanover Square. He published many addresses—he was a tireless speechifier at reunions of veterans—on battles of the Civil War (or "Slaveholders' Rebellion," as he liked to call the conflict), but although a Protestant, he also was a great student and defender of Mary Queen of Scots. A gourmet, he constantly gave dinners, often assembling old fellow soldiers. In 1881, for example, his cook prepared a fine dinner for a group of his cronies accompanied by some of the John Watts wines. After the lavish dinner and ancient wines, "Each officer rose," said a respectful account, "and recounted some gallant deed in the war in which he had participated or of which he had been an eyewitness."

The Knickerbockers were very charitable although sometimes their charity could be a little precious. Madeleine Cutting, of the family with no fewer than seven listings in the Four Hundred, went hatless for some time so she could donate to the children's hospital in Pittsfield, Mass., the money other girls were spending on what the newspapers called "fascinating pokes." Mabel Gerry, descendant and heiress of Goelets and Hoffmans, kept a careful account of all the money she spent on herself annually and at the end of the year gave an exactly equal amount to charity. Important buildings at Columbia College, Episcopal churches, and hospitals in New York bear the names of Schermerhorn, Rhinelander, Stuyvesant, Roosevelt.

Notable among the philanthropists was the Rhinelander family. Their emigrant ancestor was Philip Jacob Rhinelander, who came to the New World in 1686, following the Revocation of the Edict of Nantes, which denied religious toleration to Protestants in France. He settled in New Rochelle, New York, a haven for Huguenots as its name shows, La Rochelle being the stronghold of the Protestants in France. The Rhinelanders prospered as merchants, as sugar refiners, and, ultimately as one of the great land-owning families of Manhattan. William Rhinelander, head of the family in 1892, lived on the northeast corner of Washington Square and Fifth Avenue. He was an old man, keeping his health and his pink cheeks by plunging into a cold tub every morning in the unheated shower room in the basement of his house. His habit was chiefly unusual for being daily: few people then took a daily bath, hot or cold. Across Fifth Avenue lived his maiden sister, Miss Serena Rhinelander, famous for her piety and her contributions to the Episcopal Church. She built the Church of the Holy Trinity, the Rhinelander Memorial parish house, and a school for crippled children, all of which still exist, in a great religious complex in the style of the French Renaissance, on East 89th Street. The land was part of the original seventy-acre farm that was the summer home of her grandfather, William Rhinelander, who bought it in 1798. The church and the parish house were estimated to have cost her $500,000. Like so many Knickerbockers, Miss Serena lived a dignified life on her inherited fortune, winters in the city supervising her charities, summers at New London, Connecticut, in her spacious house shaded by much-admired old trees. One of her family, Dr. Philip Mercer Rhinelander, went into holy orders himself and became Episcopal Bishop of Pennsylvania. Rhinelander money was also responsible for Robert College in Constantinople.

Philip Rhinelander gave a party each New Year's Eve "to the Old New Yorkers," friends whose families had lived in New York for at least a hundred years. The Rhinelanders, not being Dutch, were not considered true Knicker-

Lewis Morris, third and last Lord of the Manor of Morrisania (an English royal grant), patriot, and Signer of the Declaration of Independence from New York, was the ancestor or kinsman of many members of the Four Hundred. John Woolaston painted him in 1750 at the height of his colonial splendor.

bockers by purists but were so considered by the public. As intermarriage between the Dutch and emigrants of other origins, notably the English and Scotch, continued, there were fewer and fewer true Knickerbockers. On March 12, 1879, there was a vigorous effort to broaden the base of the St. Nicholas Society. An elitist group wanted to amend the constitution to restrict the election of new members "to the descendants in the oldest male line" of present or former members. A Judge Fitch led the opposition vigorously: he wanted a Society of a thousand members "with a fifty-foot wide clubhouse on a Fifth Avenue corner." As the discussion grew heated, at least by the dignified standards of such an organization, the judge ridiculed the idea that the Society was composed of

Knickerbockers anyway. "Three out of four in this room," he remarked, "are of English descent. . . . Why there is not enough of the old Knickerbocker element in this Society to entitle us to say 'we'." His eloquence won the day: the amendment was defeated, and the St. Nicholas Society continued to try to increase its membership.

Intermarriage between the Dutch and other emigrants began in the seventeenth century and increased in the eighteenth to the point that it was rare for a prominent New York family to be purely Dutch. Seventeenth-century families not of Dutch descent who were rich and prominent included the Morrises of "Morrisania," (arrived 1670), who were English; the Livingstons (1673), who were Scottish; the Jays (1690), who were French; and the Hoffmans, whose first ancestor in America, Martinus Hoffman, immigrated from Sweden in 1657. As early as 1863, Walter Barrett, when publishing his recollections entitled *The Old Merchants of New York City*, spoke of the Knickerbocracy as "an old aristocracy in this city which is not generally understood," and defined it as a mixture of Dutch and English and Puritan stock and Huguenots.

Two of the British clans were especially notable. Dozens of descendants of the great Morris family were included in the Four Hundred. The English-born Richard Morris settled in what is now the Bronx in 1670 on two thousand acres. He became Lord of the Manor known as Morrisania. Among his descendants were Lewis Morris, third Lord of the Manor, a patriot during the American Revolution and a signer of the Declaration of Independence. The great Livingstons were not Dutch in origin either, but its members, when not marrying each other, as they often did, were connected in countless ways with the Dutch aristocracy. All Livingstons were descended either from Robert Livingston or his nephew. The wealth and connections, the public offices, the splendid war records, and the numerous family relationships created around the Livingstons a special aura which survives even today. Ward McAllister wrote: "All my life I had been taught to have a sort of reverence for the name of Livingston, and to feel that Livingston Manor was a species of palatial residence that one must see certainly once in one's lifetime."

Valedictories were always being pronounced on the Knickerbockers. In 1873 *The Home Journal* spoke of a reception, "among the most aristocratic of the day" at Mrs. George Griswold Gray's, where there were numerous "representatives of Old New York—that class of genuine Knickerbockers fast dying away." In 1870 the English writer Justin McCarthy, who obviously reveled in melancholy, writing in *The Galaxy* magazine after a trip to New York, asked his readers "What is a Knickerbocker?" and then answered the question himself. His definition of a Knickerbocker was, "one of those who had grandfathers and ancestors and are proud of them, who date back to Peter Stuyvesant and his peers and paladins. . . . who would rather be poor, if needs be, than to be mixed up with any of the vulgarity of modern wealth and who would be offended if they were mistaken for residents of Fifth Avenue." He invited his readers to "wander toward the East River until you emerge from shops and noise and traffic and modern activity into the solemn, stately monotony and majestic silence of Second Avenue, where there dwell the Knickerbockers in dignified isolation, fading grandly away . . . touching and sublime in their fall."

*The annual parades of the Coaching Club included the finest four-in-hand outfits.
Charles F. Havemeyer's blue and black coach drawn by four bay horses ended the outing
at the Claremont Inn on Riverside Drive near 125th Street on May 25, 1895.*

5

Time might hang heavy on the hands for many men of the Four Hundred. They were grandsons of Old New Yorkers, well-to-do in federal times, who became rich when the value of their inherited real estate holdings exploded with the city's growth in the mid-nineteenth century, removing any necessity for them to engage in gainful labor. Some men of the Four Hundred were diligent custodians of their family inheritances; some were naturally industrious, or embarrassed to be idle, and sought new investments and business challenges; others, in an America preoccupied with business and "getting ahead," held positions in business, but hardly pretended to work. Sidney Dillon Ripley of the Four Hundred, for example, was the grandson of Sidney Dillon, president of the Union Pacific Railroad. He himself was treasurer of the immensely profitable Equitable Life Assurance Company, owned by the family of his wife, Mary Hyde, but he seldom reported to the office. Horses were his main interest, but he also bred Brown Swiss cattle, then rare in this country ("ungainly looking animals, but as valuable as they are ugly," remarked *Town & Country* magazine), at his country place at Hempstead, Long Island, comfortably near the Meadow Brook Hunt Club, where he was an active rider to hounds. When he died in 1905, *The New York Times* remarked complacently, "Mr. Ripley held largely aloof from business, as well as from public affairs."

In their own social circles there was little criticism of men if they chose not to work. Of James Vanderburg Parker, for example, a bachelor and a permanent member of Mrs. Astor's entourage, a flimsy book of the time entitled *The Ultra-fashionable Peerage* said that he had "inherited a large fortune which has enabled him to be a lifelong man of leisure." Middle-class businessmen, and journalists, too, sneered at "Society loafers," but their wives thought loafers charming cotillion partners, and their daughters dreamed of marrying one. Hostesses like Mrs. Astor depended on unemployed or underemployed males as escorts, dinner partners, and cotillion leaders. Today, such gentlemen are known as "walkers," and they are as indispensable to hostesses now as they were then. Mrs. Astor always had such men in her entourage, which meant they were invited to every party she gave and escorted her when Mr. Astor was absent, which he usually was. In the next generation, the ambitious Mrs. Cornelius Vanderbilt (Grace Wilson), who inherited Mrs. Astor's social supremacy, used to keep a card index of "men who can lunch," which implied that they did not have a job and were thus free for her two-hour weekday luncheons, and another file of "men who dance."

Luncheons weren't given every day, and the daylight hours had to be filled by gentlemen of leisure with some sort of occupation. Sport was the answer, and never had the organized and expensive sports—coaching, foxhunting, yachting—been so important to rich Americans as they were in the late nineteenth century. Among the Four Hundred were some of the most ardent sportsmen, and to a surprising extent, sportswomen, in the United States. Their model was Britain. The Four Hundred imitated, or strove to imitate, the British aristocracy and gentry, also freed by hereditary wealth from day-to-day labor. Rich Americans were going through a period of intense Anglophilia: one commentator wrote indignantly at the time, "The frenzy for anything and everything English is grafting strange embellishments on our native stock. Pink coats and cricket pads. Broad A's and high teas." Ward McAllister, among many others, affected a British accent, and James Van Alen, Mrs. Astor's son-in-law, used not only Anglicisms but sprinkled his conversation with medievalisms like "zounds" and "forsooth" that bewildered even the British. The life of the Van Alens was as English as could be but not current English: their house in Newport, "Ochre Point," appeared to date, as the press wrote admiringly, "from the days of Good Queen Bess," with no gas pipes allowed and only wax candles for illumination. After the turn of the twentieth century the Van Alens went to live in Britain, purchasing a stately home, Rushton Hall in Northamptonshire.

The Four Hundred, men and women both, drove coaches drawn by a team of four, hunted foxes, and jumped horses like the British, but it was all a rather unconvincing performance. Traditions, which count in matters of style, were lacking. The British gentry were rural people who had hunted and shot on their own land forever. The Four Hundred were essentially an urban aristocracy. The Livingstons, the Van Rensselaers, and the Morrises had been great landowners along the Hudson, but by 1892, they, too, were city dwellers. The Astors, the Vanderbilts, and the Fish family had been New Yorkers for generations. In Britain, full-time sportsmen were not a new phenomenon and were much admired for their amateur skills. In the United States there had been plenty of shooting and fishing in the early settlements, but the quest was for food and not amusement, and sports were seldom ritualized with appropriate clothing and sophisticated equipment. American sportsmen of the second half of the nineteenth century had either to adapt British traditions or begin their own. In the event, they did both.

The most elegant sportsmen were called "dudes," a word surviving many changes of meaning in the American language during the last century. "Dude" came to mean a "tenderfoot," but in 1892, when the word was new, dudes were dandies, clothes-conscious and highly mannered in their behavior, whose primary interest was sport. The Four Hundred contained many choice specimens of the dude, among them Frederic Bronson, Winthrop Chanler, F. Brockholst Cutting and William Cutting, brothers Ogden and Robert Goelet, F. Gray Griswold, William Jay, the three Kane brothers (De Lancey, S. Nicholson, and Woodbury), brothers James P. and Joseph F. Kernochan, Sidney Dillon Ripley, Frank Knight Sturgis, William Seward Webb, and William C. Whitney.

Charles Hanson Towne, who grew up in New York, said the word "dude" was coined about 1880. "A dude was a dandy—any man who wore exquisite clothes; and we children were inclined to laugh at him as he sauntered down the street with a cane and spats and . . . a light overcoat with plaid buttons which spread, fanlike, as it left his waistline. Brown derbies were much in vogue; and of course patent-leather shoes with razor-points, and boutonniere completed the costume." Towne considered these gentlemen "epicene" and whenever he saw one "walking up the [Fifth] avenue to keep an appointment for afternoon tea, I thought, 'Alas! They toil not, neither do they sin.'" You could spot a dude when you passed him on Fifth Avenue: his high hat was pushed back well off the forehead, his shirt had a very high and very stiff collar called the "choker," and his creaseless trousers were tight. The lack of creases indicated the work of a tailor; creased trousers were invariably homemade. The cane was important, not for support or beating varlets, but because it had connotations of the British gentry. The dude took his cane into the drawing room when visiting ladies. The fashionable and much admired posture for a male caller was seated, leaning forward, his chin resting thoughtfully on the gilded head of the cane. Though worshipped and emulated by young men, especially junior clerks in stores and offices, the dude was always faintly ridiculous to other American men and subject to derision even by his contemporaries. When

Edith Wharton was giving directions for the stage production of *The Age of Inno-cence*, she declared, remembering her youth in 1880s New York, "Male actors ought to have moustaches & not tooth brush ones, but curved and slightly twisted at the ends. They should wear dark gray frock-coats and tall hats and bouton-nieres—a bunch of violets by day, a gardenia for evening dress." In the 1890s, fads for men were lavender kid gloves, black straw boaters for summer wear, and heavy watch chains swinging with lockets and seals.

Most conspicuous among the dudes were the dashing "sealskin brigade," a group of horse fanciers that included both men of the Four Hundred and raffish types not received in drawing rooms but knowledgeable about horseflesh. In the winter, they wore coats made of sealskin reaching to their ankles, with matching caps and gloves, and laid sealskin lap robes across their knees when driving their trotting horses. Only rich men could afford these accouterments. Sealskin was extremely expensive: a good coat with cap and gloves cost from $1,500 to $2,500, a year's income for a middle-class family. Fancy shops advertised sealskin coats in *The Social Register;* one was F. C. Booss & Brother at 294 Fifth Avenue between 30th and 31st Streets, which "specialized in sealskin." Dudes loved horses. Among the participatory sports, those involving the horse were by far the most popular. The horse for centuries, even millennia, has occupied a special place in the hearts of the rich and leisured. In the nineteenth century the horse was to rich men what the luxurious automobile and the private plane are to rich men today. Although the story is often told, it surely is not true that horses in the stables of O. H. P. Belmont in Newport slept on fine linen sheets—horses sleep standing up—but the fact that such spoiling was regarded as only slightly over the top says a lot about horse lovers of the time.

The sport most favored by the Sealskin Brigade was driving fine trotting horses. The trotter was harnessed to a sulky, a light carriage seating one man, or during the winter to a sleigh, popularly called a "cutter." In the late nine-teenth century the eastern United States was in a cycle of severe winters, with frequent heavy snowfalls; even today the Blizzard of 1888 is a byword. Snow lay on the ground in the city longer than it does today, when heating pipes, underground transportation, and electrical wiring help New York create its own, warmer climate. Sleighing and ice-skating on frozen ponds—there were several in Central Park—were then major sports in the city. And sleighs drawn by trotters were the last word in fashionable transportation. The family of I. Townsend Burden of the Four Hundred, notable anyway for their stylish clothes ("the fearfully and wonderfully well-dressed Townsend Burden family," a Society chronicler called them), attracted all eyes when they rode through Central Park in a peacock blue sleigh.

The racing of trotters, not called "harness racing" until about 1900, was then more important from Society's viewpoint than Thoroughbred racing. Trotters were raced on Harlem Lane (now St. Nicholas Avenue), then still a dirt road in upper Manhattan. A little later sulkies sped along the Harlem Speedway, parallel to the Harlem River. In and around New York there were seven trotting tracks by the time of the Civil War. Great emphasis was placed on the style and appearance of the horses and carriages, but speed, of course, was the purpose of the whole exercise. In 1845 a horse named *Lady Suffolk* ran a mile in two minutes, twenty-nine-and-a-half seconds, establishing the record. Expensive efforts were made to better that time. In 1892 *Nancy Hanks* ran a mile in two minutes and four seconds. Dedicated horsemen congratulated themselves and sagely ascribed the speed to lighter shoeing of the horses, lighter harness, and a "bicycle" sulky that weighed only twenty-nine pounds. Trotting was the sport of millionaires, but interest drifted downward. Famous trotters and their speeds were known by name to the multitude and each had its following. Currier & Ives, "printmakers to the American people," always alert to popular enthusiasms, issued many lithographic portraits, including four different versions of *Lady Suffolk* and six of *Nancy Hanks*.

Racing Thoroughbreds was an even more expensive sport, and one to which many American millionaires—you had to be a millionaire to own a stable—were and still are involved. The Lorillard family were among the leaders, one of the great American sporting dynasties. The term "millionaire" is said to have been coined in 1826 to describe Peter Lorillard, related to many members of the Four Hundred. In those days, the term meant total assets of a million dollars, and there were only half a dozen men in the United States who could be so described until the Civil War brought a vast expansion of fortune. The three Lorillard brothers, Peter, George, and Jacob, were descended from a very old New York family, but they were the first of their name to make great fortunes. Jacob was a tanner and currier and made a large fortune at it, but the truly immense sums were made by Peter and George, who established a business in chewing tobacco and snuff. The irreverent *Police Gazette's* "Society reporter" (actually the racy weekly had no such employee) suggested a Lorillard coat-of-arms consisting of "a cuspidor couchant with two cigars and a plug of tobacco rampant." The Lorillards aroused the ire, or perhaps the chance to exercise their wit, of both great New York diarists of their time. Philip Hone said Peter Lorillard "led people by the nose for the best part of a century and made his enormous fortune by giving them that to chew which they could not swallow." Strong wrote when Peter died, "How many cubic miles of smoke and gallons of colored saliva are embodied in the immense fortune that was his last week!"

Lorillards were absorbed with horses even more than most of their sportsmen friends. At the 1,244-acre Rancocas Stud in Jobstown, New Jersey, Pierre Lorillard kept eight stallions, eighty brood mares, forty-eight race horses in training, and forty-five yearlings. By 1875, he had established his famous racing colors of cherry red jacket for his jockeys with black hoops on the sleeves and a black cap with a gold tassel.

Saratoga, New York, was then, as now, a great horse town. The Lorillard family visited Saratoga often. When Pierre's family came to town they used to rent an entire suite of rooms across the front of the Clarendon Hotel. When the Clarendon slipped a little in social standing, the Lorillards moved over to the Grand Union Hotel, where they rented a large "cottage" on the grounds for their Saratoga sojourn. In either place the Lorillards were conspicuous. The teenage diarist from Chicago, Julia Newberry, visiting Saratoga with her mother, copied from the hotel register the entry for the Lorillard party in 1869: "three children, two maids, one man [servant], one coachman and horses ahem !!! and governess!"

The American Jockey Club, dedicated to Thoroughbred racing, was organized in 1865 by Leonard Jerome, William R. Travers, and August Belmont. Leonard Jerome, grandfather of Sir Winston Churchill, built a track named for himself, Jerome Park, in the Fordham section of the Bronx. The most famous race was the Belmont Stakes, run there from 1867 to 1889, when the track closed. Racetracks were opened at Coney Island in 1879, Sheepshead Bay in 1880 (by the Coney Island Jockey Club), in 1885 at Gravesend, and in 1889 at Morris Park in the eastern Bronx, the largest track in the country, with a grandstand seating 15,000 (it closed in 1904). Men of the Four Hundred were among the organizers of all these tracks.

Coaching, driving a coach drawn by a team of four horses, was another elite sport, probably because it was so expensive. Great skill was required: handling four spirited horses in tandem was not a sport for the inexperienced. The driver had to hold the reins in his left hand and a whip in his right hand. Colonel William Jay fathered the sport in the United States. Member of a distinguished Four Hundred family, with a long record of public service, he was the grandson of John Jay, first Chief Justice of the United States Supreme Court. He was senior warden of Trinity Church, where men of his family had served as vestrymen since 1697, a lawyer, and president of the New York *Herald* newspaper. Visiting in

At the elegant Jerome Park, Society enjoyed horseracing, including the Belmont Stakes, traveling to the northwestern Bronx in private carriages, as shown in a contemporary engraving. Trap shooting was also offered as were sleighing and ice skating in the winter months.

England in the 1870s, William Jay discovered the pleasures of coaching. The British aristocracy were trying to revive as a sport what had once been a necessity. Public coaches ("stagecoaches" because they traveled in stages) had long been superseded in Britain by the railroads, but they had left behind romantic recollections of neighing horses, rumbling coaches, and muffled-up outside passengers—Dickensian reconstructions far removed from reality. There had always been amateur "whips" (drivers), mostly rich young sporting men, who joined "driving clubs" as long ago as 1807. By 1856 the Four-in-Hand Club had been organized, and in 1870 the Coaching Club. For American horsemen the sport had pleasant associations with noblemen: the Duke of Beaufort had written the best book on *Driving* and the Marquess of Blandford, future Duke of Marlborough, was devoted to the sport. The latter regularly drove a coach as a public vehicle between London and Dorking, a distance of twenty-two miles.

Among New York sportsmen De Lancey Astor Kane was especially noted for his skill in the difficult art of driving four-in-hand teams of horses and for his attempts to revive coaching both as a sport and as public transportation.

William Jay, who loved horses, was intrigued, and with the gesture of a rich American bought the Dorking coach and shipped it to New York. In 1875 he was the prime mover in organizing the Coaching Club, of which he was president from 1876 to 1896. James Gordon Bennett, Jr., young heir of the New York *Sun* newspaper fortune and a participant in nearly every sport, Frederic Bronson, Leonard W. Jerome, De Lancey Astor Kane and his brother S. Nicholson Kane, Thomas Newbold, A. Thorndike Rice, William H. Vanderbilt, and Jay were the nine original members. Frank K. Sturgis, president of the New York Stock Exchange and Madison Square Garden and a founder of the horse show at Lenox,

Massachusetts, where he had his country place, and Newport, where he had his summer place, was one of the famous whips. Others were Robert Livingston Gerry, A. Augustus Schermerhorn (Mrs. Astor's brother), Alfred Gwynne Vanderbilt, C. Oliver Iselin, and Theodore Havemeyer (William Jay's brother-in-law), who all had Four Hundred connections. Among sportswomen a few were whips: Mrs. Thomas Hastings (Helen Benedict), wife of Thomas Hastings, architect of the New York Public Library, was sometimes called "the best four-in-hand driver in this country" and constantly took blue ribbons at the National Horse Show.

Alfred Gwynne Vanderbilt and Reginald Rives, who later wrote the history of the Coaching Club, drove public coaches on which anyone could buy a seat, with a published fare ($1.50 to $2.50), from New York to nearby towns like Ardsley or Pelham. De Lancey Kane ran a coach called "The Tallyho" from Madison Square to the Westchester Country Club. Slightly confused by British expressions, the public thought every coach was called a "tallyho," and that became a generic name. In 1876 it was announced that Kane was establishing, at a cost of $25,000, a line of English coaches to run from New York to New Rochelle. "The best horses" would be provided, and, "Mr. Kane will hold 'the ribbons' himself," the impressed *Home Journal* remarked, concluding, "This is a London fashion which deserves to be appreciated in New York. The drives are beautiful and the people will be glad of the novel opportunity presented." Actually, the people preferred taking the train to being hurtled recklessly over dusty roads by overdressed young men out for speed records. The attention and enthusiasm of the drivers waned, anyway, and the routes were soon discontinued. A few traces lingered into the twentieth century: in 1905 Robert Livingston Gerry established a coach service during the racing season between Belmont Park and the Holland House Hotel on Fifth Avenue.

In coaching, speed actually did not count as much as style. Every aspect of the coach, the horses, the driver, and the attendants was scrutinized by other members and the public. Buttons were polished, lap robes properly folded, and each horse had artificial flowers attached to his headband. Horns played by a guard announced the arrival of the coach. James Van Alen, always leading in extravagance, imported a veteran guard from England to teach Americans to "wind" the horns in the proper style. Members of the Coaching Club diligently studied the incomprehensible British coaching jargon and spoke familiarly of the ability of a driver in "thonging his whip" or "touching the near leader on the off-side under the bar." In two years from its founding, the Coaching Club had sixty members who paid a $75 initiation fee and $35 annual dues. Among them they

Numerous outdoor social gatherings were held during the annual parades of the Coaching Club, occasions for finery, not all of it equine. Mr. and Mrs. Goodhue Livingston and Mrs. Alfred Gwynne Vanderbilt dressed in the latest fashions about 1906.

drove seventeen "drags," coaches lighter in weight than the British model, and faster, but dangerous since they were more likely to tip over. The first parade of the Coaching Club was held on Fifth Avenue in 1876. Colonel Jay's coach, an English drag with canary-colored body and red undercarriage drawn by bay and chestnut "wheelers" (the back horses) and a pair of bay "leaders" (the front horses), led the procession. Jay was wearing a bottle-green coat with gilt buttons, a yellow-striped waistcoat, and a silk topper. Large crowds gathered along Fifth Avenue and cheered the handsome turn-outs. Women spectators wore "Gainsborough" hats covered with lace and clusters of long plumes, the most unsuitable possible wear for watching the hot and dusty sport. White lace dresses touching the ground were popular. The Coaching Club parades, although great favorites of both participants and observers, lasted only about twenty-five years. By that time there were too many automobiles on Fifth Avenue noisily competing for space to make room for the leisurely procession of the Coaching Club.

A few women participated in this strenuous sport: Ruth and Florence Twombly, great-granddaughters of Commodore Vanderbilt, "are the best whips in Northern New Jersey," wrote *Town & Country* admiringly, "and whenever either young woman appeared in the ring at the Morristown Horse Show there was round after round of applause."

Another favorite horse sport of the rich was polo, brought to the United States by James Gordon Bennett, Jr. The press said flatteringly that he "has done much to create a taste for and improve the character of outdoor amusements in America . . . ." He had admired the game in England, where it had been introduced from India in 1869, and early in 1876 he began to form a polo club, importing what the press called "Shetland ponies," actually standard-sized horses only referred to as "ponies." There were, of course, no trained animals in this country. He was joined by several of his sporting acquaintances (the notoriously high-handed and self-centered Bennett had few friends), including Frederic Bronson, William Jay, Pierre Lorillard, and several ladies, led by the indefatigable sportswoman Mrs. James P. Kernochan (Catherine Lorillard). The first matches were played that year at Jerome Park. Bennett, who did nothing by halves, built a polo clubhouse and placed the Delmonico family, New York's long-established restaurateurs, in charge. Shortly thereafter, the sport was introduced at the Rhode Island resorts, Newport and Narragansett Pier.

Polo was a game for country clubs. Several still-existing clubs claim the honor of being the oldest; the Westchester Country, founded in 1883, claims to be the *second* oldest. James Montaudevert Waterbury, son of a rich New York merchant, was the mover in its organization. He was a jolly soul, ingenious in planning parties. In 1889 at his country house near Pelham, he gave a circus party for 350 guests. A special train brought the guests from New York to Pelham railroad station, from which they drove to his house along roads lighted by torches. A sawdust ring was surrounded by galleries in which a Hungarian band and Lander's orchestra, the smartest in New York, played continuously. "The grand entrée was made at half-past nine o'clock," wrote a breathless reporter, "four gentlemen and four ladies mounted on matched Thoroughbreds, dashed from the anteroom and began to dance the grand quadrille on horseback." Some Society figures insisted on performing circus tricks: Winthrop Chanler injured his back doing acrobatics. Waterbury's two sons, Lawrence ("Larry") and Montgomery ("Monty") became famous polo players at the club and on the Long Island polo fields.

A country club, but more, was Tuxedo Park in Orange County, New York, in the Ramapo Mountains about forty miles from New York City. A planned community, it consisted of country houses (called "cottages" in elegant under-statement) centered around a clubhouse. Pierre Lorillard III dreamed up Tuxedo as a place where cottagers and guests could engage in sport in land-scaped surroundings. His family had been buying land in the region for nearly a century, and their holdings amounted to thousands of acres; six thousand were dedicated to Tuxedo Park. In 1885–1886, he and his architect, Bruce Price, laid out trails, put in sewerage and a water system, and erected fences and gates. Rusticity was carefully planned. In one of her novels, the Society writer Constance Cary describes "Tupelo Park," obviously Tuxedo, where her characters spend a weekend. Their arrival was "a pleasant drive enough, through a wilder-ness that had been made to blossom into something akin to the perfection of English landscape gardening. The winding roads were paved and drained and provided with lamps for gas, but overhead grew trees of the deep wood." The luxury was of the costliest kind—concealed. The twenty-two original cottages and elaborate stables surrounded a gray wooden clubhouse. You had to be a member of the club before you could buy or build a house, and as it was grace-fully stated, "The park will be freely opened to visitors, though, of course, the sporting privileges of the place are restricted to members of the association." Gamekeepers wore green and yellow liveries, the club colors, also worn by the cottagers in ties and scarves.

For the gala opening of Tuxedo Park on May 30, 1886, seven hundred guests came by train along the west bank of the Hudson River from New York. The first Autumn Ball, which became a traditional event, was held in October, an historic night in the annals of Society and of male fashion: to the horror of many guests, young Griswold Lorillard, Pierre's son, and some of his friends daringly appeared in tailless dress coats instead of the traditional white-tie evening suits. Thus was "the tuxedo," or "tux" born—at least according to one story. Like all great inven-tions, its origin is disputed. According to Tuxedo Park resident Herbert C. Pell, Pierre Lorillard's nephew, tuxedos were smoking jackets invented by an English tailor about the time Tuxedo Park opened. They were worn at dinner parties, and the custom spread. Smoking, incidentally, was as a matter of course restricted to men, and was almost exclusively of cigars. According to Herbert Pell, heir to a tobacco fortune himself, "cigarettes were considered dudish degeneracies dan-gerous to health and morals." E. Berry Wall, self-proclaimed "king of the Dudes," says in his memoirs that, "The first dinner jacket to make its appearance in the United States was sent out to me by my London tailor Henry Poole"—about 1887. Wall wore the new garment to a ball at the Grand Union Hotel in Saratoga,

Pierre Lorillard conceived of Tuxedo Park, on the Ramapo River north of New York, as a paradise for sportsmen in the autumn and winter months between the annual visits of Society to Newport. Members' houses were coyly referred to as "cottages" although they might have fifty rooms. This is the main entrance to Lorillard's own house.

where he was ordered off the floor and told that if he wanted to dance, he had to wear regular evening clothes of white tie and tails.

Tuxedo was a dressy place. In 1909 at the Tuxedo Park Horse Show, Mrs. Edwin Main Post, daughter of Bruce Price, the architect of Tuxedo, was observed wearing a handpainted chiffon gown with a cerise cloak and "a small little black hat, much like a tricorne, with a great brush of stiff, rose-colored aigrettes pointing backward." She was later famous as Emily Post, author of *Etiquette*.

Pierre Lorillard put a golf course in the park in 1889, a small race track, and an electrically lighted toboggan slide. Cold weather sports were emphasized because at first Tuxedo was primarily an autumn and winter resort; its cottagers spent the summers mostly at Newport or Bar Harbor or Lenox. There was a Tennis Club building equipped with one of the few facilities in the United States where court tennis could be played. One of the leading players was T. Suffern Tailer,

Lawn tennis achieved its first American success during Newport summers; viewing the matches was a major afternoon pastime at the Casino. Alfred Gwynne Vanderbilt, an early automobile enthusiast, like several members of his family, attended in his "machine."

son of Edward N. Tailer. T. Suffern was also a golf enthusiast who built his own private course at Newport. The Tuxedo Club held lawn tennis tournaments and gave silver cups to victors. There were rowboating and pigeon shoots, curling and ice boating. "Tuxedo was organized as a sporting community," said Pell, "and every effort was made to develop and encourage games and other sports. Deer, pheasants and wild turkey were brought in." The aristocratic game birds evinced a reluctance to stay within the precincts of the park and be shot, and the cracksman soon had to fall back on the local birds. Two-horse wagonettes provided transportation within the park; when there was a dinner or party a wagonette went from house to house picking up guests who had telephoned for the service, Tuxedo being one of the first communities anywhere to have universal telephone service.

Among the first cottagers were William Waldorf Astor, Grenville Kane, Peter Cooper Hewitt, George S. Bowdoin, Lloyd S. Bryce, Robert Goelet, Richard Mortimer, and Sir Roderick Cameron. Mortimer, heir to a fortune made in the wool trade in New York, was married to Eleanor Jay Chapman, descendant of John Jay. They were key members of the Four Hundred. Their Tuxedo Park house, which was ten years in the building, was very large and very English, "to the very lions that surmount the posts of the gateway," it was remarked. One reporter said the Mortimer place "reminds one of an old English manor house," which, no doubt, it was intended to. One side of the driveway wall was decorated, rather incongruously, with the busts of Roman emperors!

Sir Roderick Cameron was a great favorite in New York Society, a real British knight living and working in the city. He was a Canadian, his father a member of the Canadian Parliament and founder of the Northwest Fur Trading Co. Cameron came to New York before the Civil War and established R. W. Cameron & Co., a company shipping goods between the United States, Canada, and Australia. He was especially active in Australia, commissioner for New South Wales at the Philadelphia Centennial celebrations in 1876, and knighted in 1883, "for services in promoting trade with Australia." At Tuxedo Park he built an English-style shooting box from which he sought the elusive game birds. At Clifton, Staten Island, he maintained a Thoroughbred stud. His wife, Anne Fleming Leavenworth, died in 1879, but his children were popular in New York Society and counted, like him, among the Four Hundred.

Tuxedo fascinated the public and at once became synonymous with the carefree gaieties of the rich. A music hall song ran:

> "You don't know what life really is
> til you've been to Tuxedo Park."

Julia Ward Howe, however, commented dourly that it was like "the white of an egg."

Tuxedo Park had a golf course, an early one for the United States. Golf was the subject of some wit when it first became popular. When the Shinnecock Hills Golf Club opened in Southampton, Long Island, newspapers made fun of "Shinnecock swells who think they have to wear a red coat to play the game." According to legend, when Walter Breese was told by his teacher he should "keep his eye on the ball," he proceeded to take out his glass eye and place it on top of the ball. In 1885 the first amateur championship tournament of the United States Golfing Association was held in Newport.

The most English sport was foxhunting, and American sportsmen were bound to give it a try. There was a short history of foxhunting in colonial America, but the hunts were merely a miscellaneously dressed rabble mounted on untrained horses pursuing a clever animal across the unfenced fields. The sport in all its colorful formality and skill had never truly established itself in this country. Frank Gray Griswold, an heir to the N.H. and G. Griswold Company, shippers founded in 1796 and onetime employee of the Lorillards, was an accomplished sportsman who also wrote thirty-seven books. Among them were seven volumes of *Sport on Land and Water*, studies of El Greco and Sandro Botticelli, and books on wine and on opera, to which he was devoted. In the winter of 1876–1877, he established what he proudly called "the first properly turned out and hunted pack of hounds in the United States" in Jamaica, Long Island. He called the new pack "The Queens County Hunt." As the first Master of Foxhounds he had his problems—with horses, dogs, and riders. Horses had not been taught to jump, except in circuses. The hounds he had to import already trained from Ireland. He also had to curb the enthusiasm of his riders; it took a while for aggressive New Yorkers to understand that their competition was the fox, not each other. In 1882 another pack, the Meadow Brook Hunt, was established nearby, and in 1893 the two were joined with Griswold as Master of Fox Hounds.

Many women participated in these horse sports. Mrs. Burke Roche (Frances Work) won blue ribbons at horse shows, and her stables were considered to be among the finest in Society. Her father, Frank Work, a railroad magnate of the 1870s, was closely allied with Commodore Cornelius Vanderbilt. She married, very much against her father's will, the brother of the Irish Baron Fermoy. Frank Work despised noblemen, whom he considered fortune hunters. He attempted in his will to ensure that his grandchildren be brought up as Americans. In fact, Edmund Burke Roche, the elder of Mrs. Burke Roche's twin sons, did attend St. Paul's School and Harvard ('09), but he later became the 4th Lord Fermoy. By his daughter Frances, Mrs. Burke Roche became the great-grandmother of Diana, Princess of Wales. In New York and Newport, Mrs. Burke Roche lived in great style, with touches of eccentricity. Her much-admired garden in Newport, for example, was planted only with blue flowers. Unfortunately, she turned out to be as interested in her stablehands as in the horses they tended, and after divorcing the Hon. Mr. Burke Roche she married in 1905, to the horror of her family and friends, a lusty young Hungarian horsetrainer named Aurel Batonyi. Her father decided that was really too much and cut her out of his will. The Batonyis were also divorced after only four years of marriage.

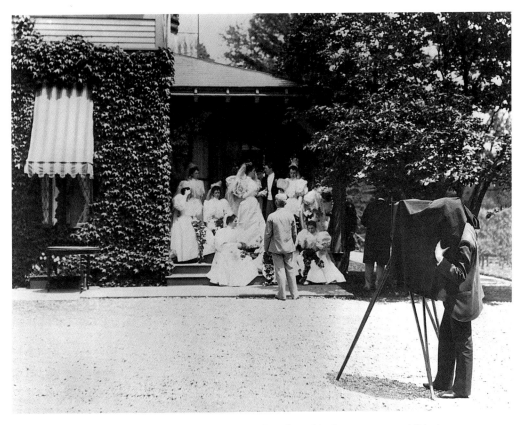

The numerous children of Sir Roderick Cameron, a Canadian shipping magnate established in New York, were popular members of the Four Hundred. In 1895 Anne Fleming Cameron married Belmont Tiffany at the Cameron home on Staten Island. A special steamer brought 150 guests from Manhattan.

An even more ardent and all-around sportswoman was Mrs. James P. Kernochan. She was Catherine Lorillard, another member of the sporting dynasty. She and her husband lived near Hempstead, Long Island, in the heart of what was then the sporting country, where she was known as a daring rider to hounds. The Kernochans were much interested in dogs, introducing one of the first packs of beagles into this country from England. Mrs. Kernochan was famous for her Irish terriers, which were allowed the run of her house and slept on the "piazza," as the porches of smart homes were called. She was president of the Ladies' Kennel Association of America. Hildegarde ("Hilda") Oelrichs, sister of Charles May Oelrichs of the Four Hundred, was "renowned for her skill and pluck in the

The Meadow Brook hounds began pursuing foxes on Long Island in 1881 and was soon the most popular hunt with the Four Hundred. Among the most fearless members was Mrs. James P. Kernochan (Catherine Lorillard), daughter of a famous sporting family and considered one of the finest riders in America.

hunting field." This intimidating young lady shot stags in Scotland at Balmacaan, home of the Bradley Martins, and in 1887 bagged a grizzly bear, a major big-game trophy, on a trip to the Rockies. Almost equally athletic was Mrs. W. Forbes Morgan, Jr. (Edith L. Hall), daughter of Valentine Hall (and aunt of Eleanor Roosevelt), who was "a daring equestrienne, a good swimmer, and an expert shot with the rifle."

To practice all these field sports, the best thing was to have your own fields. Country clubs and resorts like Tuxedo Park were all very well, but visiting there could not equal riding your own broad acres every day. Most members of the Four Hundred had a country place or places; not a few were on a princely scale. At Elm Court, his place at Lenox, William Douglas Sloane captained a baseball team composed of his gardeners that played "the citizens' team," composed of locals. Rutherfurd Stuyvesant lived, when in New York, in the family house at Stuyvesant Square and East 15th Street and devoted his time to philanthropy and

Dr. William Seward Webb and his wife Lila Vanderbilt created their private sporting kingdom around their Queen Anne house, Shelburne Farms in Vermont, where they had boating on Lake Champlain in their steam yacht Elfreida, *golf on their nine-hole private course, foxhunting, shooting, fishing, and, especially, polo.*

to managing his vast Stuyvesant properties, but he was an active sportsman. In the 1880s, he attempted to create the largest game preserve in the eastern United States on his country estate, Tranquility Farms, at Allamuchy in Warren County, New Jersey. Tranquility got its name in 1787, when the wife of the first owner, Mrs. John Rutherfurd, after enduring a long trip from New York over almost nonexistent roads, said with a sigh when she saw her farm, "This is indeed tranquility." Stuyvesant added to it another estate at Allamuchy Mountain, which he fenced in to make a deer park; a dozen gamekeepers patrolled the grounds. In his kennels lived more than one hundred fox terriers, pointers, and setters. His second wife was Austrian, formerly a Comtesse de Wassenaer, and their main residence became Paris. They also spent a lot of time cruising the Mediterranean in their yacht. In 1909 Stuyvesant died in Paris, rather dramatically: taken ill while promenading the Champs-Élysées, he was carried into the famous Le Doyen restaurant on the boulevard, where, after identifying himself, he expired.

An equally grand estate was Shelburne Farms near Burlington, Vermont, developed by Dr. William Seward Webb and his wife Lila Vanderbilt, granddaughter of Commodore Vanderbilt. The four thousand acres on the shore of Lake Champlain were not inherited by Dr. Webb, but he was buying back family land granted by the state of Vermont to his grandfather, Samuel B. Webb, a Revolutionary soldier of distinction and aide to George Washington. William Seward Webb was a sophisticated man who had studied medicine in Europe and at the College of Physicians and Surgeons in New York. Rather than practicing medicine, however, he went to work for his father-in-law, William H. Vanderbilt, and became president of the Wagner Palace Car Company, which made railroad sleeping cars.

The grounds of Shelburne Farms were laid out by Frederick Law Olmsted and a hundred-room house was built between 1887 and 1899. The facilities for sport were grand. Dr. Webb bred the all-purpose hackney, a strong stock horse that he used for draft purposes. He imported a famous sire, *Matchless of Landesboro*, from England and bred mares to him every year. The "breeding barn" was the largest barn in America. Another barn stabled three hundred horses and was large enough that indoor polo could be played in it. A nine-hole golf course with a par of thirty-six strokes was much enjoyed by Lila Webb, one of the best women golfers in the United States. Their steam yacht floated on Lake Champlain. Their son, J. Watson Webb, kept his own pack of hounds, which he bred, crossing English blood with Welsh for a keener dog. He also became one of America's great ten-goal polo players. Dr. Webb, it is not surprising, was an enthusiastic four-in-hand driver. In June of 1894 he entertained the Coaching Club, which had driven its drags from the Hotel Brunswick on Fifth Avenue in New York to Shelburne Farms, a distance of 318 miles, in four days. Dr. Webb's private railroad car kept pace alongside the coaches, truly a millionaire's touch. The whips on the trip included Dr. Webb, Alexander J. Cassatt, president of the Pennsylvania Railroad and brother of the painter Mary Cassatt, Frank K. Sturgis, Frederic Bronson, Theodore A. Havemeyer, Reginald W. Rives, William K. Vanderbilt, O. H. P. Belmont, Eugene Van Rensselaer Thayer, and William C. Whitney.

By 1895 Dr. Webb owned more than 200,000 acres in the Adirondack Mountains which he used solely for sport. He surrounded his entire private park with a fence sixty-three miles long. He was the largest single landowner in the Adirondacks, his acreage even greater than William C. Whitney's. The Adirondack and St. Lawrence Railroad, which he owned, wound its way through the mountains with private stations for the estates of himself and his friends. Dr. Webb

William Collins Whitney, who made a fortune in New York street railroads and married a Standard Oil heiress, was sometime secretary of the navy. He entertained fellow sportsmen at his nine homes in various Eastern states and was one of the prime movers in making Aiken, South Carolina, the Southern capital of the horse sports.

named his place Ne-ha-sa-ne and put it under the management of Gifford Pinchot, the forester, who had worked on Biltmore, the majestic estate in North Carolina belonging to Dr. Webb's brother-in-law, George W. Vanderbilt. Webb imported fifty elk and moose from Canada, which he put to grazing in a 20,000-acre forest. For shooting he imported blackcock (black grouse) from Germany and partridges from England; thousands of quail and pheasants were reared annually. Grand gestures came naturally to Dr. Webb: in 1893 he took his entire family on a trip to California and Vancouver, not by private railroad car, but by an entire six-car special train consisting of observation, dining, sleeping, and baggage cars, "and a car fitted up as a play-room for the children." The party was gone three months.

William Collins Whitney outdid all his fellow sportsmen in the number of places he owned to ride, shoot, hunt, and play polo. A financier in New York street railways and husband of a Standard Oil heiress, he had the necessary funds.

He was devoted to the horse sports, ran a racing stable, and owned two of the largest and finest forest preserves in the country, one called Whitney Park in the Adirondacks of 90,000 acres, and the other 10,000 acres in the Berkshire Hills of Massachusetts with an enormous house in Lenox; he was the largest property owner in the State of Massachusetts. He also owned a villa in Newport, a country place at Westbury, Long Island, a house for hunting in Aiken, South Carolina, and a house in Florida. He had a house in London and, of course, a Fifth Avenue mansion. At his estate in Lenox, October Mountain, he bred a herd of American bison much envied by his fellow sportsmen. In 1900, he gave two bulls named Cleveland and McKinley to the newly organized New York Zoological Society (the Bronx Zoo). He also gave twenty elk from his large herd to the State of New York to restock the forests of the Adirondacks. He was constantly holding sporting events at one of his houses. At Wheatly Hills on Long Island, for example, were held the National Beagle Club's field trials, with dinner for entries and their owners served in his private gymnasium.

Even when not being ridden or jumped, horses were conspicuous in Society. Those pulling the vehicles of ladies were as well known, usually by their colors or the liveries of their drivers and footmen, as the ladies themselves—Mrs. Astor's chestnuts with green-liveried coachman, Mrs. Stuyvesant Fish's strawberry roans, the various Vanderbilt ladies with black horses and maroon liveries. There was an enormous variety of carriages: O. H. P. Belmont drove a spider phaeton, Orme Wilson, Mrs. Astor's son-in-law, a victoria. Mrs. Herman Oelrichs (Theresa Fair), who had enormous Nevada mining wealth and was a law unto herself, drove in Central Park in a daumont, designed especially for visiting, with liveried footman perched up behind from whence they jumped down to deliver calling cards at the houses of friends.

The horse was shortly to be rivaled by the new automobile. The Four Hundred led the way in automobiling: even Mrs. Stuyvesant Fish maneuvered an electric wagonette around the Newport lanes. The proud owners were called "the automobility." The first automobile show in America was held in 1899 in New York, and was attended by numerous members of the Four Hundred. By 1901 *Life* magazine could declare "A man who would now win the parvenu's bow must belong to the automobility." There was not really a word for the place you kept your vehicle; "garage" was not in use for several years. When in 1900 the novelist Paul Leicester Ford, an early enthusiast, built a new house at 37 East 77th Street, newspapers described it as having "a room for the storage of automobiles on the street floor." At the turn of the century there were still only about

13,000 automobiles in the United States, which shows that automobiling was still a rich man's sport. Edward Wharton, husband of the novelist, was news in 1904 when in his new machine he drove from The Mount, their house in the Berkshires, to Hartford and returned whole.

In 1904 a versifier satirized the new rage with a parody of *The Charge of the Light Brigade*:

Half a block, half a block
 Half a block onward
All in their motobiles
 Rode the Four Hundred
"Forward!": the owners shout
"Racing car!" "Runabout!"
 Into Fifth Avenue
 Rode the Four Hundred
"Forward!" the owners said
Was there a man dismay'd?
Not, though the chauffeurs knew
 Some one had blundered.
Theirs not to make reply,
Theirs not to reason why,
Theirs but to kill or die
 Into Fifth Avenue
Rode the Four Hundred.

Members of the Vanderbilt family were leading "automobilists." William Kissam Vanderbilt ("Willie K."), an expert driver himself, established the motor raceway on the Jericho Turnpike on Long Island in 1900 and donated the Vanderbilt Cup for speed. He gave his son Harold, aged eight, a gasoline-driven tricycle and himself drove a Locomobile. Dave Hennen Morris, who was married to Alice Vanderbilt Shepard, was elected president of the Automobile Club of America in 1904. Mrs. Clement C. Moore was married to the grandson and namesake of the clerical author of the same name who wrote "The Night Before Christmas." Mr. Moore's income from West Side Manhattan real estate permitted them to live in Paris and travel in the winter to Egypt. In 1900 she began to take a great interest in automobiling and claimed to be one of the first American women to own a "motor." Beatrice Bend of the Four Hundred married the most ardent automobilist of all, Cortlandt Field Bishop, heir to a vast New York City real estate fortune. He was a man without paid occupation who was a book collector, a sportsman, a bal-

At 15 East 67th Street (midblock on left) lived Cortlandt Field Bishop, heir to a New York real estate fortune and a notable collector of rare books, and his wife who was Amy Bend of the Four Hundred.

loonist, and, most ardently of all, an automobilist. His wife enthusiastically joined him in motoring. At Lenox, where they had an enormous house called Ananda, signs had been erected by the township reading "Automobiles not allowed," for fear they would scare the horses. Bishop and his wife pursued a vigorous campaign against these signs, which he finally had removed. They took long automobile trips to Europe; in many parts theirs was the first automobile seen. They even took a car to North Africa and into the Sahara, where, the newspapers reported, "their big car frightened the camels into running away, but had little or no terrors for the natives."

A humbler sport was bicycling, the craze for which came in two halves: in the 1870s a simple bicycle known as a "boneshaker" was seen on the streets, followed by the famous high wheel machine that has entered legend. In the second wave, in the early 1890s, the "safety" bicycle, low-wheeled and suitable for ladies, appeared, and bicycling became one of the greatest American enthusiasms: clubs were formed that had badges and caps and sashes and organized expeditions to the suburbs and beauty spots. Real enthusiasts aimed to achieve a "century," that

Astor money enabled James Van Alen to lead a life of mansion-building (Wakehurst, above, in Newport) and expensive sporting pleasure. When the federal income tax was instituted in the U.S. he was so insulted that he moved to Europe.

is, a 100-mile trip on a cycle. Bicycling at night was popular, and along the new Riverside Drive "a myriad of twinkling headlights moved in a glowing, shifting, dreamy maze," as one historian put it. Mrs. Stephen Van Rensselaer Cruger (Julie Grinnell Storrow) was a favorite of the press, which even ran stories when she fell off her bicycle while "taking an afternoon spin on her wheel last week in Central Park." Fortunately, there were no spectators to this humiliating tumble because, "It has been the custom of Mrs. Cruger, like many others in the fashionable world, to convey her wheel in her carriage to a secluded place in the park, and there pursue the exercise." The Duke of Marlborough, betrothed to Consuelo Vanderbilt, took up the sport in New York where he was arrested for "scorching," or riding recklessly, on his bike. In a very different level of Society, young Alfred E. Smith, later governor, was so adept at gliding without pedaling that he became known as "the coaster king."

An entire culture of dressing grew up with the sport. The shorter skirts that women wore while cycling provided freedom from the constricting fashions of Victorian time. Cycling costumes were quite expensive and one could have a

James Van Alen married Emily Astor, eldest daughter of William and Caroline Astor, over the furious protests of the bride's father, who hated the groom's father. Challenges to duels were issued but in the end William surrendered to Emily's tears and the wedding came off.

cycling "habit" tailored. Mrs. John Jacob Astor, a devotee, wore a habit of dark blue cloth with a full-skirted coat cut like an eighteenth-century riding coat with wide cuffs and pocket flaps of buff velveteen. "The coat is double-breasted," *Town & Country* reported, "tight fitting, and buttoned with cut-gold buttons, and a lace ruff about the throat."

You could spend a lot of money on coaching, and polo was certainly not cheap, but the really big money was required for yachting, especially after the introduction of steam yachts in 1881. Sailing boats for pleasure was a long tradition in New York with its superb bays and tidal rivers, going back to Dutch days; the word "yacht" is itself Dutch. Organization of the sport began when the New York Yacht Club was founded on July 30, 1844. A syndicate of club members built *The America*, which in 1851 won the celebrated victory over the English Royal Yacht Squadron entry and began the international competition for *The America*'s Cup, which is still staged. The first oceangoing yacht race started on 11 December 1866, from New York to England. The last two decades of the nineteenth century were boom times for the building of yachts: there were twenty-three steam yachts in the New York Yacht Club's squadron in 1882, but by 1900 there were 189.

From the first, the New York Yacht Club required not only seamanship and, of course, money, but the proper social credentials. The unpopular Jay Gould, who was felt to have given capitalism a bad name, was a yachtsman but was never invited to join the club. Instead, in 1883, when his steam yacht *Atalanta* was ready, he joined the American Yacht Club, founded the same year. A generation having wiped the stain off Gould money, his son was later asked to join the New York Yacht Club. The list of the Four Hundred contains about 169 family names. Sixty-seven of these were represented in the New York Yacht Club in 1892, including Astors, Cuttings, Goelets, Havemeyers, Iselins, Kanes, Posts, Potters, Roosevelts, Schuylers, Stokeses, Vanderbilts, and Whitneys. Members wore a handsome badge that the club had made by Tiffany & Co. from 1873 on. It consisted of "a foul anchor, with a circle of gold bearing the name of the club and the date of its organization, the whole surmounted by the Signal Flag of the New York Yacht Club, on a gold plate."

A curious convention dictated that the decorations on these yachts should remind one of the sea, as though the passengers had to be reminded that they were sailing. Hence, the lighting fixtures were concealed by crystals in the shape

Yachting was Society's most expensive sport and high position in the New York Yacht Club was eagerly vied for by men of the Four Hundred. The annual cruise of the yacht club fleet to Newport was a highlight of each summer. Here the fleet lies in Newport Harbor in August, 1888.

The three Kane boys, great-grandsons of John Jacob Astor, had the means to devote their lives to sport. Woodbury Kane stood out as a footballer, crickter, cross-country rider, and polo player. During the Spanish-American War he was one of Colonel Theodore Roosevelt's "Fifth Avenue Boys" in the Cuban campaign.

of turtle-shells and the salt cellars and pepper pots on the dining table were tiny terrestrial globes. Naming the yachts was a matter of grave discussion. Grace (Wilson) Vanderbilt, seeking a name for a new yacht beginning with the letter "V" (the Vanderbilts liked to give "V" names to their private railroad cars and yachts), once asked friends at a party to make suggestions. One brave guest suggested *Vandal*. Grace ignored the suggestion with *sang-froid* and after more discussion settled on *Vanitie*!

One of the grandest of the new steam yachts belonged to William Astor, Caroline's elusive husband. Launched in 1884, the *Nourmahal* was 235 feet long and described by an awed press as "a floating palace" (*all* big yachts were described as "floating palaces"), and "a veritable queen of yachts." The suggestive meaning of the name, which the press delicately refrained from translating, was "Light of the Harem" and it came from the poem *Lallah Rookh* by Thomas Moore. The main saloon, staterooms, and bathrooms were finished in solid hardwood and the entire vessel lighted by electricity, a novelty at the time, with electric bells for service calls in all rooms.

The first member of the Four Hundred to become "Commodore" (president) of the New York Yacht Club was Woodbury Kane. Great-grandson of the first John Jacob Astor, he attended Harvard, where he was a football player, a cricketer, a tennis player, and a polo player. When he graduated, he spent some time in the Far West riding with cowboys. One of his cowboy friends mourned when he left, "Too bad, too bad; he was a good guy and could handle a horse, too, and now it seems he has turned into a Society man, and leads cotillions, whatever they are." During the Spanish-American War Kane was one of the band of "Rough Riders" organized by his friend, Assistant Secretary of the Navy, Theodore Roosevelt. The sons of Hamilton Fish and I. Townsend Burden were also Rough Riders.

The preeminent yachtsman of the period was Ogden Goelet, descendant of a French Huguenot family established in Manhattan in 1667, very large New York landowners, second only to the Astor family. The Goelets had originally been ironmongers. The envious said the Goelets had "learned how to turn iron to gold." More importantly, they early on bought a pasture for their cow, forty or fifty acres, along Fifth, Lexington, and Fourth Avenues and held on to the land. Ogden Goelet spent much of his time in Britain, leasing the enormous Wimborne House in London, where he entertained Alexandra, Princess of Wales. He also lived at 606 Fifth Avenue, and at Newport the Goelets had a villa called Ochre Court. During his yachting career, Ogden Goelet owned many vessels, culminating in the huge steam yacht *Mayflower*, which was 320 feet long and was built in Glasgow in 1896. He enjoyed his colossal yacht only a year; he died aboard the *Mayflower* during the races at Cowes on the Isle of Wight in 1897. His daughter and heiress, with a dowry estimated at $3 million, was Mary ("May") Goelet. After looking over all the British dukes, she announced her engagement to the 8th Duke of Roxburghe. "Socially," wrote *The Home Journal*, "a stupendous amount of importance and interest" lay in the wedding, which took place at St.

Robert Walton Goelet's yacht, the Nahma, *was sailed in numerous European regattas, including those at Kiel, Germany, where the vessel was admired by Kaiser Wilhelm II. After Goelet's death, his widow, Harriette Louise Warren, continued to cross the Atlantic in the* Nahma *and cruise the Mediterranean, where the immense yacht was sometimes mistaken for a warship.*

Thomas Episcopal Church on Fifth Avenue in 1903. "Without the church there was clamor and rabble, but the guests seated within were soon forgetful of the crowds and confusion in the streets, where the frenzied excitement of the women suggested the fury of a mob during the French Revolution," wrote *The Home Journal* in alarm. "The bridesmaids in their Marie Antoinette attire experienced some tremblings much like those of the ill-fated queen."

Ogden's brother, Robert Walton Goelet, and his wife, Harriette Louise Warren, were also yachting enthusiasts. Their yacht, the *Nahma*, inevitably described as "a floating palace," received Kaiser Wilhelm II as a guest; he was said to be "delighted with its appointments." Eerily like his brother, Robert also died aboard his yacht, while it lay in Cannes harbor. His widow continued to yacht, occasionally showing up in Newport. The *Nahma* was so big that once when, with Mrs. Goelet on board, it was passing through the Dardanelles, the Turkish garrison took alarm and prepared to fire, thinking the vessel was a warship. When the mistake was realized, the Sultan was apologetic and sent Mrs. Goelet an order of the Ottoman Empire to make amends. For less distant travel Robert Walton Goelet had constructed for him the *Aunt Polly*, a houseboat that was "a complete summer residence afloat." Two-storied, its bedrooms and private baths had all the interior work made of notched pine, giving it an Adirondack camp atmosphere.

C. Oliver Iselin of New Rochelle, N.Y., descendant of Swiss bankers, had a family dedicated to yachting. He defended The *America*'s Cup four times. His equally enthusiastic wife sailed with him in 1899 on their yacht *Columbia* for the international tryouts. At their house "All View," on the extreme tip of Premium Point at the entrance to New Rochelle, they maintained a veritable sporting community, "a sort of little Tuxedo," *Town & Country* wrote. There Mrs. Iselin taught her children to sail and drew plans for model boats they could try out on the lake in Central Park.

The Goelet family, heirs to vast New York real estate, were leading yachtsman. Ogden Goelet had the steam yacht Mayflower, *320 feet long, built for him in Glasgow in 1896 but died a year later. He was an active member of the New York Yacht Club and the donor of several handsome silver trophies.*

One of the grandest weddings of the Gilded Age united Mary ("May") Goelet, daughter of the yachtsman Ogden Goelet, to the 8th Duke of Roxbughe in 1903. The Goelet money refurbished Floors Castle, the duke's Scottish home, which still contains much French eighteenth-century furniture that came from Mary Goelet.

A "perfect sporting gentleman," much admired in his time, was Winthrop Astor Chanler, born in 1863. Great-grandson of John Jacob Astor I, he was one of the famous "Astor orphans," the ten children of Magdalen Ward Chanler, granddaughter and part-heiress of John Jacob Astor. She and her husband died comparatively young, and their three girls and seven boys were cared for by trustees at Rokeby, a Hudson River estate near Rhinebeck. The children were called "the Astor orphans," although they were, of course, really the Chanler orphans. They were famous for their rowdiness and general resistance to discipline and education; their trustees seem to have been intimidated by their charges. The boys were sportsmen. Lewis Chanler sailed a sloop on Lake George, played polo on Long Island, and hunted in England. (He had attended Cambridge University, where he was president of the Cambridge Union). He practiced criminal law and also had an interest in politics, serving as supervisor of the town of Red Hook, New York, and a member of the New York State Assembly. He had a place in Tuxedo Park. Robert Chanler was also a member of the Assembly. He built Chanler Park along the post road near Rokeby with a grandstand, baseball field, shooting range, and track. He was rather better known as an artist. Even his wife said that Winthrop ("Wintie") and his siblings "had no incentive to work or to choose a profession . . . the boys didn't know how to take orders or to keep regular hours." Relieved by his inheritance of the necessity of paid labor, he was always free to adventure in any part of the world. Adventure usually took the form of sport.

He was extremely handsome: in his youth he was a "B.Y.M.," or "beautiful young man." His future wife, who was also his first cousin once removed, Margaret ("Daisy") Terry, was the daughter of Luther Terry, an expatriate American painter in Rome, who painted neo-Old Master canvases. She described her future husband when they first met in Europe: "He was twenty years old and very good looking: hazel eyes full of a merry light, irrepressibly curly brown hair, an air of great good breeding and courage in his handsome face. . . ." He was attractive to women and once sighed to a pretty young woman, "Oh, for the larger customs of the East." Chanler graduated from Harvard in the class of 1886. He was a friend of Theodore Roosevelt; when Roosevelt was president of the police board of New York during 1895–1897, Chanler often accompanied him on his rounds of the city. Chanler, and perhaps Roosevelt, another keen hunter, seemed to regard criminals as big game. Owen Wister, the novelist (*The Virginian*), one of Chanler's close friends, wrote rather sadly, "Roosevelt may perhaps have been ready to help Chanler harness his alert and restless mind to some sustained occupation. That was never to be." He was content to be, as he was sometimes called, "The Golden Butterfly."

Chanler was one of the original members of the Boone & Crockett Club, founded by Theodore Roosevelt and ten of his big-game hunting friends in December 1887. The founders thought of themselves as conservationists who wanted to prevent "market hunting" and "game hogs" (hunters only interested in securing large bags) from decimating the remaining big game in the United States, thus preventing dedicated hunters from carrying out what they considered the traditions of the sport. Chanler, along with Philip Schuyler of the Four Hundred, was also on the committee of the club that led to the establishment of the New York Zoological Society, which opened in late 1899.

The Astor money enabled Chanler and his large family to live in luxury in many parts of the world—Rome, Newport, Tuxedo, New York. "Wherever thrills were to be had," wrote Maude Howe Elliott, a cousin of his wife's, "there was Wintie in the thick of them." In the winter of 1891–1892, he and Daisy and the family (there were seven children) were living in a house on West 34th Street belonging to the Astor estate, not far from William and Caroline Astor's house. They had a cottage in Tuxedo Park. Daisy hated Tuxedo, where she found the clubhouse "big [and] ugly" and mainly devoted to poker playing by the men. A convinced and argumentative convert to Catholicism, she campaigned for the building of a Roman Catholic church in the park. When the resolutely Episcopalian park refused that demand, she had a chapel built just outside the gates.

Chanler hunted the moufflon, a wild sheep with curved horns, shy and hard to stalk, and therefore much sought by hunters, in Sardinia in 1889. In 1902 he went to Naan, Ireland, with his friend Charles Carroll of the Four Hundred for the fox hunting. Carroll was the great-grandson of Charles Carroll of Carrollton, last surviving signer of the Declaration of Independence; his maternal grandfather was the New York banker Royall Phelps. He and his wife, Suzanne Bancroft, granddaughter of George Bancroft, the historian and diplomat, lived mainly in Paris and Biarritz. They also pursued foxes at Pau in southwestern France.

Pau was an unusual place, filled with upper-class Britons, many of them living there to save money. Sir Richard Francis Burton, the explorer, spent his childhood there when his parents "retreated to the Continent for economy's sake." The British expatriates had started foxhunting, for which the country around was suitable. They were joined by Americans attracted by the climate and the sport. Frank Gray Griswold spent some time there. Rene La Montagne, member of a colonial New York family, goaler of the Rockaway Hunt Club, spent "two rattling good seasons at Pau," commented *The Home Journal* in 1889. "The country around Pau is stiff, and his experience there got him in good condition for the Long Island rail fences." The Carrolls were members of the horsey set in France: in 1901 Charles was elected a member of the Jockey Club, a signal honor as very few, if any, Americans were members. When they were in Ireland Chanler and Carroll hunted with the Meath Hounds five days a week. On the sixth day, they went out with the Ward Staghounds. They hunted until the first frost came in November. Later, when he was living in Rome, Chanler organized the Roman Foxhounds that hunted the Campagna.

Chanler served in the Spanish-American War as a member of "The Cowboy Regiment" known as the "Rough Riders." He was shot in the right arm. In 1900 he went to Morocco to investigate some oil wells, although his qualifications as an oil geologist were not obvious. Actually, he spent his time shooting wild pigs, jackals, wildcats, pigeons, ducks, and, when nothing else was available, hares. Four years later, he and his family moved to the Genesee Valley in upstate New York, where he bought Sweet Briar Farm and organized the Geneseo Hunt, of which he became master.

Winthrop Chanler was not the only one who essentially devoted his life to sport. Eleanor Robson Belmont, whose husband August Belmont II, was a major figure in the horse world, recalls in her memoirs that they had a house in Hempstead, Long Island, then the center of polo in the United States; Nursery Farm of three thousand acres in nearby Babylon, L. I.; a bungalow in Lexington, Kentucky where they had a stud farm; a cottage, The Surcingle, in Saratoga for the races that had its own private training track; a quail shooting place at Garnet, South Carolina; a Newport "cottage" called By-the-Sea, which required sixteen servants indoors, four men in the garage, three in the stable, and gardeners as required by the season; and of course a Fifth Avenue residence. Their private railroad car, the *Mineola,* carried them to all these places and also to Canada to hunt moose and to kill salmon on the celebrated Restigouche River. August Belmont, in addition, bred fox terriers and was president of the American Kennel Club, chairman of the American Jockey Club, vice-commodore of the New York Yacht Club, and president of the Meadow Brook Club. He played polo there with his three sons, who were known as "Battery B." The Belmont racing colors were scarlet and maroon and those colors were carried into their everyday life: the liveries of their male servants were a maroon coat with scarlet piping and silver buttons with the Belmont crest, worn with knee breeches of black satin. All their carriages were painted maroon with a scarlet stripe on the wheels.

Constance Cary (Mrs. Burton Harrison), although a Confederate whose husband
had been Jefferson Davis's private secretary, after the Civil War became a prominent
figure in New York Society and won respect for her novels, plays, and memoirs.
She was a leader of the "Upper Bohemia" part of Society.

6
Authors, Architects, and An Astronomer

onsuelo Vanderbilt, Duchess of Marlborough, took refuge from a grim marriage in "sociological work." On a trip to New York in 1908 her mother, Mrs. O. H. P. Belmont, gave a dinner in her honor at the newly opened Plaza Hotel. Following the dinner was a lecture on "The Modern Issue," which was interpreted as "the responsibilities of wealth." *Town & Country* remarked complacently, "Those people who deny the existence of a serious-minded social world should have seen how tractably, even cheerfully, all the well-known bachelors submitted to this mental nourishment."

The Four Hundred received very few such compliments. They had an unhappy reputation as light minded at best or frivolous at worst. If you praised a man like Elisha Dyer, Jr., or Thomas Cushing by calling him "a noted cotillion leader," it was difficult to take him seriously. The fatuous comments of Ward McAllister on behavior hardly emphasized accomplishment. Newspapers chronicling the Four Hundred in the detail now devoted to movie stars and rock singers, relished extravagance and frivolity, and loved quarrels and rivalries. The antics of Mrs. Stuyvesant Fish and Mrs. Hermann Oelrichs enthralled their readers and they never tired of descriptions of Goelets's yachts or the Newport competition of the Vanderbilt wives. The clothing of the ladies was fascinating, too, in an age when dress was elaborate and specialized; the first issue of *Vogue*, which appeared in 1892, inventoried the trousseau of Consuelo Vanderbilt, about to marry the Duke of Marlborough, in such detail that even her monogrammed underwear was described and pictured.

Three intellectual ladies depicted New York Society as mindless and pleasure-seeking: Margaret ("Daisy") Chanler, Edith Wharton, and Constance Cary.

Edith Wharton dwelled on the philistinism of the New York in which she grew up; the most serious intellectuals among her characters collect snuff boxes. Daisy Chanler, an American who had spent her childhood in Rome among expatriate artists and writers, "saw the United States with foreign and unfriendly eyes" when she was brought to New York as the bride of Winthrop Chanler. In her two volumes of memoirs that became standard references on the Gilded Age, she deplored the lack of culture in New York circles. Like her close friend Edith Wharton, she was not charitable about her contemporaries. "As a society," she wrote of the New York circle she knew in the 1890s, "it seemed flat and arid, a Sahara without lions or lion hunters [distinguished people were lions and their hostesses lion hunters]. The Four Hundred would have fled in a body from a poet, a painter, a musician, or a clever Frenchman." Constance Cary, who published many books under her married name, Mrs. Burton Harrison, and also wrote plays and nonfiction books about Society, ridiculed the lack of sophistication among New York's social strivers; her novels abound with New York Society types committing cultural gaffes.

The circle of the Four Hundred was not Proustian. One searches memoirs in vain for the kind of conversation that was going on simultaneously at the fictional dinner table of the Duchesse de Guermantes. The Four Hundred's table talk was not memorable. Charles Francis Adams wrote of millionaires as a class: "a less interesting crowd I do not care to encounter. Not one that I have ever known would I care to meet again either in this world or the next; nor is one associated in my mind with the idea of humour, thought, or refinement." Visiting foreigners weighed in. The haughty Lord Curzon sneered at New York: "The men busy, sallow, straw-hatted, perspiring . . . a city whose entire existence appeared to be the apotheosis of business, with but the smallest concessions to sentiment, aesthetics, or romance." This vigorously negative view did not prevent his marrying an American heiress, Mary Leiter of the Four Hundred, daughter of a self made merchant and a mother famous for her grammatical errors. Curzon used her money to restore his dilapidated stately home, Kedleston, in England.

Despite wealth, travel, and familiarity with Europe, New York Society *was* in some ways unsophisticated. Publicly at least, it showed a prudish face; every tiresome and unrealistic "moral" convention of the American middle class was observed: when Mrs. Douglas Cruger opened her new home at 120 West 14th Street she adorned the entrance hall with classical statues she had accumulated during a long sojourn in Europe. Guests at her first parties professed themselves horrified at the nudity of the marbles though surely those frigid white figures inspired no lustful thoughts in her guests. "To save their blushes," Mrs. Cruger agreed that when she gave a party the offending parts of the statues would be covered with pocket handkerchiefs.

New York Society supported "culture," was generous with donations, and joined boards but was not, it is pretty plain, interested in being emotionally or intellectually involved. Lectures, which required only keeping awake, were easy and popular. Peter Marié, who professed to unite the arts with social life, founded the Thursday Evening Club, which first met at his house on 37th Street. Members listened to authorities on diverse subjects; the aim was "intellectual intercourse and improvement of the mind by lectures." Marié, always ingratiating himself with the ladies, designed a mock coat-of-arms for the new organization: two blue stockings crossed. While not specifically stated, the proper social background was necessary for membership, or *de rigueur* as the members would undoubtedly say. By 1903 criticisms were heard that the intellectual content was diluted, and a critic thought lectures were all right in their place—before lunch—but in the evening after dinner all should be "bright and gay," the implication being that intellectual enquiry was exhausting and could not possibly be amusing. Nevertheless, the club still exists. Constance Cary Harrison thoroughly approved of the Thursday Evening Club of which she wrote, "To this club have belonged successive generations of the more conservative families of New York. Its waiting list is long and elected members step serenely into place conscious that neither fleeting time nor fickle fashion can disturb their dignified tenure of privilege." The Harrisons entertained the club with programs of readings by Society authors in their home at 83 Irving Place. The address just off Gramercy Park was in the heart of Upper Bohemia: Elizabeth Marbury and Elsie de Wolfe would conduct their famous salon on Irving Place; Robert Chanler, the artist among the "Astor orphans," lived nearby. O. Henry, who was unknown to the Four Hundred, lived at 55 Irving Place. A typical evening included a sketch by Mrs. S. Van Rensselaer Cruger (Julie Grinnell Storrow) entitled "The Moujik." She had traveled in Russia, where according to her, a Russian prince had passionately pursued her, a claim that left the other ladies either indignant about possible impropriety, or envious of her adventure. Mrs. Frederic Rhinelander Jones (Mary Cadwalader Rawle), always standing on the ramparts of literature, read one of her poems. The program was followed by supper for the hundred guests.

In the early 1880s, a study club for women named Causeries de Lundi after the famous column of literary criticism published each Monday by the Parisian critic Charles Augustin Sainte-Beuve was founded by Mrs. Hamilton Fish, Mrs. John Jacob Astor, Mrs. John Kean, and other ladies including at least two professional writers, the novelist Mrs. Schuyler Crowninshield and Miss Justine Bayard Erving, the historian and critic. Causeries de Lundi met regularly to talk about books for more than forty years. The Entertainment Club, also all women, met at the Waldorf-Astoria Hotel "to study topics of the day." The ladies' minds were not exclusively focused on current events: at a lecture on Alaska, Mrs. Rhinelander Waldo, mother of a Deputy Police Commissoner of New York, wore a low-cut gown, an innovation not well received by the other members, who considered the attire "too dressy." The dispute among the ladies reached public print and sparked strong opinions. Mrs. Waldo wrote to the newspapers indignantly, "It was intimated to me that the club was displeased with my attire. I was informed that the president of the club had received thirty-three letters from young women who took exception to the cut of my gown." So at the next evening Mrs. Waldo wore a black shawl over her shoulders but still heard mutterings that "I was getting to be 'actressy' in my manner." So she dropped the shawl but wore a blue gown to which exception was also taken: "I received scores of complaining letters," wrote Mrs. Waldo, whose presence was clearly not desired at all. She retired from the field and devoted herself to building an eccentric neo-French Renaissance house on the southeast corner of Madison Avenue and East 72nd Street, turreted and loaded with outdoor statuary, which is still standing and occupied by a Ralph Lauren store. Women were the backbone of these organizations partly because they were forbidden to join, or even visit, most of the city's numerous other clubs, which had all-male memberships. The first real women's club was the Sorosis, organized in 1868, but mainly professional women joined and it didn't interest Society; the first women's club with a Four Hundred membership, the Colony, did not come along until 1903.

Among the city's literary hostesses was Mrs. Frederick W. Whitridge, who conducted one of New York's few salons. She came honestly by her interests: she was the daughter of the English poet and educator Matthew Arnold. In her house at 16 East 11th Street gathered literary figures, nicely balanced with Society. Across the street at number 21 was another literary house, presided over by Mary Cadwalader Rawle Jones. She was forty-two when McAllister listed her name along with that of her husband, Frederic Rhinelander Jones, whom she had married in 1870, when she was twenty. He was an heir to the Chemical Bank of New York, founded by his relatives, the Jones and Mason families. His sister, Edith Newbold Jones, became famous as Edith Wharton. Mary Jones was of colonial Pennsylvania

One of New York's most literary hostesses was Mary Cadwalader Rawle (Mrs. Frederic Rhinelander Jones), sister-in-law and close friend of Edith Wharton. She entertained her literary friends, who included F. Marion Crawford, Henry James, and Henry Adams in her little house at 21 East 11th Street.

stock; the important part of the name, to which she always called attention, was "Cadwalader," a revered one in Philadelphia. Her friend Henry James and others called her "Mary Cadwal," and she passed the name on to her daughter, Beatrix Cadwalader Jones, who also appeared among the Four Hundred. The slender, dark-haired Mary was always called Minnie by her sister-in-law Edith Wharton. The Rawle–Jones marriage was never happy but the couple stayed together until 1905, when they began divorce proceedings that soon were bitter. Fred, who never had a profession, died in Paris in 1917, estranged from Minnie, from their daughter Beatrix, and from his sister Edith, who although she lived nearby hadn't seen him for years and complained that she was obliged "to go through the motions" of mourning. Although Minnie and Fred were incompatible, she formed a steady friendship with Edith, who was bored, as she liked to say, by the company of most women. She helped Edith with her refugee work in France during World War I and acted as her business agent in New York. In return, Wharton extended financial assistance, of which Minnie always stood in need.

Minnie's house at 21 East 11th Street was visited by many *littérateurs.* Daisy Chanler said the house was "full of books and old engravings" and "an island of refuge" for F. Marion Crawford, Henry James, John La Farge, Augustus Saint-Gaudens, John Singer Sargent, and Theodore Roosevelt. On the second story were two rooms called by Minnie "the author's suite," where she put her writers when they came on visits. She was especially close to Henry James. Millicent Bell, writing of Henry James, said, "All his feeling for Old New York seemed sometimes to concentrate upon his vision of Mary Cadwalader Jones." Daisy Chanler found "all the books of the day on the table, all those of the past, well bound, standing shoulder to shoulder in ordered ranks along every available wall space." Like most people in Society, Daisy Chanler liked Minnie, who truly loved literature and excelled as a hostess. "She has stood and fought for good English, good manners, good citizenship," wrote Mrs. Chanler, who learnedly and typically—she was a little inclined to show off her Continental education—called Minnie "the typical Bee-Woman praised by Pindar."

Minnie herself wrote. In 1900 she published *European Travel for Women,* based on her extensive travels on the Continent. She recommended taking along warm underwear, a portable rubber bathtub, and a bottle of brandy. Giving advice and assistance was very much Minnie's forte. She was an active worker in and for hospitals in New York and led a campaign for a badly needed school of social work at Blackwell's Island in the East River. The other side of Minnie was that she was *too* busy and her interest in the affairs of her friends, though kindly meant, was often seen as meddling. In 1908 her friend Henry Adams wrote from Paris about her: "She is in a tub of trouble and distress . . . Poor woman! She is always in trouble, chiefly owing to what she calls her 'gaffs' which means her nervous restlessness and craving to do good to everybody—or to tell everybody how much she would like to do them good if she could." He continued, "Her energy is restless and tireless and she hankers for a job." He occasionally gave her small employments himself: the same year she was bidding on Chinese porcelain for him at an art auction.

One of her principal visitors was the novelist Francis Marion Crawford, a cousin of both Ward McAllister and the Chanlers. He was the son of Thomas Crawford, an expatriate American sculptor in Italy, and Louisa Ward and was Daisy Chanler's half-brother. He was Julia Ward Howe's nephew, a great favorite of hers and of her brother, the lobbyist and host "Uncle" Sam Ward. Crawford had grown up in Italy and made that country his home for most of his life. He was sent, however, to St. Paul's School in New Hampshire for some American

Francis Marion Crawford, a nephew of Julia Ward Howe and a cousin of Ward McAllister, was connected with the Four Hundred in many ways. One of the most successful writers of his time, he laid most of his melodramatic novels in Renaissance Italy and with their proceeds bought an Italian castle for himself.

education before attending Cambridge University. He visited Boston, and his Aunt Julia introduced him into her refined circle where poetry in Greek was quoted during receptions. In New York, on the other hand, Uncle Sam Ward entertained him at his famous dinners and evenings at the theater, no doubt more exciting for a young man than reciting Greek. Crawford was handsome and aware of his looks. He was vain and boasted of his physique: he once told Minnie Jones that "he had the exact measurements of a certain classic statue in the Louvre," which turned out to be that of Antinoüs. A more objective observer in the press described him as "a large man, with a fresh, florid complexion and ener-

getic blue eyes . . . [who] looks like a healthy Englishman." His looks and sophisticated background (he spoke half a dozen languages) brought him to the attention of the celebrated Isabella Stewart Gardner, hostess, art collector, and dis-
turber of the social peace in Boston. There has been much speculation about their
relationship: he was handsome and young; she was flamboyant but very plain and
fourteen years older. Although they were certainly close friends for a while, there
is no evidence of a love affair, which seems unlikely for other reasons than age
difference—both, for instance, claiming to be profoundly religious, Crawford a
convert to Roman Catholicism, Gardner an Anglo-Catholic. Crawford eventually married Bessie Berdan, daughter of an American diplomat, and settled in
Sorrento, where he exhausted his assets in building and maintaining a castle he
couldn't afford.

He was a prolific and successful novelist who knew his audience well.
When he arrived in the States for a visit in 1892 he was interviewed on ship-
board where he told the press, "I am a thorough American and will speak of the
United States as 'home.' . . . I think there is a richer field for the novelist in the
United States than in Europe. There are more original characters to be found
here, and they are in greater variety." He was man of his time so far as prudery
was concerned: "It is true," he said solemnly, "that to be successful in any degree
today, a writer in English must bear in mind that he is writing for women,
mainly for young women, and wholly for respectable women. . . . The subject of
sex must be always entirely excluded from successful novels, for the reason that
they are intended to be read by young women." His prudent stories were laid
in Renaissance Italy or in contemporary New York (*Katherine Lauderdale* and its
sequel *The Ralstons*, for example, the action of which largely occurs in the Fifth
Avenue neighborhood of his friend Minnie Jones's house). He was a slow
starter: until he was twenty-eight years old he hadn't done much of anything
except spend money from his mother's steadily diminishing fortune, and his relatives constantly complained of his indolence. After his first successs, *Mr. Isaacs*,
a story he heard in India (where he had gone to study Sanskrit!) he never slowed
down, publishing sixty-six books in the twenty-eight years between 1881 and
1909, many of them in more than one volume.

When Crawford visited New York his publishers, Macmillan, put him up in
a penthouse in their building at 66 Fifth Avenue, but he spent most of his free
time at Minnie Jones's nearby house. He kept a carpenter's kit in an upstairs room
and repaired anything around the house that had been broken, specializing in
injured umbrellas. In return, Minnie always gave him his favorite dessert, rice

pudding topped with strawberries. When the creative mood was upon him he wrote five thousand words a day, Sundays excepted. His writing habits were fixed: he arranged his worktable so that the light fell on the paper from his left. He sat with his side to the table, his right arm resting on it and the paper parallel with its length. The temperature in the room had to be sixty degrees. When writing one of his books he lived entirely on crackers and dried apples. He relaxed by fencing. He was eccentric, melancholy, always worried about money, and a believer in astrology. His perennial lack of money was easily explained: the expenses of his villa in Sorrento, called the Villa de Renzis when he bought it and named by him the Villa Crawford, consumed what he made from his steady writing. The little stone castle overhung the sea and was always about to slide into it; a seawall had to be erected at enormous expense to shore it up. Frank and Bessie and their four children lived in great state with many formally attired menservants: "White ties were bought by the boxful," his cousin Maude Howe Elliott wrote.

Minnie Jones was a reliable friend for Crawford: she even wrote a book for him, a lightweight account of Bar Harbor in a series Scribner's was publishing on American summer resorts that Crawford had undertaken, but couldn't find time to write. He revised Minnie's manuscript and when the book was published under his name in 1896, gave her the royalties. Minnie had a house in Bar Harbor called Reef Point, looking out over Frenchman Bay, that she and Fred Jones had built in the 1880s. Bar Harbor was considered more intellectual than Newport, which was not saying much, and many of Society's more serious members summered there—Constance Cary Harrison, for example. Minnie took a great interest in Bar Harbor, especially in its cleanliness; she was active in the Village Improvement Society and presented the town with a handsome pushcart "to be used in gathering waste-paper from the streets."

Few Society women had professions; they were actively discouraged from working for money. Beatrice Bishop, whose mother was Amy Bend of the Four Hundred, remembered her mother telling her she should never work for pay because it would deprive someone of a job who actually needed the pay. A notable exception was the Four Hundred's Beatrix Cadwalader Jones, Minnie and Fred's only child, who not only entered a profession but, in fact, developed a new one. From childhood she loved plants. She studied botany at Harvard's Arnold Arboretum and traveled with her mother and sometimes with her aunt Edith Wharton, an ardent gardener, to the famous gardens of England and the Continent. She then looked out for clients to commission gardens from her. One

Lewis Morris Rutherfurd of the Four Hundred was America's greatest astronomer in the late nineteenth century, making important discoveries in the heavens with a photographic telescope he invented. He photographed his son Rutherfurd Stuyvesant (who reversed his name to inherit the Stuyvesant estate) and his bride-to-be Mary Pierrepont about 1863.

of her first commissions was the garden at Wakefield in Newport, built by William and Caroline Astor's son-in-law, James J. Van Alen. Then there was the garden for Emily Vanderbilt Sloane's enormous Elm Court at Lenox, Massachusetts. From private clients she moved to designing for institutions, especially colleges and universities: Yale, Princeton, and Stanford among them. *Town & Country* noted approvingly, "Her landscape gardening is so far from being an ephemeral fad that she hangs out her 'shingle,' inviting competition with all the 'mere men' who are classed as landscape architects." Greatly respected for her accomplishments, Beatrix Jones was not one of the easiest members of the Four Hundred. Very aware of her patrician background, she had the same chilly manner for which her aunt Edith Wharton was only too famous; she did not suffer fools gladly. As her list of important commissions lengthened, she became quite bossy and sometimes astonishingly high-handed with her clients. Without having previously shown any interest in marrying, she suddenly at the age of forty-one married Max Farrand, a Yale professor and distinguished authority on the United States Constitution. They divided their later years between California, where Farrand became director of the Henry E. Huntington Library, and the house at Reef Point, Bar Harbor.

The Four Hundred counted one internationally distinguished scientist among them, the astronomer Lewis Morris Rutherfurd. He and his wife were part of the "Second Avenue set," considered the staidest, but most aristocratic, circle in New York Society. They lived in a large brick house at 175 Second Avenue on the corner of 11th Street, property that had come down through the Stuyvesant family, a part of the Governor's farm or *bouwerie*, surrounded by numerous kin. Margaret (Chanler) Rutherfurd, always called Daisy, descended from Peter Stuyvesant as well as from John Winthrop, first governor of the Massachusetts Bay Colony, and Robert Livingston, first Lord of Livingston Manor. Rutherfurd himself was twice (his parents were first cousins) the great-grandson of Lewis Morris, signer of the Declaration of Independence. He was a graduate of Williams College who also attended law school and was a member of the Peter Augustus Jay and Hamilton Fish (also a Stuyvesant descendant) law firm for a short time. Blessed with large independent means, Rutherfurd turned to his real interest, astronomy. He was one of the first astronomers to pursue "celestial photography" and developed a unique spectroscope for taking photographs of the heavens. The house on Second Avenue had its own observatory with a thirteen-inch refracting telescope, one of the best in the United States. He used to invite his friends to drink tea and watch the heavens. George Templeton Strong spent the evening there in 1859: "Rutherfurd was watching the movements of a little miserable, loafing comet, like a detective policeman. . . . It looked like a distant street lamp dimly seen through the fog by a near-sighted man, a small, amorphous, hazy blotch of faint light." Another time, "the sky was cloud [and] the planets didn't 'receive'." When asked to explain how he became an astronomer, Rutherfurd said, "I cannot. My family contained no one else with an aptitude for mathematics. Only in college did I learn that people counted on their fingers. I was surprised, supposing all children counted in their heads as I had done."

His trailblazing scientific endeavors never prevented Lewis Rutherfurd from leading an active social life. When he was a young man and wanted to call on Julia Ward (later Howe), her strict father prevented his calling at their great Bond Street house "because he belonged to the fashionable world." The Rutherfurds had a musical household: Lewis and Daisy sang duets and took the children to rehearsals of the Philharmonic Orchestra on Friday afternoons. Opera stars like Christine Nilsson, then at the height of her renown at the Metropolitan Opera and a great favorite of New York Society, came to 175 Second Avenue to sing for them and their guests. At the same time, the Rutherfurds' active social life did not keep him from his telescope, often in company with his wife. When one of his nieces asked if "Aunt Daisy" helped in his work, he replied, "Yes, indeed. Many and many a night your aunt stood handing me slides as I experimented with light." Rutherfurd was large and stately and wore his silver hair rather long; he looked just the way nineteenth-century America liked its men of science to look. He and his wife divided their time between Second Avenue, Tranquility, the old Rutherfurd estate in New Jersey, and Edgerton, their house in Newport. At each house they entertained. Mrs. Rutherfurd was very popular as a hostess. Constance Cary Harrison said of her: "No parties seemed more agreeable to me, more an exponent of the best New York could do in the way of uniting gentle people all of a kind, than Mrs. Rutherfurd's. That pair presented the unusual combination of an uncommonly beautiful woman married to a uncommonly handsome and distinguished man. Mrs. Rutherfurd was a law-giver in her circle and no weak one; she invited whom she pleased, as she pleased, and an offender against her exactions came never any more. But she had the prettiest way in the world of putting people in the appropriate place."

A Society woman who wrote professionally was Mrs. Stephen Van Rensselaer Cruger (Julie Grinnell Storrow), a grandniece of Washington Irving. Her husband, who was in the real estate business, was descended from the two mayors of New York named Cruger. She used the name "Julien Grant" for novels, her own

Mrs. Stephen Van Rensselaer Cruger (Julie Storrow Grinnell) wrote breathy romance novels and books of travels in which she slyly recounted the powerful effect she made on amorous foreign princes. She claimed to come honestly by her literary talent, being the grand-niece of Washington Irving.

name for travel books. Julie Cruger was a lady of style. When she was presented at the British Court in 1894 she wore primrose velvet lined with yellow satin with a petticoat of ivory satin embroidered in silver and gold sequins and the customary (required, in fact) white plume in her hair and veil. She was liberally besprinkled with diamonds. At Bayville on the North Shore of Long Island she built Idlesse, a country home in the American colonial style overlooking Long Island Sound. She later moved to "a fine old mansion" in the Georgetown neighborhood of Washington, D.C. To create the true colonial atmosphere she tabooed gas and electricity, and the house was lighted only by candles. *Town & Country* remarked admiringly, "When the mood for writing is upon her, Mrs. Cruger shuts herself away from everybody and works eight or nine hours a day, but when her book or story is finished she becomes again the woman of fashion and grande dame."

Also a writer, and later a well-known lecturer was Julia Dent Grant, the youngest person on Ward McAllister's list, sixteen years old in 1892. She was the granddaughter of President Ulysses S. Grant and was being presented to American Society, having already made her debut in Europe, when her father was ambassador to Austria. Her appearance on McAllister's list is surprising: her grandfather had been president, but the family was neither aristocratic nor rich, and not really New Yorkers. General Grant had failed in business before the Civil War, and throughout his life lacked financial sense. When he left the presidency, Grant and his wife Julia had moved to New York, taking a house at 3 East 66th Street presented to him by public subscription; the citizens of New York also made him a cash present. He and his sons joined a brokerage firm organized by Ferdinand Ward called Grant & Ward, hoping to capitalize on the ex-president's fame, although his record in handling money should hardly have inspired confidence in their investors. The Grant family were poor judges of character: Ward absconded with $15 million, leaving the Grants with a loss of $500,000 and nearly destitute. They survived on a loan from William H. Vanderbilt and an advance from Mark Twain's publishing house of $20,000 for Grant's *Memoirs,* which he was writing although already stricken with the cancer of the throat that was to kill him. The president's eldest son, Frederick Dent Grant, helped with research. Mark Twain, who dealt with him, said Fred had "a curious, rather bored, monotone voice." Twain did not like Fred and even confessed to being afraid of him. Grant died while his book was still in manuscript and it was edited by Frederick. Sold door to door by subscription, Grant's *Memoirs* was one of the greatest successes in American publishing history. The first check sent by the publishers to the family came to over $300,000.

The youngest member of the Four Hundred, Julia Dent Grant, granddaughter of President U.S. Grant was only sixteen years old when Ward McAllister put her on his list. Married a few years later to the Russian Prince Cantacuzene, she survived the Russian Revolution of 1917 and was the last surviving member of the Four Hundred when she died in 1975.

Frederick married Ida Marie Honoré, niece of Mrs. Potter Palmer, social ruler of Chicago. In 1889 President Harrison named him minister to Austria. Daughter Julia made her debut in Vienna, bowing before the Emperor Franz Joseph at the age of sixteen. "My hair was not put up on my head," she said, "for my mother thought me too young, but my braid which was heavy and shiny, was twisted by myself and fastened in a great bundle low on the nape of my neck."

("Putting her hair up" was a sign that a girl had made her bow to Society.) She wore a gown of soft white ruffles of transparent gauze with a stiff satin waist covered with clear crystal beads, white satin slippers and, for the first time in her life, long gloves. Frederick, who was no more liked in Austria than he was in the United States, soon brought his family back to New York, where he rented a house on West 73rd Street. He joined the police department. "We found American Society rather liked European traditions," wrote his sophisticated daughter Julia. "It was still in the phase where people composing it were limited in number and were acknowledged as those names distinguished in colonial or revolutionary history." She was sponsored at a Patriarch's Ball by Mrs. William Rhinelander Stewart (Annie Armstrong), who possessed those qualifications. Apparently becoming acquainted with Ward McAllister at the Patriarchs, Julia then made it onto his list. On a visit to Europe, she met Prince Michael Michailovitch Cantacuzene, a Russian nobleman who claimed descent from the medieval emperors of Byzantium. They were married in Newport, at Beaulieu, a house that her aunt Mrs. Potter Palmer was renting, first in a Greek Orthodox ceremony, then with the rites of the Protestant Episcopal Church. Her grandmother's gift to her was a magnificent pearl, diamond, and emerald necklace that had been given to her by the citizens of Mexico City when she and the ex-president were on a trip around the world. From then on she was known as Julie Feodorovna Cantacuzena. The prince took her to his family's estate at Bourmoka in Russia, which was both primitive and luxurious. And remote—fifty miles from a telegraph. They were caught there by the Russian revolution of 1917. They escaped, and back in the West Julia began writing and lecturing about her experiences in Russia.

There was a type of educated New Yorker who participated in the cultural life of the city, but didn't inconvenience themselves in the cause. Egerton Winthrop, a descendant of John Winthrop, colonial governor of Massachusetts, and born to wealth, was, according to his friend Edith Wharton, a prize example of the type. He had lived in Paris after his first wife's death but returned to New York in 1885, settling in a house on East 39th Street that he decorated in the French Renaissance style. He languidly practiced as a lawyer. Egerton Winthrop lives in the words of Edith Wharton, who was about the age of his children. When she was a young woman, encompassed on all sides, as she saw it, by her Philistine relations, she was introduced to the ideas of Darwin and Huxley, as well as to the French Naturalist novelists by Winthrop, and he traveled with her in Italy. He acted as her lawyer during her divorce from Edward Wharton in 1913. The character Sillerton Jackson in *The Age of Innocence* and the *Old New York* sto-

Julia Dent Grant became well-known in the 1920s for her books and lectures on the Russian Revolution. She and her Russian husband, Prince Cantacuzene, had had hair-raising adventures escaping from the Bolsheviks.

ries is modeled on Winthrop. He was a cultivated man, but fussy and absorbed in the minutiae of Society. Wharton saw even her closest friends with a cool eye: when Winthrop died, Wharton referred to him as "my dear and good and wise friend whom everyone misunderstood but the few people near him." And she wrote to Henry James of Winthrop, "Never, I believe, have an intelligence so distinguished and a character so admirable been combined with interests for the most part so trivial . . . he lived his life in dilettantish leisure." He was not unique in Gilded Age New York.

In 1892 Washington Square was a backwater of Society where a few old families, noteably the Rhinelanders, the Duncans, and the Danas survived in dignified somnolence. Still rich and respected, they no longer counted for much except socially. Edith Warton, who scorned the neighborhood, described it unforgettably in Custom of the Country.

7
Citizens

While Ward McAllister reverenced the Livingstons and discoursed freely on the advantages of colonial ancestry, on his list were many families like the Burdens, the Coopers and Hewitts, the Cuttings, the Haddens, Havemeyers, Frelinghuysens, Howlands, the Kernochans—rich and valued citizens of New York, whose eminence did not go back to New Amsterdam. New York Society was never so exclusive as it dreamed it was: the ranks were open to a newcomer if he or she worked at acceptance and had money to spend; doors could be forced provided one did not mind a few snubs while forcing them. The newer fortunes came from shipping and manufacturing, railroads, and banking. The Burdens and the Coopers were iron manufacturers, the Haddens and the Howlands ship owners, the Havemeyers sugar refiners.

Businessmen have always been respected in New York. In the early years of the nineteenth century they were an instantly identifiable class. Profession and position were easily distinguished by clothing: the old merchants wore black trousers, a swallow-tail coat, wide black stock, low open waistcoat, and a thick linen shirt. Though rich, they prided themselves on dignified but simple living: Mrs. Peter Lorillard, wife of the great tobacco baron, who lived at 40 Chatham Street, had plenty of servants, but when she had guests she herself "would hand around the apples, cracked hickory nuts, and nice things she always kept on hand." Frugality was a prime virtue. It often degenerated into stinginess: certain families—the Goelets in their earlier generations are a good example—were famous for their reluctance to part with money. So were the Lorillards until the third generation, when Pierre Lorillard discovered the joy of spending money in the world of coaching and hunting and founded Tuxedo. The merchants were

169

solid and responsible men, very different from the corner-cutters of the get-rich-quick Gilded Age that followed. Isaac Roosevelt, ancestor of several of the Four Hundred, was a sugar refiner—an amazing number of Four Hundred fortunes began with sugar—on Queen Street during the American Revolution, and from 1786 to 1791, was president of the Bank of New York across the street. "It is said that he would go each morning to his place of business," Allan Nevins wrote in his history of the bank, "and help his son and partner prepare for the work of the day, and then at ten o'clock would walk across the street to the bank to perform his duties as president." Steadfast Protestants, often Evangelicals, most of the old merchants were pious. They founded bible societies, Sunday schools, and orphanages. They insisted on decorum in their rich but austere homes along Bond Street (where Caroline Astor grew up) and around Washington Square. Isaac Sherman, who made a fortune in wholesale cooperage (barrel-making), scorned worldly vanities: he forbade his family to attend the theater and allowed no card-playing in his house. He left $10 million to his daughter Cornelia, who married Bradley Martin of the Four Hundred and became one of the most extravagant hostesses of the end of the century. Many spendthrift members of the Four Hundred were the children and grandchildren of these industrious and thrifty merchants.

The great mercantile houses of New York in the early nineteenth century were N. L. and G. Griswold (known to their rivals as "No Loss and Great Gain Griswold"), importers of rum, sugar, and tea; the Aspinwalls, "commission merchants," who sold cargoes of almost any commodity on which they could profit; LeRoy, Bayard, another great trading house; Archibald Gracie & Co., ship owners; G. G. and S. Howland, who owned the Liverpool packet ships and eventually merged with the Aspinwall firm; and the Grinnells, owners of whaling ships. Catherine Ann Griswold married Pierre Lorillard; Meredith Howland married Adelaide Torrance, a Vanderbilt; Julie Grinnell married Stephen Van Rensselaer Cruger; Daniel Le Roy married Susan Fish, a descendant of Peter Stuyvesant, marriages that melded the patroons, the Knickerbockers, and the old merchants. Legend has it that in New York as in England "being in trade" was a barrier to social advancement. That is only partly true: it was being in *retail* trade, shopkeeping, that constituted the barrier. No shopkeepers were to be encountered among the Four Hundred although many had grandfathers who had kept shop. New York's greatest nineteenth-century retailer was Alexander Turney Stewart, whose mammoth department store on Broadway at Ninth Street was world famous. Although he and his wife, Cornelia (Clinch) Stewart, lived across 34th Street from William and Caroline Astor in a white marble house much grander than the Astors', there was no social familiarity between the families.

The Stewarts' enormous fortune enriched the Four Hundred eventually, however: it went to Mrs. Stewart's nieces and nephews among whom was J. Clinch Smith, a clubman who went down on the *Titanic*.

New York was a great port, renowned for its harbor, a main source of the city's great wealth. Ships like those of Howland & Aspinwall traded with Cuba and Mexico, entered the Mediterranean, and developed the very lucrative Pacific trade. Their bottoms carried an astonishing array of goods: furs (the origin of the Astor fortune), ironware, salt, brandy, "domestics" (textiles), fireworks, and gunpowder, each ship was "a country store on a mammoth scale." With their regular sea routes established, the more adventurous shippers sought other sources of wealth. W. H. Aspinwall, whose grandchildren were among the Four Hundred, left the active management of Howland & Aspinwall in 1850 to organize the Pacific Railroad and Panama Steamship Co. This project was born of the California Gold Rush: Panama was a quicker route by far to the gold fields than crossing the plains and mountains by wagon. You took a ship from New York to Panama, transferred to a train, crossed the Isthmus, and met another ship on the Pacific side bound for San Francisco. The eastern terminus of the line, built in 1855, was named Aspinwall. With part of his vast wealth from shipping W. H. Aspinwall bought paintings; he was a major patron of living American artists. The gallery in his house on 14th Street was open one day a week for viewing by "those who have more taste than money."

The evangelical tradition lingered for generations. John Langdon Erving was a young man in 1892, when he appeared on McAllister's list. Descended from the Van Rensselaers and very well-connected with the old merchants, he was amiable, high minded, and so involved in good works he was known as "Sunbeam" Erving. He faithfully attended the Madison Square Presbyterian Church on East 24th Street. The minister there was the fifty-year-old Dr. Charles H. Parkhurst. On Valentine's Day 1892, just two weeks after Ward McAllister released his list, Dr. Parkhurst, long concerned with municipal sin and new president of the Society for the Prevention of Crime, mounted his pulpit and delivered to his astounded congregation an Old Testament denouncement of bribe-taking police who allowed brothels, gambling parlors, and opium lairs to flourish in Manhattan. Such charges, which were quite true, were not new, but Dr. Parkhurst, hitherto rather mild in his sermons, delivered them with a mighty outrage that roused the respectable classes of the city. Parkhurst did more: he attacked Tammany Hall, the headquarters of Manhattan's Democratic Party and the font of corruption, which he characterized as a "lying, perjured, rum-soaked and libidinous lot." To make himself quite clear, he called the Tammanyites "polluted harpies that under the pretense of governing our city are feeding day and night on its quivering vitals." A grand jury demanded he document his charges. Unable to furnish proofs, he and John Langdon Erving and a private detective, all disguised rather unconvincingly as "bloods" with mustachios and caps, visited bordellos, drug dens, and illegal taverns throughout Manhattan. Amid the open debauchery, Parkhurst and "Sunbeam" Erving found ample evidence of police corruption. Keepers of brothels and other illegal establishments, as they expected, routinely bribed the police and the politicians. Headlines blazed Parkhurst's findings. Although his enemies in the city administration ridiculed Parkhurst's mission and accused him and his friends of enjoying themselves in the brothels and saloons under guise of indignation, Parkhurst's revelations brought a reform party into City Hall three years later that reorganized the police force; Theodore Roosevelt, Jr., the future president, was chairman of the new Police Board.

The Stokes family descended from Thomas Stokes, who came to New York from London in 1798 and made a fortune as a merchant. He was pious, supported Protestant missions, and was a founder of the American Bible, the New York Peace, and the American Tract societies. His son James married Caroline Phelps, an heiress of the great metals firm, Phelps, Dodge Co. Their son, Anson Phelps Stokes of the Four Hundred, was a partner in that firm and also in the banking house of Phelps, Stokes & Co. He was said to own half a million acres of land in the state of Connecticut. His fortune was estimated at around $75 million. A remarkable tradition of philanthropy ran in the family. Anson's daughters Caroline Phelps Stokes and Olivia Eggleston Phelps Stokes donated a dormitory to Yale, St. Paul's Chapel to Columbia University, a school to Booker T. Washington's Tuskegee Institute, a building to Robert College in Constantinople (founded by the Robert and Rhinelander families of the Four Hundred). Stokes benefactions have continued to the present day, the main conduit being the Phelps Stokes Fund, set up in 1911 with a bequest from Caroline, which is mainly devoted to expanding educational opportunities for those in need. The Phelps Stokes family were conscientious and religious (several of Anson's sons, grandsons, and great-grandsons became high-ranking Episcopal clergymen), but not austere; they enjoyed the good things of life, which they owned in abundance. Their summer home, Shadowbrook, in Lenox, Massachusetts, was noted for its size (over one hundred rooms) and its unstinting hospitality. Anson Phelps Stokes was a dedicated yachtsman and published an account his adventures in *Cruising the West Indies* in 1902.

Also rich and philanthropic and jolly were the descendants of Peter Cooper. Peter Cooper was the most respected New Yorker of his time; in the

*Napoleon Sarony, one of
New York's best portrait
photographers, caught Peter
Cooper, the grand old citizen
of New York, at the peak
of his career in business and civic
betterment. Cooper's descendants,
who included inventors,
collectors, philanthropists,
and writers figured largely
in the Four Hundred.*

long history of the city he may be its most universally esteemed citizen. When he died in 1883, the Cuban patriot José Martí, then an exile in the city, wrote that "he lived the Sermon on the Mount," and there were innumerable other commendations. However you wanted to improve New York, you could count on Peter Cooper: he gave money, he chaired innumerable civic betterment meetings, he was a leader in the campaigns for better fire and police protection for the city, for better sanitation, for public education, and improved conditions in prisons. In 1859 he established The Cooper Union for the Advancement of Science and Art, the only private, full-scholarship college in the country. He himself had attended school only fifty-two days in his poverty-stricken youth. Self-taught, the classic tinkering American, Peter Cooper invented lots of new machines, some obviously useful (a grass mower) and some that never caught on (a musical cradle). At different times he was a cabinetmaker, a grocer, and a man-ufacturer of glue at a factory on East 34th Street. He was, more importantly,

Abrams Stevens Hewitt, Peter Cooper's son-in-law, opposed the Tweed Ring's domination of New York and won the mayoralty of the city in 1886 against the young Theodore Roosevelt and the single-taxer Henry George. Like Peter Cooper he fought corruption and struggled to improve services in the burgeoning city. He was long chairman of the family's Cooper Union for the Advancement of Science and Art.

owner of a great ironworks in New Jersey and a major financier in the laying of the Atlantic Cable.

His son, Edward Cooper, was mayor of the city in 1879, and Peter's daughter Sarah Amelia married Abram Hewitt, who was mayor in 1886 (he defeated the young Theodore Roosevelt, Jr.). Despite their lack of a colonial pedigree, the Coopers and their connections featured largely in the Four Hundred. They even entered the ranks of European royalty when in 1924 Eleanor Green, Peter Cooper's great-granddaughter, married Prince Viggo of Denmark, grandson of Christian IX. Peter Cooper's grandson, Peter Cooper Hewitt, as a youngster accompanied his grandfather to lectures at the Cooper Union. Old Peter always took an air cushion that he had invented for sitting on the hard benches of the Great Hall; it was young Peter's duty to follow his grandfather carrying it. The audience generally rose when the little procession entered, and lectures did not begin until the cushion was inflated and the old gentleman comfortably seated. Peter Cooper Hewitt continued the family tradition of inventing by producing an early incandescent light. He showed signs of promise even as a boy by devising a system of silk threads suspended over lower Lexington Avenue, where the Coopers and Hewitts lived, to knock top hats off pedestrians. He and his pals haunted nearby Gramercy Park where they hoisted benches to the top of the flagpole in the center and put firecrackers under the park watchman's seat.

Eleanor Gurnee Hewitt and her sister Sarah Cooper Hewitt, daughters of Abram and Sarah Amelia Cooper Hewitt, founded in 1896 the Cooper Union Museum of Art and Decorating for use by professional designers and design workers, bestowing on it historic textiles, drawings, prints, and decorative arts and making it one of the major museums in the world for the study of the decorative arts. Eleanor, called "one of the dignified representatives of the social regime of old New York," lived with her sister at 9 Lexington Avenue in a house bought for their parents by Peter Cooper. When old Peter died in 1883, Abram Hewitt had the house done over by Stanford White with "Moorish" ceilings and carved oak walls; perched on the stair banister was a stuffed peacock, then a sign of advanced taste. He kept fourteen servants. In 1907 his daughters used the house next door to build a ballroom half a block long. Their home in the country was the old Cooper family place, The Forges at Ringwood Manor, New Jersey, near the ironworks, later given by the family to the state of New Jersey and now Ringwood State Park. None of the Coopers were stuffy. Ex-mayor Hewitt and his wife and daughters liked to dress up as much as anybody in Society, giving one party to which "their guests are expected to come dressed as vegetables." Ladies trimmed their gowns with imitation kitchen gardens, and the gentlemen were given headdresses representing beets, cabbages, or cauliflowers. The idea came from the "plant parties" given at Versailles by Louis XVI and Marie Antoinette. The English art historian Roger Fry, who was serving as a curator at the Metropolitan Museum of Art and was anti-American, met Sarah Hewitt at a dinner in 1906. He found her "age about fifty, looks like an English old maid— a fright and a frump, one thinks, but I have quite lost if not my heart at least my head to her, for she is immense fun." He found her "passionately devoted to the eighteenth century," possessor of a fine library, and a collector of Tiepolo draw-

The Coopers and Hewitts shared a double house, repeatedly enlarged and redecorated at 9 Lexington Avenue near Gramercy Park. The family, despite its reputation for high-minded endeavors, was not stuffy and added a ballroom where imaginative costume balls were given.

ings. The Coopers and Hewitts were all rich and generous: Frederick Cooper Hewitt gave more than $4 million to New York Hospital, the Metropolitan Museum of Art, and Yale University.

Annie and Arthur Leary were a special case in New York Society: the only Irish Catholics on McAllister's list, with a fortune from retail trade. James Leary, their father, was a hatter and made a large fortune from a fashionable New York emporium devoted to selling men's hats. He had an old-time connection with John Jacob Astor, from whom he bought furs, largely beaver skins. Most men's hats were made of beaver skin. It was a good business to be in: men of all classes never went out hatless. Old Leary had his shop in the Astor House hotel on Broadway and Vesey Street. The shop's front window was eye-catching long before "dressed" windows became common. Phrenology, the "science" of "reading" the bumps on a skull and determining all sorts of physiological and psychological characteristics from them, fascinated the public. The phrenologist passed his hands over the patient's head and determined how large were the bumps of "envy," or "kindness," or whatever quality. The size of a head was thought to indicate brain power: the bigger the head, the stronger the mind. Leary preserved the wooden blocks carved as hat-forms for his customers and displayed the largest in his shop window, without, it appears, any complaint from the possessors of these mighty domes. His showpieces were Daniel Webster and General James Watson Webb, whose cranial dimensions fascinated passersby. Webb, a fiery newspaper editor and frequent duelist, was the father of Alexander and William Seward Webb of the Four Hundred.

Annie Leary, also of the Four Hundred, James's daughter, born in 1833, lived at 1032 Fifth Avenue, at Pelham, New York, and at Newport. She was among the leading Roman Catholic ladies in New York and for her benefactions to Catholic charities received the papal title of countess from Pope Leo XIII in 1902. New York newspapers loved to refer to her as Countess Leary: the combination of a noble title with a washerwoman's name was irresistible. Very few Americans had been ennobled; they usually had to marry titles at great cost. Countess Leary was jolly and companionable. She had a surprising friendship with Henrietta ("Hetty") Howland Robinson Green, "the Witch of Wall Street." Hetty was the heiress of an old New Bedford, Massachusetts, whaling and shipping fortune that she, blessed with an uncanny skill in investing, had multiplied many times over. She was generally thought to be the richest woman in the United States, owning railroads stocks innumerable. The uncomplimentary name, " Witch of Wall Street" came from her utter neglect of her appearance and her unsavory habits. She lived mainly on leftover oatmeal which she reheated on the radiators in brokerage offices, seldom washed or changed clothes, and lived in two rooms of a dilapidated boardinghouse in Hoboken, New Jersey. She had a husband, Edward Green, rich in his own right, but they seldom were under the same roof (although there were two children) since he could not bear her pursuit of money to the exclusion of a comfortable existence.

The countess was the only person who could drag Hetty from her boardinghouse. Their friendship went far back: Annie had been a bridesmaid at the Green's wedding. Years later, the countess came to the rescue of the couple's only daughter Hetty Sylvia Ann Howland Robinson Green, known as Sylvia, who had been born in 1871. Hetty, hating to spend money, was content to let her only daughter share a drab boardinghouse existence with her. Annie Leary, worried about the girl's future, somehow inveigled Hetty into permitting a coming-out dance for Sylvia at the Leary house and even got Hetty into an evening gown. She was less successful in getting Sylvia married, however; she did not marry until 1909. One of the greatest heiresses in America, indeed the world, she married no

Arthur Leary, son of a hatter, entered Society as a clubman and dancing partner. He lived on Fifth Avenue a few doors from his sister Annie at number 1032. Both were ardent Roman Catholics; Annie was created a countess by the pope for her gifts to New York Catholic charities.

fortune hunter. Matthew Astor Wilks was a great-grandson of John Jacob Astor, rich, and at least twenty-five years older. He was a Society figure of whom little is known, although McAllister included him in the Four Hundred, no doubt on account of the Astor relationship. He died in 1926 at his home at 7 West 81st Street, leaving an estate of $1.5 million. He had signed an antenuptial agreement, renouncing any claim on his wife's enormous fortune. Sylvia survived many years, and having inherited the fortunes of her mother and her childless brother, left $100 million when she died in 1951 in her twenty-room duplex apartment at 988 Fifth Avenue. Her estate was divided into 140 shares, each worth $641,155.93, and was notable because every cent went to charity; it was then the largest American estate ever left entirely for charitable purposes.

Her piety did not prevent Countess Leary from living a high-style life and entertaining vivaciously and extravagantly, to the distress of her nieces and nephews, her future heirs, who saw their inheritances vanishing. *Town & Country* remarked benignly, "Miss Leary is an ideal hostess and takes the greatest interest in the lighter side of life." She gave dinner parties constantly. The company was sometimes oddly assorted; she could never quite understand the intricate structure of Society—or space. At her house in Newport, the dining table ran through two drawing rooms, turned at a right angle, and ended on the piazza. The interior of her house was odd, too, because she tied bows of red ribbon on clocks, chandeliers, fruit baskets, almost anything that could be ornamented. She tied bows on herself, too, and wore a red wig, usually with a white bow or a diamond star as a highlight. Her dresses were invariably white, high in the back but with a square décolleté in front; there was always a white jeweled ribbon around her throat. She loved prelates. When a cardinal came to visit her she prepared a throne for him in her drawing room. She entertained the Neighborhood Amusement Club at her house with "an Eighteenth Century Musicale" at which minuets were performed. Maude Howe Elliott, who knew the countess from Newport summers, said, "She was a gracious old lady, eccentric in appearance and tenacious about the use of her title." In Newport she lived—and entertained constantly—in a house on the corner of Bellevue Avenue and Pelham Street, which became after her death the Elks Club of Newport.

Alexander McTier Hadden, an heir to the Aspinwall shipping fortune, managed to combine the "social labor of leading cotillions" for the Four Hundred with an active concern for the poor. Like "Sunbeam" Erving, he was a high minded young man genuinely anxious to help the underprivileged, a heritage, no doubt, from their pious grandfathers. He also organized a bible study group called The Round Table. Religious endeavor was not uncommon among upperclass New Yorkers: Cornelius Vanderbilt II taught Sunday school (he met his wife, Alice Gwynne, there), and members of the Stokes and Dodge families among others produced several generations of missionaries and clergymen. Hadden was fortunate in his wife because he married Maude ("Minnie") Miner, a professional social worker said to be the first woman probation officer in the United States.

Cornelius Vanderbilt II's sister, Mrs. Elliott F. Shepard (Margaret Louisa Vanderbilt) gave the Margaret Louisa Home to the Young Women's Christian Association in memory of her daughter. The home's restaurant served breakfast and luncheon for twenty cents each, dinner for thirty-five cents. Some days more than a thousand women and girls took meals there. "The Saturday customers include young women on the way to matinees, whose careful mammas will not allow them to take luncheon alone in a more public place," *Town & Country* wrote approvingly. Some newspapers, always anxious to find examples of rich people's thrift, implied rather nastily that women from Fifth Avenue patronized the Margaret Louisa to save a little money.

Summer camp for the Four Hundred was the season between July and September at Newport, Rhode Island. On cramped lots rose their massive houses, fully equipped and staffed for the few weeks spent there. Richard Morris Hunt, Society's favorite architect, designed the grandest house, Cornelius Vanderbilt II's The Breakers.

8

Venusberg

When her cousin Walter Van Rensselaer Berry stayed with Edith Wharton at her home in Lenox, she wrote to a friend after his departure: "He came to us for two days, and is now in the Venusberg—Newport!" Wharton had spent many summers at Newport herself and disliked it; she said in her frostiest manner, "I did not care for watering-place mundanities." When she called the resort "Venusberg," she certainly did not have in mind the erotic retreat of *Tannhauser*; she was thinking of Newport's frivolity, the absence of any real occupation, and the exhausting pursuit of amusement. Newport, Rhode Island, a small town on a flat sandy island called Aquidneck, had little to recommend it in the way of natural beauty, only a few narrow beaches and no promenade where one could take the air and be admired. The rocky cliff walk that encircled much of the island was not suitable for leisurely strolls. The climate was windy and wet and the season quite short, only from the Fourth of July to mid-September. Nevertheless, during the second half of the nineteenth century Newport drew rich New Yorkers—and a few visitors from other parts of the country—in increasing numbers, people happy to spend fortunes to mingle with each other for six weeks on the chilly coast of New England and to build little palaces that they saw only once a year. While at Newport, they dressed just as elaborately as they did in New York (but in lighter colors) and entertained just as lavishly and in the same stiff manner as they did in the city.

Ward McAllister's cousin, Julia Ward Howe, who became the rather surprising matriarch of the colony, recalled finding the town, when she first visited in 1832, "a forsaken, mildewed place, a sort of intensified Salem, with houses of rich design, no longer richly inhabited." Newport was then between two golden ages. In colonial times it had been a prosperous seaport lined with the elegant houses of rich merchants. Trade was stagnant by the time Howe arrived and never recovered, and the mansions, some of the finest ever built in America, slowly decayed. But after the Civil War, Newport renewed itself and became the premiere American summer resort.

A season at Newport in the Gilded Age was supposed to be six weeks of relaxation and amusement. By the standards of the twentieth century there was little of either. Social striving affords no relaxation, and social striving is what Newport was all about. Amusements seem to have been fairly joyless, perhaps because they were obligatory and confined by rules. On Saturday nights at the Ocean House, the principal hotel, there was a "hop," an informal dance without quadrilles or cotillion. Crash (a cheap, coarse fabric used for towelling) was laid over the carpeted floor for dancing. A memorable feature was Richard Peters of the Four Hundred giving an exhibition of the cancan. That was about as daring as Newport got, at least publicly. Mainly, the women called on each other, or at least left cards. They talked of who was in Society and who was not and how far newcomers had progressed toward the Promised Land. They discussed engagements, possible engagements, broken engagements. They ran over lists of eligible young men and maidens; there was always a shortage of the former and an abundance of the latter. They discussed clothes and jewels and the staple topic of the rich at all times, The Servant Problem. Men gathered at the Reading Room, which was really a clubhouse and not a library, and talked about horses and, their wives suspected, loose women.

Old-timers remembered Newport as a "Southern resort" because so many rich Southerners used to escape the heat of the South, especially the low country along the Carolina and Georgia coast, by spending the summer there; Ward McAllister's parents from Savannah were among them. There were not many visitors at any time, and as George William Curtis wrote, "The quaint little town dozed quietly along its bay." The atmosphere was "cold roast beef New England" and quite intellectual. George Bancroft, the historian, and Julia Ward Howe were the leading lights of the community. Lewis Morris Rutherfurd, the astronomer, and his family summered there; they were among the first members of the Four Hundred to do so. Literary discussions over the teacups followed by charades were the style of entertainment. In 1874 Julia Ward Howe and a group of her intellectual friends organized the Town and Country Club, which got up amateur theatricals, readings, and such heavy-duty amusements as translating the

Julia Ward Howe, who wrote The Battle Hymn of the Republic, *was the doyenne of Newport. During her long life she saw Newport evolve from a small-town summer retreat for authors and professors into America's premiere summer resort. At the end of her career she gave a party for Oscar Wilde during his 1882 visit to Newport.*

"Mother Goose" rhymes into seven languages, including Greek and Latin. Even at the first meeting of the club, uneasy members mentioned "the growing predominance of the gay and fashionable element in Newport." Before Julia Ward Howe died in 1909, she had seen the transformation complete. Most of the cottagers were well-to-do but not in the millionaire class. Even if rich, ostentation was not their style; they scorned footmen in powdered hair. George Bancroft's simple rose-covered house at 64 Kay Street was later lived in by Charles Oelrichs of the Four Hundred and his family. A daughter of the Oelrichses, Blanche, described her childhood summer home as a "yellow wooden house across from a poultry dealer."

In August, 1891 the interest of the yachting set was focused on the race for the Goelet Cup. The handsome Iroquois was one of the entrants.

Economically, Newport in its second golden age just got by; its inhabitants were glad of summer jobs as gardeners and maids. The town "sustained a feeble trade in coals," Mrs. John King Van Rensselaer wrote, and there was a chewing gum factory open to visitors. Otherwise, "the chief industry," again according to Mrs. Van Rensselaer, "was the investigation of social credentials." Trade was neglected "while the migratory population concerns itself with the more spectacular business of granting, or withholding, social recognition." Social acceptance was the most important thing in life to the summer people. Blanche Oelrichs recalled once finding a fine lady in pink taffeta and lace crumpled up on the stairs of their house, "weeping bitterly because my good-natured mother had failed to procure for her an invitation to somebody's ball."

In 1865 Paran Stevens of Boston, a great hotel man who managed the Tremont House in Boston and the Fifth Avenue Hotel in New York, was already building a house in Newport. August Belmont, the New York financier, did much to make Newport a desirable summer residence. In 1868 he was famous for his stylish stagecoach in which he drove along the Newport avenues "propelled by four blood bays, with two 'tigers' [footmen] seated behind, with folded arms . . ." in English Regency style. Mrs. Belmont, born Caroline Slidell Perry, daughter of the naval hero Matthew Calbraith Perry, was noted for her beauty and her stylish dressing: "The plumes in her hat were half as big as Mr. Belmont," wags said. She was an accomplished hostess, much more popular than her unrefined husband. Mrs. Van Rensselaer said that at Newport Mrs. Belmont "eliminated from social enterprises the last hint of rural flavor. She came prepared to make the colony a center of fashion. She succeeded and thereby abolished the old charm and tranquility of the resort." Ward McAllister was saying, "Newport was no place for a man without money." Already in 1873, Pierre Lorillard rented a villa in Newport called The Rocks, belonging to E. D. Boit, Jr., of Boston, for $6,000 for the season, an enormous sum and "the high water mark in rents" according to contemporary reports. Lorillard deserted Newport when he developed Tuxedo Park.

In the early days of Newport simplicity had been regarded favorably, but in the 1880s, as Blanche Oelrichs wrote, "The quiet intimacies, the simple gaieties of my parents and their naive coterie of friends were giving way before an influx of millionaires and their wives. . . ." Inevitably, there was mourning for the old days. George William Curtis, the editor and essayist who died in 1892, wrote sadly of this Newport of his final years: "And this whirl of fashionable equipages . . . this confused din of dancing music, scandal, flirtation, serenades . . . this singing, dancing, and dawdling incessantly: this crushing into a month in the country that which crowds six months in town – these are the foot prints of fashion."

The greatest loss was probably intellectual: gone were *conversazione* among highbrows. Newport between the 1870s and the early years of the new century was resolutely Philistine. Tessie Oelrichs (Theresa Fair), for example, heiress with her sister Virginia, known as "Birdie" (Mrs. William K. Vanderbilt, Jr.) of a vast Nevada mining fortune, lived more or less apart from her husband, Herman Oelrichs, in her Newport mansion, Rosecliff, where she was noted as a good housekeeper—literally. She liked to scrub the marble floors herself, watched by her fascinated housemaids. Unfortunately, she had no other interests. Her niece Blanche wrote sadly of her Aunt Tessie, "Gardens, music, literature were all names to her, not means of sustenance, nor was there any standard abroad in the Newport of those days gradually to correct her ignorance." Despite her money and her social position, she is one of the saddest figures of Newport. She was deaf and missed a great deal of conversation, and in middle-age her mind began to give way. Loud disputes with others became common: one of Harry Lehr's star turns was a one-man sketch of a quarrel between Tessie and a neighbor lady called "The Widow Campbell." But Tessie for many years led festivities at the resort. In 1899 the social event of the first week in September was an automobile parade, one of the earliest held in the United States. Tessie's high, open car was twined about with white and pink hydrangeas with twelve white doves (stuffed) placed gracefully among them. From the mouths of the doves flew streamers of delicately tinted satin ribbons. An arbor of yellow artificial wisteria with bows of wide white satin ribbons was built over the chassis. This flowery juggernaut won first prize, a large silver bonbon box, for the best decorated automobile.

If ever there was a place where parties were the machines for social propulsion, it was Newport. Parties were given to impress the neighbors. "You don't give parties to enjoy yourselves," said Tommy Cushing succinctly, "but to advance yourselves." Newcomers were convinced the path to acceptance lay in giving ever more lavish and frequent parties, "Haroun-al-Raschid entertainments," one commentator wrote scornfully, in which simple occasions were transformed into events. William K. Vanderbilt and his wife Alva opened a new barn on their estate with a ball in the attached carriage house. Like Ward McAllister's *fêtes* and other bucolic entertainments in Newport, it had a distinct Marie Antoinette air: the ladies carried long shepherd's crooks of white and gilt; the columns of the carriage house were decorated with stacks of newly cut cornstalks tied with ribbons, interspersed with floral horsecollars, horseshoes, and yokes. "Supper was served," according to *The Home Journal,* "at small tables in the stalls, the eating troughs being filled with flowers." At one of Tessie Oelrichs's parties at Rosecliff, the cotillion was led by the inevitable Harry Lehr and Elisha Dyer, Jr. There was a "butterfly conflict," in which tissue paper butterflies with iridescent bodies to which were attached burrs, were thrown at the dancers, immediately sticking to frocks and evening coats. Tessie got the idea from the throwing of blossoms at the Battle of Flowers in Nice each year. Mrs. Stuyvesant Fish was not likely to be behind. At one of her dinners the table centerpiece was a miniature lake with ferns and aquatic plants, goldfish swimming, and little yachts sailing. Each yacht bore the names of contesting boats in the recent trials to choose the defender of *The America*'s Cup. But entertaining at Newport constantly teetered on the brink of bad taste: at one of Alice (Gwynne) Vanderbilt's musicales at The Breakers, the dinner table's much-admired centerpiece was "a large parrot made of seven hundred pieces of candied sugar and almonds. A chain of silver almonds hung around the neck and fastened one foot to the solid candy pedestal below." Decorations no doubt served as "conversation pieces" in a society not given to verbal inventiveness.

Life at Newport was governed by a strange distaste for the sea. Children of the Four Hundred remembered being taken by their governesses to various beaches, especially the elect Bailey's (properly known as the Spouting Rock Beach Association) and allowed to remain in the water for exactly twenty minutes. When they emerged, they immediately had large hats clamped on their heads "for fear of sunstroke" (surely rare in chilly New England) and were blanketed until they could change their clothes for fear of the sun falling directly on their skins, which was thought unhealthy at any time.

Prudery prevailed when it came to entering the water. In 1910 the committee at Bailey's Beach ruled that long stockings were required for ladies at all times. Miss Elsie Clews, a New York heiress, caused a great scandal and received a serious warning from the house committee when she went in bathing without stockings. Other Four Hundred resorts were equally prim: when the pool at Northeast Harbor, Maine, opened in 1898 a neat sign read "Ladies in bathing suits are requested not to lounge in the sun, as it may cause just criticism." The newspapers took malicious pleasure in describing the costume that Harry Lehr wore at the beach. The suit, the paper wrote, was "décolleté in order to expose the whiteness of his snowy neck, and the trunks abbreviated so as not to deprive his admirers of a full view of his shapely limbs which will be modestly incased with silken hose. A chic sun-bonnet will protect his peach-blow complexion." Men's bathing trunks reached to below the knees; as a great concession the sleeves of their shirts reached the elbow. As for the ladies, bathing dress was designed to preserve modesty. Mrs. Stuyvesant Fish in the early '90s wore a bathing suit consisting of a full dark green satin skirt with a flounce and piping of white satin. White satin and lace lined a pointed vest and there was also lace on the belt and collar and on the wrists of the sleeves. This outfit was worn with bloomers, stockings, and sandals. Old Mrs. Kernochan ("Kate" Lorillard) was easily identified during her dips because to all the above she added a jacket with full sleeves and a Mother Hubbard bonnet tied under the chin.s There was, of course, little swimming that could be done in such an outfit; wading near the shore was about the limit of aquatics. No wonder the usual word for a sea bath was "a dip."

Indoors, amateur theatricals (the players preferred to call them "private" theatricals) were as popular in Newport as they were in New York; usually, each play was performed at the Casino for two nights. In 1881 the comedy *False Colours* starred Elisha Dyer, Jr.; the Cushing brothers Tom and Robert; the inevitable Peter Marié; Catherine Howland Hunt, wife of Newport's favorite architect, Richard Morris Hunt; and, surprisingly, Julia Ward Howe, already past sixty, who loved dressing up and acting. The Cushings had no professional obligations and were always ready for high-jinks. His friends thought Tom, always wearing the latest fashions and with his mustaches carefully waxed, had the look of a suave Frenchman. A monocle rounded out his elegance. His wife, Fanny Grinnell, was elegant, too: her bonnets were the admiration of all Newport; there was a rumor that Tom himself trimmed them. Towering hats weighted with flowers and feathers and held in place with long and menacing hatpins and embroidered veils were among the major art works produced in Newport. Their total unsuitability in a place as windy as Newport did not prevent ladies from wearing them at sporting events, garden parties, and the beach.

Tableaux, or "living pictures," in which costumed players stood still, not uttering a word, were posed by Benjamin C. Porter, the portrait painter, one of the Four Hundred, and a popular Newport resident in the summer. Porter had a studio on Pelham Street. He was very fashionable as a portraitist who delighted in rich fabrics and jewels. Maud Howe Elliott said he was "a whimsical, amusing man, a great favorite in society." Elliott, whose own husband was an artist but not so successful, thought that Porter "had more than he could do; his work suffered."

Newport had clubs, some of them sedate family organizations, others freespirited and frolicsome. The Clambake Club was organized by James Otis, Brockholst Cutting, Charles M. Oelrichs, and other companionable spirits. The purpose was to eat clams, play baseball, shoot clay pigeons, and drink, all away from the eyes of the guardians of ritual, their wives. The Archery Club, on the other hand, was prim and primarily female; archery was deemed peculiarly suitable for young women. One of the most memorable scenes in *The Age of Innocence* is an archery contest on a golden day in Newport. The founder of the Archery Club was Lewis Morris Rutherfurd at his estate Edgerton on Harrison Avenue facing Narragansett Bay and sloping down to the water. De Lancey Kane's daughters were among its most active members.

Newport at its best seems represented by the Coaching Club of New York parading during the short summer season. Blanche Oelrichs remembered rushing to the gates when she heard the horn that announced the parade. The four-in-hands were "dappled by the sun and rich summer shade, the lovely high-stepping horses straining their tensely groomed bodies under the flashing harness. . . ." The ladies aboard "really resembled bizarre snowdrifts of lace, taffeta, and silk . . . the gentlemen in frock coats and gray tall hats, who seemed always to be wearing the most impeccable boutonnieres."

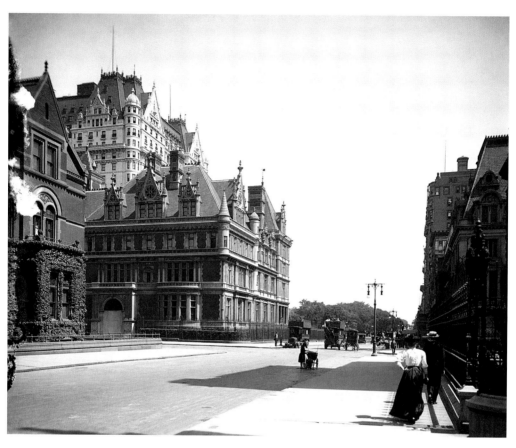

George Browne Post, himself a member of the Four Hundred, was the architect for Cornelius Vanderbilt II's house on the northwest corner of Fifth Avenue and 57th Street, which was eventually extended north to 58th Street, making it the largest townhouse ever built in America.

9

After the Ball

The hit song of 1892 was Charles K. Harris's pleasantly mournful *After the Ball*. More than six million copies of the sheet music were sold, and the song instantly became a standard. Harris, America's most successful songwriter, told an interviewer he wrote songs on topics currently absorbing the public. In the 1890s plays about Society were popular: he cited *The Second Mrs. Tanqueray* and *The Crust of Society* as inspiration for *After the Ball*. The song also echoed the melancholy that settled on the United States the year after the Astor ball; the Depression of 1893 was a serious one. While it would be incorrect to contend the Four Hundred felt much effect from a depression, there was a generally doleful atmosphere.

Two months after the publication of Ward McAllister's list, Mrs. Astor, at the height of her renown and authority, was besieged by a series of family scandals. Of her four daughters, one, Emily Astor Van Alen, had already died. The third daughter was Charlotte Augusta Astor, thirty-four years old in 1892. Since 1879 she had been married to J. Coleman Drayton, who had a distinguished South Carolina family background. They lived in an Astor house in New York and had an estate in New Jersey. There were four children. Charlotte Augusta, perhaps bored with the sedate life of a young matron, fell in love with a New Jersey neighbor of good social credentials, Hallet Alsop Borrowe. This was no affair of sighs and handholdings. As Society, and soon the newspapers, discovered, the couple enjoyed lusty and quite indiscreet encounters in various hotels in New York. Coleman Drayton soon found out, too, and, backed up by the enraged William Astor, challenged Borrowe to a duel, not once but repeatedly. Borrowe, not very gallantly, removed himself to England. Charlotte Augusta, having settled some of her ample trust funds on husband and children, followed him; then Drayton and William Astor, breathing threats of disinheritance, followed *her*. The newspapers, to the horror of Mrs. Astor and her circle, gleefully covered the scandal in rich detail. Borrowe bowed out, and Charlotte and her father went to Paris. While there, William died of a sudden heart attack on April 25, 1892. Charlotte Augusta brought her father's body back to New York and long mourning justified the family secluding itself. When the mourning ended, Caroline Astor had her daughter by her side when receiving guests. In 1894 Charlotte Augusta sued Drayton for a divorce, asserting—as did Borrowe—against all evidence, that no adultery had taken place. Drayton got the four children and substantial funds, Borrowe disappeared, and Charlotte Augusta settled in England, where she soon found another man, George Ogilvy Haig. He was a Scot, a member (but not of the moneyed branch) of the family that distilled Haig & Haig whiskey; he was one of the many brothers of Field Marshal Earl Haig of First World War fame. He died in 1905, but Charlotte Augusta, emulating her mother, was a popular London hostess until her death in 1920.

The second Astor daughter, Helen, who had married James Roosevelt Roosevelt, died in 1893. Her husband, always called "Rosy," never had a profession, although he had a decorative appointment in the American Embassy in London, where his wife died. Their son, James Roosevelt Roosevelt, always called "Taddy," was destined to cause his grandmother more embarrassment. His behavior was erratic and he was a failing student at Groton School, where his antics constantly embarrassed his half-uncle, the conventional Franklin Delano Roosevelt. Taddy came to New York after a useless term at Harvard and ran with a crowd that was definitely not Four Hundred. In 1900 he married a prostitute named Sadie Messinger. Newspapers found out and ran flaming headlines like "Astor Scion's Bride Won in Dance Hall." His grandmother Astor was said "to have taken to her bed." Taddy never reformed, ignoring his grand relations and working as an automobile mechanic. He and Sadie lived in Forest Hills, where she died in 1940, and he eighteen years later, leaving his entire estate of $5 million to the Salvation Army.

Caroline and William's only son, John Jacob IV, was generally considered a social liability. He was large and awkward and his walk was invariably described as "shambling." He was unkindly known in Society as "the golden Caliban." He was an unlikely bridegroom for a beautiful young Philadelphia debutante, but Ava Lowle Willing, descended from colonial Pennsylvania gentry who were only moderately rich, accepted him. The wedding was held in state in Philadelphia; Mrs. Astor was pleased. John Jacob, according to his cousin Winthrop Chanler,

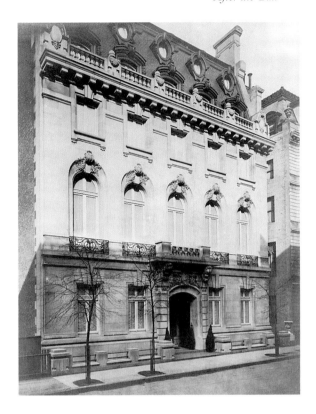

3 East 64th Street, which still exists, was designed by Warren & Wetmore for Mrs. Astor's youngest daughter Caroline ("Carrie") and her husband Marshall Orme Wilson. They kept up the Astor tradition of grand parties into the Jazz Age. Mrs. Wilson did not die until 1948, fifty-six years after her name appeared on the list of the Four Hundred.

"had no friends," and there was difficulty in getting enough guests to attend his bachelor dinner. "Not one of the men would cross the street to shake hands with him for his own sake," Winthrop wrote to his wife in Europe, "but the mother is such a social power and has done so much for them that they are only too glad of the chance." Chanler, who frankly disliked his cousin, spoke of his "ridiculous appearance and manners." Yet in some ways John Jacob was a man of parts, especially for a millionaire: he was an inventor, not of crackpot rich man's toys, but of solid devices such as a bicycle brake and a marine engine; he wrote an early science-fiction novel called *A Journey to Other Worlds*; he served as an officer in the Spanish-American War (he liked to be referred to as "Colonel" henceforth); and he was the builder of the St. Regis and Knickerbocker hotels, notable New York buildings then and now. Ava was haughty, selfish, and unfaithful. From the start, she and John Jacob quarreled, and when she took up bridge with an enthusiasm that bordered on obsession, he retreated to the yacht *Nourmahal*, exactly as his father William had. They were waiting only for his mother to die so they could part and were divorced in 1909, less than a year after her death. Ava soon married again, to Lord Ribblesdale and began a career as international hostess. John Jacob married unsuitably an eighteen-year-old girl named Madeleine Talmadge Force. In 1912, he and Madeleine sailed for home on the *Titanic's* maiden voyage. Madeleine, who was pregnant, was saved and gave birth to a son later that year; John Jacob went down with the ship. His estate was proved at $107 million.

William Astor's nephew, William Waldorf Astor, had never been fond of his "Aunt Lina," primarily because she occupied the place in Society that he felt belonged to his wife. Like so many of the Astors an aloof, unpopular man, he loudly disassociated himself from his scandal-making relations. He did worse. When his father, John Jacob Astor III, died in 1890, he announced that he was tearing down the paternal home at 33rd Street and Fifth Avenue, next door to Mrs. Astor at 350, and building New York's finest hotel, which he named after himself, the Waldorf. Naturally, Caroline could not endure living next door to a public institution. She, her son and his wife joined forces and commissioned a new house at 840 Fifth

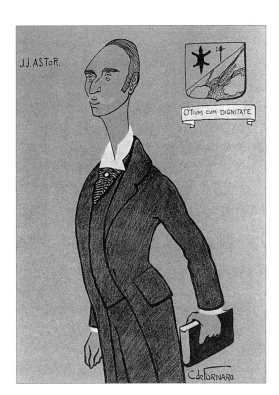

Mrs. Astor's only son, John Jacob Astor IV, was homely and clumsy; behind his back he was called "The Golden Caliban." His vast wealth did not prevent him from seriously pursuing mechanical inventions, writing science fiction, and serving in the Spanish-American War.

When she was sixty-five years old, Mrs. Astor was forced by the advance of commercial establishments to desert 34th Street and move to 65th Street and Fifth Avenue where Richard Morris Hunt built a double house with majestic interiors like the room above for her and her son and daughter-in-law. She died in this great house.

Avenue at 65th Street, choosing Society's favorite architect, William Morris Hunt. Number 350 was demolished and her son built a hotel, which he called the Astoria, on the site. In the interest of making money he even joined the hotel to his hated cousin's, forming the first Waldorf-Astoria, the finest American hotel of its time. Eventually, the Empire State Building rose on the site. On February 2, 1895, Mrs. Astor gave a farewell dinner at number 350. On February 13 she sailed for Europe on the *Teutonic*, keeping to her schedule as always. "Shortly afterwards her mansion, richest in hospitable traditions of all the homes in New York, will be demolished to make way for a magnificent hotel," announced *Town & Country*, fully conscious of the passing of a New York landmark.

The leveling of 350 was another sign that the Gilded Age was over. Society, more extravagant than ever, was loosening up. Parties given by Mrs. Astor's own circle, even by her relations, were becoming outlandish; stateliness had departed. Gone indeed were the days when giving a masked ball was regarded as a questionable enterprise. In 1905 Carrie and Orme Wilson, Mrs. Astor's daughter and son-in-law, gave a "headdress dinner" at which members of the Four Hundred were asked to appear in "striking" hats. On Mrs. Edmund L. Baylies's head there "rested a basket of flowers which in no way impeded the quick movements that accompany her vivacious manner," wrote a newspaper. Carrie Wilson wore a pansy-colored gown with a pansy headdress "suggesting the flower that signifies thought." The petals of the flower had been painted yellow and purple, with crystals sparkling on them. Mrs. John R. Drexel appeared as "Night" with a blackbird on her head. Bad taste was encroaching on even the most elegant entertainments. In 1895 Edward M. Curtiss gave a dinner in honor of the actress Kathryn Kidder, who had made a great success in *Madame Sans-Gêne*, a play set in the age of Napoleon. The dance favors were purple and white Napoleonic hats filled with bons-bons, which was tasteful, but the soup had floating in it miniature billboards inscribed "Mme Sans Gene," the sweetbreads, a popular dish at the time, were decorated with empire wreaths made of truffles, and the Roman punch served halfway through the meal was suds in a wash-tub. When Mr. and Mrs. John Innes Kane, Astor relations, opened their new home at 610 Fifth Avenue in 1909, some of the guests called the house-warming a "resurrection party"; many people there had not been seen in years. Society reporters said that conservative people were being lost to Society because they were "overwhelmed by the tidal wave of wealth and loathe to accept invitations because unable to return courtesies in the prodigal style of the day."

Ward McAllister was spared the abandonment of his ideals of dignity and order. He died in 1895, symbolically the same year that Mrs. Astor left 350 Fifth Avenue. He and his family had remained on East 19th Street, now rapidly becoming a social backwater. His funeral took place at Grace Church and the funeral procession proceeded along Fifth Avenue. Not many of the Four Hundred attended; fashionable society never lingers over departed leaders. Many, anyway, had disapproved of him as an indiscreet windbag, baring social secrets that they would prefer to be inaccessible to the mob. Several gentlemen, among them Harry Lehr and Frederick Townsend Martin, aspired to the succession. Martin professed to be amused when he was called "The Ward McAllister of to-day," but he was known as a "promoter of social intercourse" in New York, Newport, and—a new field of operations—Palm Beach, where *Town & Country* asserted, "He has always been a leader, and the season was hardly natural without him." He did resemble Ward McAllister in writing a fatuous book of memoirs; his was entitled *Things I Remember*.

Ward McAllister died on January 31, 1895, fittingly two days after Mrs. Astor said farewell to 350 Fifth Avenue, where McAllister had admired and chronicled her triumphs. He was buried at Grace Church, the Four Hundred's favorite, on a snowy day.

The depression did not halt the parties: "Even before the costume ball given by Mr. and Mrs. Bradley Martin in February 1897 at the Waldorf-Astoria the newspapers proclaimed that [the] dress ball . . . will be not only the event of the fashionable season, but an event of New York's social history." Anticipation ran high. You could put on your costume and be photographed at the Rockwood Studios, 1440 Broadway, or at your residence, day or evening, against "back-grounds of epochs suitable for photographing the guests of the great social event." Customers were assured that the photogenic light was quite harmless. At the ball, a thousand guests were adequately waited upon; there were about 350 waiters and maids and men in the dressing rooms. The Bradley Martins spent $30,000 on the ball; their guests are said to have spent $150,000 on their costumes. Even after a storm of criticism broke over this extravagance in bad times, they were not without defenders. "Daisy" Harriman, for example, had her own theory of economics; she said,

"I think the Bradley Martin balls that added to the gaiety of nations and set money in circulation were far more pious enterprises than unostentatious hoarding." Dr. William S. Rainsford, rector of St. George's Episcopal Church at Stuyvesant Square, disagreed, denouncing the Bradley Martin ball from his pulpit the following Sunday. He was a spoilsport about Society's amusements—surprising since he was one of the favorite pastors of the Four Hundred and counted J. P. Morgan among his parishioners. Valerie Burkhardt Hadden felt so guilty about having worn an elaborate Louis XV costume to the ball that she had the heavy lace underskirt made into a vestment for Randolph Ray, rector of the Anglo-Catholic Church of the Transfiguration ("The Little Church Around the Corner").

Long before her death Mrs. Astor had remarked, "Many women will rise up to take my place when I am gone." Truly, a vacant throne invites aspirants, but not many were courageous enough to try for the succession to Mrs. Astor. Mrs. Ogden Mills (Ruth Livingston) had every qualification except personality—the same combination of colonial ancestry on her side and millions of dollars on her husband's. She appears to have anticipated her accession when in 1901 she added a ballroom to the Mills house in Manhattan. She could well afford it: her father-in-law's estate was probated at between $50 and $60 million. "Teenie" Mills considered herself the arbiter of the most exclusive circle within the circle of the Four Hundred. Daisy Harriman said that she was "a great stickler for form." She and her husband had a small "set" of young couples who were avid, not to say fanatic, bridge-players. They met constantly at house parties, a form of entertainment much favored by the Millses. Ruth had inherited a family mansion at Staatsburg, New York, originally built by her ancestor New York Governor Morgan Lewis early in the early nineteenth century. Stanford White completely transformed the house, making it one of the most luxurious country houses in America. The view over the grounds to the Hudson was—and is—superb, although it is doubtful that the Millses or their guests spent much time looking at the view; they rarely lifted their eyes from the cards. It is generally accepted that the house and the household inspired the account of the Trenors, characters in Edith Wharton's *The House of Mirth*. Mrs. Mills was amazingly elegant. In 1906 she was observed at the opening of the Metropolitan Opera in a tight-fitting gown of black velvet with white lace sleeves; on her bosom rested a massive spray of diamonds with a string of pearls extending to the right shoulder. Her requisite diamond tiara was "of extraordinary height," compared by reporters to the crown of a peacock "only there were more points, each tipped with a large pearl." She spoke in a drawling voice, very supercilious. Harry Lehr, who had probably suffered from her pointed

The extravagant costume ball given by Mrs. and Mrs. Bradley Martin of the Four Hundred in 1897 marked a major change from the sedate affairs hosted by Mrs. Astor. Guests such as these hastened to be photographed in their costumes and even gave interviews to the press about the party. Mrs. Astor never in her life talked to a reporter.

remarks, once said that, "She has reduced rudeness to a fine art." Greetings to her guests were particularly distant: she languidly extended a limp hand with a far-away expression as though she were not quite certain who they were, and then appeared to forget their presence. (The same technique is used by Proust's Madame de Villeparisis). She could never have succeeded the cordial Mrs. Astor.

Another possible successor to the Astor throne, or rather divan, because that is where Caroline reigned in her ballroom, was Mrs. Stuyvesant Fish, born Marion ("Mamie") Graves Anthon. Her career embodied the last days of the Gilded Age. Like Caroline Astor, she had few personal attractions, a good figure with a slender waist that she showed off in the tightly laced fashions, but a horsey face with an expression that grew grimmer and grimmer as the years passed. False curls hung beneath immense picture hats secured by long pins, and she was usually veiled. There was nothing conciliatory about her manner, and it is small wonder that most of her contemporaries, including guests, servants, and children were afraid of her. She was irreverent and strangely bitter, a woman who performed the rituals of Society without really believing in them, bossy and demanding and well aware of her power to belittle with her quick and merciless words. In a society that aimed at gentility and was generally soft-spoken and in which women were supposed to be more or less retiring, she was the flamboyant exception. She was of a different generation (Mamie was twenty-three years younger) and a polar opposite to Mrs. Astor, who took her position in Society and everyone else's seriously and who never considered the rituals of Society trivial. She was plainly bewildered by Mrs. Fish, and although they entertained each other for decades and certainly considered themselves friends, they were never intimates.

Mamie was no democrat. Although she professed to scorn Society's values, she did not throw open its doors to newcomers. At Newport Mamie and Tessie Oelrichs and Mrs. O. H. P. Belmont (Alva Smith) were known as "the social strategy board"; they united in repelling undesirables from their charmed circle, but they had their own rivalries as hostesses among themselves and for years feuded triangularly. The rivalry showed itself in who they entertained and how well. They did not compete architecturally. Mrs. Fish's Crossways was a handsome colonial style structure but not palatial (Robert Van Cortlandt once pretended to have forgotten the name of Mamie's house: "Is it Crosspatch?" he drawled. "If it is," said Mamie quickly, "it's a patch *you'll* never cross."); nor was Mrs. Belmont's By-the-Sea, especially eye catching, whereas Tessie Oelrichs, an heiress of the Comstock Lode, owned the magnificent Rosecliff. Although she would team up with Mrs. Oelrichs and Mrs. Belmont to keep out upstarts, Mamie was plenty competitive with other hostesses in giving memorable parties. She brought the chorus of *The Merry Widow* to Newport to entertain her guests, had Vernon and Irene Castle, the much-admired dancing team, give an exhibition and lessons to her friends, and hired the hefty comedienne Marie Dressler to amuse her guests; Dressler made her entrance sliding down the stairway on a silver tray. Mamie liked theme dinners: all the guests dressed as Mother Goose characters, for instance.

Her husband, Stuyvesant Fish, was a Knickerbocker, a descendant of Governor Stuyvesant, and one of the heirs to his great colonial estate on the east side of Manhattan. Like his brothers Hamilton and Nicholas, he went to a school in Switzerland in 1857. His parents were rather nonchalant about their children, as upper-class parents were in those days. Once returned to New York, Stuyvesant was sent to Charlier's School on East 24th Street and then boarded at Churchill's School for Boys at Sing Sing, New York. Two of his friends there were William Seward Webb and James J. Van Alen, later Caroline Astor's son-in-law. He had a

In 1892 Mrs. Stuyvesant Fish, Society's tart-tongued terror, presided over the largest house in Gramercy Park, number 19, which still exists. In 1898 Stanford White built for her 25 East 78th Street, which also exists today, where she had at her command the largest private ballroom in New York.

significant career in business: in 1871 he went to Chicago to work for the Illinois Central Railroad and eventually became its president. He was a big, silent man who held by many of the old traditions of the Knickerbockers; he would not, for example, play cards on Sunday. Like William Astor, he actively disliked his wife's entertaining. Unlike Astor, however, he did not go in for yachts and feminine company; after his retirement from the railroad, he whiled away his time in the country at Garrison, New York, where he especially enjoyed raking leaves and making bonfires of them. He was not without a sense of humor: in 1903 he received a letter from a friend offering to arrange a visit to the Pope in case he was in Rome. Stuyvesant replied that the letter "will be most useful if I go as far as Rome, where I have not been since Pius IX blessed me as a boy six or seven years old. Perhaps his successor will be as kind. Like vaccination, these things should be repeated occasionally through a lifetime."

Mamie's background was not humble but it was far from the Knickerbocracy. She was descended from George Christian Anthon, a German doctor who emi-

Mrs. Stuyvesant Fish prided herself on simplyfing the rituals of Society, for instance reducing dinners to an hour from three or four. The interiors of her house in Newport, Crossways, and 25 East 78th Street had comparatively restrained furnishings.

grated to Canada in 1757 and moved on to New York in 1786. He was quite successful and soon involved himself in the affairs of Columbia College, where from 1796 to 1815 he served as trustee. Two of his sons were lawyers, one also a distinguished collector of coins; another, Henry, was rector of St. Mark's-in-the-Bouwerie. Charles was a student and teacher of Greek and Latin; he taught the classics at Columbia College for years. Although the Anthons were learned in several fields, there was something rather odd about many members of the family; Mamie's strange personality may have had deep roots. When they were especially eccentric, the family was said by acquaintances to be "behaving anthonically." Mamie's own father, William Henry Anthon, was a criminal lawyer; her childhood home was at 56 Irving Place between East 17th and 18th Streets, a few steps from the large townhouse on Gramercy Park that she was to inhabit after her marriage. He was not successful, and when he died in 1875, his wife was in such straitened circumstances she had to give up the Irving Place house and move to Astoria. It was years before the family recovered. Perhaps because of her family's troubles, Mamie, although belonging to a family notable for its scholarship, seems to have received almost no education. All her life she had trouble with reading and writing; however, there is no indication that her lack of education embarrassed her.

Her match with Stuyvesant Fish was based on true affection. He adored her. Just before she died in 1915, he wrote, "In looking back over the many bitter and sweet but ever pleasurable memories of long years of married life, I can recall no moment when I failed to be thankful for my action and above all for my choice." Her patient husband was occasionally the victim of Mamie's wit: once when she was coughing he asked if he could get her something for her throat. She replied, yes, "that diamond and pearl necklace that I saw today at Tiffany's." She died "without a murmur and in no pain, dying as she always said she wished to, without a day's illness." At her funeral, lines from her favorite poem by Matthew Arnold were read: "Strew on her roses, roses and never a spray of rue."

In the last decade of Mrs. Astor's life both she and Mrs. Fish fell under the unwholesome influence of Harry Lehr, a malicious and opportunistic homosexual from Baltimore who insinuated himself into New York Society at the very end of the nineteenth century. Some people thought of him as Ward McAllister's successor as the Arbiter. Lehr himself said, "I begin where Ward McAllister left off. He was the voice crying in the wilderness who prepared the way for me. . . ." While McAllister took a serious view of Society and thought of himself as being in a sacerdotal position, Lehr liked to call himself "The Funmaker." He was a German-American, son of a tobacco importer. He claimed that his family was socially prominent; few, if any, Baltimore bluebloods supported the claim. He was born in 1869. His father died when he was seventeen years old, and he went to work in a bank. About that time he began to invent himself as a man of fashion. His first great success was playing female roles in amateur theatricals. When The Paint and Powder Club in Baltimore put on a show he appeared in a stunning gown of "white silk with low square corsage, puffed sleeves and white gloves, and bodice ornamented with open green iridescent work." When complimented on his work he said ambiguously, "I shine at both ends." Lehr spent most of his time, at least his accountable time, with the ladies of New York and Newport. Most husbands ignored his existence, but some liked him in an offhand sort of way. A century later he would have been known as a "walker," the homosexual who has nothing more to do than escort ladies to parties their husbands refuse to attend, plan those parties, dress up, and gossip. Mrs. I. Townsend Burden, formerly Evelyn Moale of Baltimore, introduced him into New York Society. He was taken up by Mrs. George Gould, the former Edith Kingdon, an actress. She was not the best protective arm, as the Goulds were only slowly penetrating Society. From Edith Kingdon Gould, Harry Lehr moved on to Tessie Oelrichs, Alva Belmont, and finally to the greatest of them all, Mrs. Astor. His social success was certainly not founded on physical attractiveness. Nearly every account of him uses words like "piggish" or "his porcine appearance." Blanche Oelrichs thought his personality "theatrical [and] effeminate." He had a mincing step and a clown's laugh that bordered on hysteria and struck more than one observer as sad. He was empty-headed and uneducated; unlike Ward McAllister, he could never have quoted Dante in calling Mrs. Astor "the Mystic Rose."

Lehr lived on air when he arrived in New York. His clothes, even his underwear, were made by good tailors in return for his recommendation to his rich acquaintances. Black, Starr and Frost, the great jewelry firm, lent him studs and tiepins and rings (men then wore more jewelry than they do today) on the same basis. He lived rent free in an apartment at Sherry's with Thomas Wanamaker of the Philadelphia department store family, described by Elizabeth Drexel as "his best friend." He got railroad passes from the Fish and Vanderbilt families; Mrs. Clarence Mackay let him send wires and cables over her husband's telegraph lines. He needed a rich wife. Edith Gould introduced him to a young widow, Elizabeth (Drexel) Dahlgren, an heiress of the great Drexel banking fortune of Philadelphia. She, judging from her two books of memoirs, was the naïve daughter of a domineering and rigidly Roman Catholic mother who not only denied her house to divorced persons, but refused to allow the very word "divorce" to be uttered in her presence. Elizabeth brought Harry to meet her mother, he amused the old lady, and she saw no objection to her daughter's remarriage since she was a widow. So it came to pass that Mrs. Dahlgren and Mr. Lehr were married in high Roman Catholic state. The marriage went no farther than the altar and was never consummated. On their wedding night he refused to sleep with her and told her that he never would. "I must tell you the unflattering truth that your money is your only asset in my eyes. . . . You are actually repulsive to me."

Harry Lehr was introduced to Caroline Astor by Elisha Dyer, Jr., at Newport. (How bitterly Dyer must have regretted that introduction when Lehr began to replace him.) Caroline took to him at once and under his influence her behavior became positively giddy. Perhaps her liking for fun that Frank Crowninshield (but nobody else) mentioned was finally coming out. Shortly after they became friends he persuaded her to attend the Bradley Martin ball. That was only the first step. Caroline, who was now nearly seventy years old, was taken to dine by Harry in public at Sherry's restaurant on Fifth Avenue—on a Sunday evening. A Sunday evening dinner out for a lady who had observed all the restrictions on Sunday entertaining from her youth! The earth-shaking event was actually reported in the newspapers: Mrs. Astor calmly enjoying her dinner listening to the ragtime orchestra in the same dining room with the actress Lillian Russell. Other diners, some of whom had apparently come only to see this great event, Grace (Wilson) Vanderbilt among them, were aghast. A newspaper reporter wrote, "I am sure it was the Lehr–Astor party whom they came to see, and I wonder if the great star cast enjoyed it. I think they had stage fright." He concluded by writing solemnly, "I never dreamed it would be given to me to gaze on the fact of an Astor in a public dining room!"

But Mrs. Astor was obviously in the last years of her long reign, so Harry set his sights on Mrs. Stuyvesant Fish as her likely successor and his new chief patroness. He and Mamie were kindred souls, funny but bitter, quick with repartee, and quite unkind. Mamie did not mind putting down Harry himself: after his wedding she told him, "Your favorite flower must be the marigold." Together, they played empty-headed pranks: Harry Lehr once arranged with the orchestra at a dinner given by James Van Alen to interrupt the dinner four times by playing "The Star-Spangled Banner" so that the food would get cold and conversations interrupted when the guests stood at attention. He and Mamie coated a dachshund with flour and set the dog loose among ladies in ballgowns so that he would ruin their gowns. Lehr gave a dogs' dinner in which the pets of his friends were invited to a scrumptious repast. It is pleasant to note that Elisha Dyer, Jr.'s dachshund so overtaxed its capacities that it fell unconscious by its plate and had to be carried home. That dinner received a great deal of bad publicity for its frivolity and expense; in defense, Elizabeth Lehr insisted that the dogs had not fed on rare viands but only liver and rice.

The successor of Mrs. Astor as Queen of Society was neither Ruth Livingston Mills or Mrs. Stuyvesant Fish, but Grace Wilson Vanderbilt. Her father, Richard Wilson, was a man of obscure lineage, a Southerner who emerged after the Civil War as a leading railroad man. The glittering marriages of her siblings to a Goelet, an Astor, and a member of the noble Herbert family of England had paved the way for her to marry a Vanderbilt even though the parents of Cornelius ("Neily") Vanderbilt III bitterly opposed the match since they considered Grace "fast." After the marriage was accomplished and a sort of armed truce reached between the Wilsons and the Vanderbilts, Grace began to emerge with social ambitions. Unlike Caroline Astor, she was pretty, a fluffy blonde with a svelte figure attractive to men, and eager to please. She appeared essentially frivolous but underneath an indecisive and helpless manner lay a determination to be the premiere hostess of America that fully equaled Mrs. Astor's. She succeeded. Unlike Caroline Astor, she was not interested for the most part in entertaining the remaining Knickerbocracy, from which she did not spring. She was up to the minute and loved to invite people who were newsworthy to her house, visiting royalty and nobility, ambassadors, and American politicians. She fancied that when she presided over a table of ambassadors and senators she had some effect on events.

Caroline Astor's final years after her fling with Harry Lehr were sad. There were signs that her mind was going. Although no reports were issued as to her health, she apparently had a stroke in December 1905, and thereafter she was confined to a wheelchair and not seen in Society. To the last, she was the queen, however, and although the press could be sarcastic about her unruly descendants, it never failed to treat her with the greatest respect. Surrounded by her surviving children and her faithful butler, Thomas Hade, she died amid the grandeur of 840 Fifth Avenue on October 30, 1908, a month past her 78th birthday. The size of her estate was not revealed, but she left over $2 million in bequests to children, charities (especially the Asylum for the Destitute Blind), and servants (Thomas Hade received $5,000). The remainder was divided between her daughters Carrie Wilson and Charlotte Haig. She was buried next to her husband and other Astors in Trinity Cemetery on West 155th Street.

The public and the press were in no doubt that Caroline Astor's passing was epochal. She was described then, as now, as a unique figure: "The last of the leaders of society, the last of its mentors . . . ," *Town & Country* intoned. Single-minded and determined, *the* Mrs. Astor had secured for herself a lofty and unquestioned position at a time when women of her class disdained seeing their names in the newspapers, and she had maintained her authority for three decades. Ward McAllister, with his undeviating respect and ceaseless proclamation of her social supremacy, had helped. Never a man to underestimate himself, surely even he would be surprised that his phrase "the Four Hundred" is still heard, and that, largely on account of it, he has secured a place in the reference books. In 1906 O. Henry published *The Four Million*, his collection of stories about middle-class New Yorkers with a title that satirized McAllister's Four Hundred; readers immediately took the allusion. Nor, a century later, is the phrase lost on the public: popular magazines update lists of the Four Hundred every year. But it is the first Four Hundred, the creation of Caroline Astor and Ward McAllister, who hold our attention for the true glimpse their lives give us into the Gilded Age in New York.

The First Four Hundred: Biographical Sketches

Ward McAllister's list abounded in inaccuracies: names were mispelled or incomplete and many spouses omitted or, worse, included although they were dead. There were vague references to "Miss Greene" or "Miss Hoffman." The rule was that only the eldest unmarried daughter of a family carried the title "Miss," with no given name, but in this as in other things, McAllister was inconsistent and ignored the rules he claimed to honor. The many reprints of the list have perpetuated these errors. In the following revision the names of the first Four Hundred are printed in bold face exactly as the newspapers printed them in 1892, followed by identifications and corrections. Many of the listed were related; cross references in bold face indicate important connections. Some people were socially prominent in their time, but left little trace in the records, not even obituaries in the New York newspapers. In locating these elusive figures, genealogies, club lists, and the *Social Register*, first published in 1887, have been indispensable.

ALLEN, FRED H. FREDERICK HOBBES ALLEN (1858–1937), lawyer and economist, was born in Honolulu, studied in Germany, and graduated from Harvard (1880). He was secretary of the Hawaiian Legation in Washington and later a New York lawyer. Despite being middle-aged, he served in the American Flying Corps in World War I and was awarded the *Legion d'honneur*. In June 1892, he married Adele Livingston Stevens (died 1939), daughter of Frederic W. Stevens and great-granddaughter of Albert Gallatin, first U.S. secretary of the treasury. He represented the United States at economic conferences in Europe; he and his wife lived in Paris for some years. Adele had many connections to the European nobility: her mother, Adele Livingston Sampson (died 1912), divorced Frederic Stevens and married Maurice de Périgord-Talleyrand, 4th duc de Dino, whose first wife had been the **Marquise de Talleyrand**.

APPLETON, MR. AND MRS. F. R. Francis Randall Appleton (1854–1929), Harvard 1875, was a lawyer with Robbins & Appleton, N.Y., and an overseer of Harvard University. In 1884 he married Fanny Lanier (died 1958), sister of **James F. D. Lanier.**

ASTOR, MR. AND MRS. JOHN JACOB Born in 1864, he was the last child and only son of **Mr. and Mrs. William Astor.** In 1891 he married Ava Lowle Willing (died 1958) of

John Jacob Astor IV and his young second wife, Madeleine Talmadge Force, were passengers on the maiden voyage of the Titanic *in 1912. Astor was drowned, Madeleine was saved, and a few months later gave birth to John Jacob Astor VI, who inherited only a small portion of his father's estate of nearly $107 million.*

Philadelphia. They had two children, W[illiam] Vincent Astor (1891–1959) and Alice Muriel Astor (1902–1956) before divorcing in 1910. In 1911 John Jacob married Madeleine Talmadge Force (1894–1940). He went down on the *Titanic* in 1912, and their only child, John Jacob Astor (1912–1992), was born after his death.

ASTOR, MR. AND MRS. WILLIAM   Astor's full name was William Backhouse Astor (1829–1892). He was the grandson of John Jacob Astor (1763–1848), an emigrant from Germany who founded the Astor dynasty in America. His wife, Caroline Webster Schermerhorn (1830–1908) was the sister of **Mrs. Benjamin Sumner Welles**. The Astors were the parents of **John Jacob Astor, Mrs. Marshall Orme Wilson and Mrs. James Roosevelt Roosevelt**.

BALDWIN, MISS   Louise R. Baldwin (died 1950) was the daughter of **Christopher Columbus Baldwin**. In 1908 she married William B. Bristow (died 1955).

BALDWIN, C. C.   was Christopher Columbus Baldwin (1830–1897), father of **Louise Baldwin** and **C. C. Baldwin, Jr.** He was a banker and president of the Louisville & Nashville Railroad, from which he made a large fortune in the 1880s.

BALDWIN, C. C. JR.   (died 1924), son of C. C. Baldwin, referred to himself as C. Columbus Baldwin. He graduated from Harvard in 1893, and married Mary E. Pease (died 1930).

BARBEY, MRS.   was Mrs. Henry I. Barbey (died 1926), born Mary Lorillard of the great tobacco dynasty; she was the sister of **Mrs. James P. Kernochan** and **Mrs. Lawrence Kip**. Her husband (1832–1906) was a financier and a director of the Buffalo, Rochester & Pittsburg Railroad. They built one of the earliest residences in Tuxedo Park, founded by Mrs. Barbey's family.

BARBEY, MISS   Eva Barbey (died 1943) was the daugher of **Mrs. Barbey**. In 1903 she married a French nobleman, Baron André de Neuflize (1875–1926).

BARCLAY, MR. AND MRS. JAMES L.   James Lent Barclay (died 1924), heir to an old New York mercantile fortune, married Olivia Mott Bell.

BAYLIES, MR. AND MRS. EDMUND L.   Edmund Lincoln Baylies (1857–1932), Harvard 1879, was descended from the Revolutionary general Benjamin Lincoln and was a member of the Society of the Cincinnati. He was a partner in the law firm of Carter, Ledyard & Milburn and prominent on New York City boards, including the Metropolitan Opera and the Cathedral of St. John the Divine. In 1887 he married Louisa Van Rensselaer (died 1945), daughter of **Mrs. Alexander Van Rensselaer** and sister of the **Misses Alice** and **Mabel Van Rensselaer**. She received the *Legion d'honneur* for her work with disabled French veterans during World War I.

BEND, MISS AMY (1870–1957) was the daughter of George Hoffman Bend (died 1900), one-time president of the New York Stock Exchange, and sister of **Beatrice Bend**. In 1899 she married Cortlandt Field Bishop (1870–1935), an heir to the vast New York real estate fortune of the Wolfe family.

BEND, MISS BEATRICE (1874–1941) was **Miss Amy Bend's** sister. At the age of forty-three, she married Henry Prather Fletcher (1873–1959), sometime chairman of the Republican National Committee and U. S. ambassador to Mexico.

BERRYMAN, MISS was Georgiana Berryman (1866–1946), granddaughter of Stephen Whitney of New Haven, one of the richest men in the United States. In 1895 she married H. Casimir de Rham (1855–1916). They lived at 24 Fifth Avenue, formerly the home of the Brevoort family and scene of many of New York's great social occasions.

BISHOP, MISS was Mary Cunningham Bishop (1865–1948), eldest daughter of **Heber Bishop**. She never married.

BISHOP, HEBER Heber Reginald Bishop (1840–1902) was a Massachusetts boy who at the age of twenty-one went to Cuba, where he made a fortune in sugar refining so rapidly that he was able to retire at the age of thirty-six. He settled in New York and became director of various western railroads and the New York City elevated railroads. In 1862 he married Mary Cunningham. Among their children was **Mrs. James F. D. Lanier**.

BOWDOIN, GEORGE S. George Sullivan Bowdoin (1835–1913) was a partner at J. P. Morgan & Co., and a director of many railroads. In 1863 at Irvington-on-Hudson he married Julia Irving Grinnell (1837–1915), grandniece of Washington Irving.

Heber Bishop was not of aristocratic lineage, and Ward McAllister patronized him although including him and two of his four daughters (shown here) in the Four Hundred. Bishop, however, had a very successful business career and in his house at 881 Fifth Avenue displayed the notable collection of jade which he gave to the Metropolitan Museum of Art, of which he was for many years a trustee.

Mr. and Mrs. Lloyd Stephens Bryce entertained on a large scale at 1025 Fifth Avenue, their home across from the then new Metropolitan Museum of Art. Mrs. Bryant was Edith Cooper, grandaughter of Peter Cooper and member of a family famous for imaginitve hospitality.

BOWDOIN, TEMPLE (1863–1914), son of George S. Bowdin, Columbia College 1885, was also a partner at J. P. Morgan & Co., and a yachtsman. In 1894 he married Helen Parish Kingsford (1860–1912), grandniece of **Mrs. William Astor**.

BRONSON, MR. AND MRS. FREDERIC Frederic Bronson (died 1900) was a member of the Coaching Club, one of the earliest polo players in the United States, and a founder of the Westchester Polo Club. His wife was Sara Gracie King (1851–1931), descended from Archibald Gracie (1755–1829), New York merchant and shipowner whose summer home, Gracie Mansion, is now the residence of New York's mayors. After Bronson's death his widow married, in 1914, Adrian Iselin (died 1935), brother of **Columbus O'Donnell Iselin**.

BROWN, HAROLD (1863–1900), member of the great Brown shipping dynasty of Providence, R. I., married Georgette Wetmore Sherman (died 1960), daughter of **William Watts Sherman**.

BROWN, WILLIAM HAROLD referred to himself as W. Harold Brown (died 1913).

BRYCE, MR. AND MRS. LLOYD Lloyd Stephens Bryce (1851–1917), nephew and namesake of the famous archaeologist John Lloyd Stephens, received a Jesuit education in this country, then graduated from Oxford in 1874. A Democrat, he was a congressman (1887–1889), advocating a single-tax platform, and was United States minister to the Netherlands, (1911-1913). He also wrote four genteel works of fiction of the type known as "silver fork novels." He married Edith Cooper (died 1916), daughter of **Edward Cooper**, mayor of New York. Their vast Georgian Bryce House at Roslyn, Long Island, designed by Ogden Codman in 1901, is now the Nassau County Museum.

BULKELEY, EDWARD The proper spelling is Bulkley. Edward H. Bulkley (died 1908) was a retired stockbroker, a member of the family that established Bulkley, Dunton & Co., New York, paper merchants. He married Margaret Stewart.

BURDEN, MISS Evelyn Moale Burden, daughter **Mr. and Mrs. I. Townsend Burden**, died unmarried in 1965.

BURDEN, MR. AND MRS. I. TOWNSEND Isaac Townsend Burden (1834–1914), an heir of the Burden iron manufacturing company of Troy, N. Y., married Evelyn Byrd Moale (1847–1916). Their son William Armistead Moale Burden (1877–1909) married Florence Vanderbilt Twombly (1881–1969), daughter of **Mr. and Mrs. Hamilton McK. Twombly**.

BURNETT, GENERAL AND MRS. HENRY L. Henry Lawrence Burnett (1838–1916) served as a brigadier general in the Civil War. A lawyer, he was a judge advocate in the trial of President Abraham Lincoln's assasination conspirators. His wife, Agnes Suffern Tailer (died 1933), was the daughter of **Mr. and Mrs. E. N. Tailer**.

CAMERON, THE MISSES were the daughters of **Sir Roderick Cameron**: Margaret ("Daisy"); Isabel (died 1906, unmarried); Catherine N. (died 1924), married, in 1912, Judah Howe Sears; and Anne F. Cameron (died 1919), who married **Belmont Tiffany** in 1895.

CAMERON, DUNCAN Duncan Ewen Cameron (died 1926), son of **Sir Roderick Cameron**, married Mary Turnure (died 1906).

CAMERON, SIR RODERICK Sir Roderick William Macleod Cameron (1825–1900) established a line of clipper ships between New York, Australia and New Zealand. He was British consul in New York, knighted in 1883. He was a founding governor of the American Jockey Club and built one of the first cottages at Tuxedo Park.

CANNON, MR. AND MRS. HARRY Henry White Cannon (1850–1934) was descended from Peregrine White, the first child born in the English colonies in North America. He was United States comptroller of the currency, president, and then chairman of the board of the Chase National Bank (1886–1904). His wife was Jennie O. Curtis (died 1929). They built a summer home called As You Like It at Cannon's hometown, Delhi, N.Y., in the Catskill Mountains.

CARROLL, MR. AND MRS. CHARLES A member of the famous Carroll family of Doughoregan Manor plantation, Ellicott City, Maryland, and great-great-grandson of Charles Carroll of Carrollton, Signer of the Declaration of Independence, Charles Carroll

The three Misses Chanlers were descendants of John Jacob Astor. Elizabeth Winthrop Chanler, the eldest, married John Jay Chapman, the writer and polemicist. She was painted in 1893 by John Singer Sargent.

The eccentric John Jay Chapman, who at Harvard stuck his hand in the fire during a disappointment in love, maiming himself for life, was descended from notable Abolitionists and reformers. He began his career working for populist causes, including municipal reform in New York . After World War I he turned to the right and became an apologist for the Ku Klux Klan. In later life he wrote studies of Greek and Roman authors.

In a daguerreotype made about 1845 Peter and Sarah (Bedell) Cooper are shown with their children Edward, who like his father became mayor of New York City and Sarah Amelia, who married Mayor Abram Stevens Hewitt. Ward McAllister included both in his Four Hundred.

(1865–1921), Harvard 1887, lived on family trusts. His wife, Suzanne Bancroft, was granddaughter of George Bancroft, the American historian and diplomat.

CARY, MR. AND MRS. CLARENCE Clarence Cary (died 1911) was the great-grandnephew of Thomas Jefferson and the grandson of Thomas, 9th Lord Fairfax, a Virginian who never assumed his English title. Cary married Elizabeth Miller Potter (died 1945). His sister, the writer Constance Cary (1843–1920), one of the most astute and quotable observers of the social scene in the Gilded Age, married, in 1867, Burton Norvell Harrison (died 1904).

CAVENDISH-BENTINCK, MRS. was Elizabeth Livingston (died 1943), daughter of Mrs. **Maturin Livingston** and sister of **Mrs. Ogden Mills**. In 1880 she married William George Cavendish-Bentinck (1854–1909), grandson of the 3rd duke of Portland.

CHANLER, MR. AND MRS. WINTHROP Winthrop Astor Chanler (1863–1927) was the great-grandson of John Jacob Astor. He was educated at Eton College and Harvard. His wife, who was also his cousin, Margaret Terry (1862–1952), called "Daisy," wrote memoirs of their life in many parts of the world. Among their numerous children was Theodore Ward Chanler (1902–1961), the composer.

CHANLER, THE MISSES were the three unmarried sisters of the above who in 1892 were being presented to Society by their sister-in-law Daisy. As "Astor Orphans," they were considerable heiresses. They were Elizabeth Winthrop Chanler (1866–1937), who in 1898 married the reformer and essayist John Jay Chapman (1862–1933) as his second wife; Margaret Livingston Chanler (1870–1963), who served as a nurse during the Spanish-American War and in 1906 married Richard Aldrich (1863–1937), principal music critic of *The New York Times*; and Alida Beekman Chanler (1873–1969), who married Christopher Temple Emmet (1868–1957), a lawyer descended from the famous family of Irish patriots.

COOPER, MR. AND MRS. EDWARD Edward Cooper (1824–1905) was the son of Peter Cooper (1791–1883), inventor and philanthropist, founder of The Cooper Union. A graduate of Columbia College, he entered politics. A Democrat, he served as mayor of New York (1879–1881). In 1853 he married Cornelia Redmond. Their daughter Edith Cooper married **Lloyd S. Bryce**.

COSTER, HARRY was Henry A. Coster (died 1917). He married Mary L. Coles (died 1923) and lived at St. Adresse in Westchester County, N.Y.

COSTER, WILLIAM B. (died 1945), a partner in Morgan Drexel and a member of the Union Club, married Martha G. Gray (died 1947).

COTTENET, RAWLINS Rawlins Lowndes Cottenet (1866–1951), known as "Rollie," was a man-about-town, heir to a brokerage fortune but mainly devoted to the arts, a fine musician who composed many songs, and a member of the board of the Metropolitan Opera for forty-two years. He owned The Rosary, Society's favorite florist, on lower Park Avenue. He never married.

CROSBY, MISS Angelica Schuyler Crosby, daughter of the below, married John B. Henderson, Jr., Harvard 1891.

CROSBY, COL. J. SCHUYLER Great-grandson of Alexander Hamilton, John Schuyler Crosby (1839–1914) was a soldier who served as aide-de-camp to General Sheridan in the Civil War and later fought in Indian campaigns under General Custer. He was governor of Montana Territory in 1882–1884 and active in the preservation of Yellowstone National Park. In 1863 he married Harriet Van Rensselaer (died 1912).

CROSS, MR. AND MRS. JAMES Richard James Cross (1845–1917), born in Liverpool and educated at the Marlborough School, was a banker with the firm of Morton Bliss & Co from 1875–1899. His second wife, whom he married in 1885, was Annie Redmond (died 1920). They lived at 6 Washington Square North.

CRUGER, MR. AND MRS. S. VAN RENSSELAER Descended from two eighteenth-century mayors named Cruger, Stephen Van Rensselaer Cruger (1844–1898), a Union lieutenant-colonel in the Civil War, managed his family's real estate fortune and was comptroller of Trinity Church. He married Julie Grinnell Storrow (1849–1920), grandniece of Washington Irving.

CUSHING, MISS EDITH (died 1921), only child of **Thomas F. Cushing**, married, in 1903, Blair Fairchild (1877–1933), Harvard 1899, the American composer. The Fairchilds spent most of their life in France; he was awarded the *Legion d'honneur* in 1919.

CUSHING, THOMAS F. Thomas Forbes Cushing (died 1902), father of **Miss Edith Cushing** was a leader of Newport society and a governor of the Newport Casino. He married Fanny Grinnell, grandniece of Washington Irving.

Among the many military men in the Four Hundred John Schuyler Crosby had an outstanding record in both the Civil War and the Indian wars in the West. His wife, Harriet Van Rensselaer, was the granddaughter of Stephen Van Rensselaer, The Last Patroon. They were the grandparents of Harry Crosby, the expatriate poet of the 1920s.

CUTTING, MRS. BROCKHOLST was Marion Ramsay (died 1912), wife of Francis Brockholst Cutting (1805–1870), mother of **F. Brockholst Cutting** and **William Cutting, Jr.**

CUTTING, F. BAYARD. McAllister gave the name incorrectly: it was Robert Bayard Cutting (died 1918), Yale 1897.

CUTTING, F. BROCKHOLST Francis Brockholst Cutting (died 1896), was a member of a group of sporting bachelors who called themselves "The Dudes." Brother of **William Cutting, Jr.**

CUTTING, MR. AND MRS. W. BAYARD William Bayard Cutting (1850–1912), graduated from Columbia College in 1869 and the Law School in 1871, and was a trustee of Columbia University, director of the Metropolitan Opera and the Metropolitan Museum of Art, and president of the Union Club. He left an estate of nearly $11 million. His estate, Westbrook, at Great River, Long Island, landscaped by the Frederick Law Olmsted firm, is now the Bayard Cutting Arboretum. His wife, whom he married in 1877, was Olivia Murray (1855–1949).

CUTTING, ROBERT L., JR. Robert Livingston Cutting (1867–1910) was a lawyer. Prominent in amateur theatricals, to the horror of his family, he married an actress, Minnie Seligman (died 1915) and went on the stage himself.

CUTTING, WILLIAM, JR. William Brockholst Cutting, Jr. (died 1911), son of **Mrs. Brockholst Cutting** and brother of **F. Brockholst Cutting**, was also a "Dude" and a member of twelve clubs who lived at the Waldorf-Astoria Hotel.

DANA, MR. AND MRS. PAUL Paul Dana (1852–1930), Harvard 1874, was the son of Charles Anderson Dana (1819–1897), editor of the influential *New York Sun*. Paul followed him to the *Sun* beginning in 1880 and when his father died became editor-in-chief. He retired in 1903. Mrs. Dana was Mary Butler Duncan (died 1922). They were the grandparents of Ruth Draper (1884–1956), actress and monologuist.

DE FOREST, MR. AND MRS. GEORGE B. George B. de Forest (1848–1932), was a noted book collector; after his death his collection was sold to J. P. Morgan for the considerable sum of $200,000. He was a member of eleven clubs. In 1882 he married Anita Hargous (died 1932), sister of **Mrs. Duncan Eliott.**

Olivia Murray married W. Bayard Cutting, railroad executive and one of the most prominent New Yorkers of his time. They were the grandparents of Iris Origo, authority on Renaissance Italy.

Nineteenth-century American men had a strange predilection for four or five-hour public dinners which concluded in a gale of toasts and speeches. The most accomplished after dinner speaker was Chauncey Depew, railroad man and U.S. senator.

Depew worked most of his life for the Vanderbilt family and his home was on West 54th Street, a few steps from the great row of Vanderbilt houses on Fifth Avenue. He composed his speeches in his "Egyptian" study. An exotic stuffed bird was considered a most desirable ornament to an important room; Depew's was an albatross.

DELAFIELD, MISS Elizabeth Ray Delafield (1872–1923), daughter of **Dr. and Mrs. Francis Delafield**, was active in the missions of the Episcopal Church and worked with the wounded in France during World War I.

DELAFIELD, DR. AND MRS. FRANCIS Francis Delafield (1841–1915), Yale 1860, Columbia M.D. 1863, was a physician and pathologist at Bellevue Hospital and a professor at the College of Physicians and Surgeons. In 1870, he married Katherine Van Rensselaer (died 1901).

DEPEW, MR. AND MRS. CHAUNCEY M. Chauncy Mitchell Depew (1834–1928), Yale 1856, worked for the Vanderbilt family for his entire career. His devotion to their interests carried him to the presidency of their New York Central Railroad and, finally, to the U.S. Senate from New York. He was famous for the wit of his afterdinner speeches, of which he delivered a truly astounding number. His wife, whom he married in 1871, was Elise Hegeman, who died in 1892.

DE PEYSTER, MR. AND MRS. FREDERIC J. Descendant of Abraham de Peyster, mayor of New York in 1691, Frederic James de Peyster (1839–1905) a lawyer (Columbia Law, 1862), was president of the Archaeological Society, the St. Nicholas Society, the Society of Colonial Wars and chairman of the New York Society Library. He was married to Augusta McEvers Morris (1851–1911), sister of **A. Newbold Morris** and member of a family established at Morrisania in the southwestern Bronx since 1670.

DYER, MR. AND MRS. ELISHA, JR. Elisha Dyer, Jr. (1856–1917) was the son and grandson of governors of Rhode Island and descended from William Dyer, one of the seventeen purchasers of Rhode Island in 1638. A graduate of Brown University, he was president of the Popp Compressed Air and Electric Power Co., but was mainly a cotillion leader, considered the best-dressed man in Newport. In 1891 he married Sidney (Turner) Swan (died 1933), a widow descended from the first families of Maryland.

ELLIOTT, MR. AND MRS. DUNCAN   The name was actually Eliott. Duncan Eliott (1863–1919), Columbia 1884, was in the real estate business. He married Sallie Hargous (died 1934), who after his death marrried first **Woodbury Kane** and second, Captain Douglas Gill.

ERVING, LANGDON John Langdon Erving (died 1934), in his youth was a municipal reformer known as "Sunbeam Erving." Afterwards, he worked for the Mexican Cable Co. In 1904 he married Alice Hanchet Rutherford (died 1955).

FISH, MR. AND MRS. HAMILTON, JR.   Fish (1849–1936) was descended from Peter Stuyvesant. Graduating from Columbia College in 1869, he went into politics and became a member of the New York State Assembly. His wife was Emily N. Mann (died 1899).

FISH, MR. AND MRS. STUYVESANT   Stuyvesant Fish (1851–1923) brother of **Hamilton Fish, Jr.**, was president of the Illinois Central Railroad for nineteen years, then president of the American Railway Association. In 1876 he married Marion Graves Anthon (1853–1915), known as "Mamie," the celebrated wit and hostess. They lived at the still-standing 19 Gramercy Park, then in 1897–1898 had Stanford White build them a much admired Italian Renaissance palazzo at 25 East 78th Street, which is also still standing.

FORBES, H. DE COURCEY   The name was properly De Coursey. He lived in Paris and died there in 1920, unmarried.

FRANCKLYN, MR. AND MRS. C. G.   Charles G. Francklyn (died 1929) was a stockbroker. He married Susan Sprague Hoyt in 1869. They lived at 5 Washington Square and were among the first New Yorkers to make Southampton, L. I., a fashionable summer resort.

FRELINGHUYSEN, THEODORE (1860–1928) was the son of Frederick Frelinghysen (1817–1885), United States Secretary of State. In 1885 he married Alice Dudley Coats (died 1889), daughter of Sir James Coats, Bart., of J. & P. Coats, Ltd, and became treasurer of the Coats Thread Co. He and his second wife, Elizabeth (Thompson) Cannon (died 1967), owned a cottage in Tuxedo Park and a house at 60 Fifth Avenue.

FURMAN, J. C. was a broker who lived in Pelham, N.Y.

GOELET, MR. AND MRS. OGDEN. Ogden Goelet (1846–1897), brother of **Robert Goelet**, left an estate of more than $80 million to his wife Mary ("May") Wilson (1854–1929), daughter of Richard T. Wilson and sister of **Grace, Marshall Orme**, and **Richard T. Wilson, Jr.** Their daughter Mary (1878–1937) married, in 1903, Henry John Innes-Kerr, 8th duke of Roxburghe (1876–1932).

GOELET, MR. AND MRS. ROBERT   Robert Goelet (1841–1889), brother of **Ogden Goelet**, in 1879, married Harriette Louise Warren (died 1913), sister of the architect Whitney Warren.

GRANT, MISS Julia Grant (1876–1975), was the granddaughter of President Ulysses S. Grant and was born in the White House. Her father, Frederick Dent Grant (1850–1912) was U.S. ambassador to Austria-Hungary. Her mother, Ida Marie Honoré (1854–1930), was the sister of the celebrated Chicago hostess, Bertha (Honoré) Palmer (Mrs. Potter Palmer, 1849–1918). In 1899 Julia married Prince Michael Cantacuzene (1875–1955). She was the last surviving member of The Four Hundred.

GREENE, MISS Of the many Misses Greene in New York Society, this was probably Annie D. Greene (died 1940), who married Guy Bates, Columbia 1906.

GREENE, ALISTER (1855–1923) was a lawyer but did not practice; instead he devoted himself to "legal research" and club life.

GRISWOLD, FRANK GRAY (1854–1937) was a member of one of the great shipowning families of New York, a sportsman, and a writer on sports. In 1907 he married Josephine (Houghteling) Canfield (died 1937).

GURNEE, AUGUSTUS C. Augustus Coe Gurnee (died 1926), Harvard 1878, descended from a French Huguenot family, a stockbroker, lived at 763 Fifth Avenue and at Bar Harbor. He died at Baden-Baden.

HADDEN, ALEXANDER M. Alexander Mactier Hadden (died 1942) married Maude Miner (1880–1967), a Smith College graduate of 1901, who was a social worker.

HADDEN, JOHN A., JR. John Aspinwall Hadden, Jr. (1858–1931), married Marie Torrance (1858–1923), a granddaughter of Commodore Cornelius Vanderbilt and sister of **Mrs. Meredith Howland**, who was very rich, leaving an estate of nearly $3 million after large gifts to the Metropolitan Museum of Art.

HALL, MISS was Elizabeth Livingston Hall (died 1941), eldest unmarried daughter of **Mr. and Mrs. Valentine G. Hall**, who married Stanley Mortimer (died 1932), brother of **Richard Mortimer**.

HALL, MR. AND MRS. VALENTINE G. Valentine Gill Hall (1834–1880), son of an Irish immigrant who had made a fortune in New York real estate, married Mary Livingston Ludlow (1843–1919). Their daughter Anna Rebecca Hall (1863–1892) married, in 1883, Elliott Roosevelt (1860–1893), brother of President Theodore Roosevelt, and was the mother of (Anna) Eleanor Roosevelt (1884–1962) who married, in 1905, Franklin Delano Roosevelt (1882–1945), later president of the United States, half-brother of **James Roosevelt Roosevelt**. Another daughter, Maud, married Lawrence Waterbury, son of **Mr. and Mrs. James M. Waterbury**.

HAVEMEYER, MR. AND MRS. CHARLES F. Charles Frederick Havemeyer (1867–1898), brother of **Mrs. Clarkson Potter**, was a member of Havemeyer & Elder, Sugar Refiners. He married Camilla Moss (died 1900).

HAWKES, ROBERT F. Robert Forbes Hawkes (died 1940), Yale 1887, a physician in New York, in 1905 he married Alice Silliman Belknap (died 1971).

HEWITT, MR. AND MRS. PETER COOPER Grandson of the great philanthropist Peter Cooper (1791–1884) and son of Abram Hewitt (1822–1903), Mayor of New York. Peter Cooper Hewitt (1861–1921) was a director of the family's iron works, the Ringwood Co. Mrs. Cooper (married 1887, divorced 1918) was Lucy Bond Work (1860–1934), sister of **Mrs. Burke Roche**.

HOFFMAN, MISS Of the sixteen Misses Hoffman listed in the *Social Registers* of the time, McAllister probably was thinking of Helen F. Hoffman (died 1951), who married Dr. William Kinnicutt Draper, Harvard 1885.

HOFFMAN, MRS. CHARLES P. was correctly Eleanor Vail (died 1903) who married Charles Frederick Hoffman (1830–1897), an Episcopal clergyman like many of his family.

HONE, ROBERT, JR. (died 1927) was the son of the president of the Republic Fire Insurance Co. and the grandson of Philip Hone, mayor of New York and keeper of the famous *Diary*.

Eleonora Iselin was the wife of the sportsman De Lancey Astor Kane, famous for his four-in-hand driving. Together they engaged in many sporting activities and took advantage of the location of their home on Long Island Sound to train their children in boating from an early age. She was painted by Thomas Dewing.

Howland, Meredith (1833–1912), an heir to the Howland shipping fortune, married the granddaughter of Commodore Vanderbilt, Adelaide Torrance (1846–1932), sister of Mrs. John A. Hadden. The Howlands lived mostly in France where Mrs. Howland became a Parisian hostess and indefatigable bridgeplayer. They had no children.

Howard, Mr. and Mrs. Thomas Thomas Howard Howard (1862–1904), a descendant of Governor Peter Stuyvesant, was newly married at the time of the list, having wed, on January 19, 1892, Rose Post (died 1949).

Irvin, Mr. and Mrs. Richard Richard Irvin was a banker. Mrs. Irvin was Mary Morris (died 1918); at the time of her death she was president of no fewer than eight charitable organizations, as well as one of the original governors of the Colony Club.

Iselin, Mr. and Mrs. Columbus Columbus O'Connell Iselin (died 1934) was the son of Adrian Iselin (died 1905), a Swiss who founded a banking house in the United States. His sister Eleonora Iselin was the wife of **De Lancey Astor Kane.** His wife was Edith Colford Jones (died 1950).

Iselin, Isaac spent most of his life abroad and died in France in 1906.

Jaffray, Miss Helen F. Jaffray (died 1929), daughter of **Mrs. William Jaffray**, married Walter Abbott (died 1919), Harvard 1888.

Jaffray, Mrs. William was Helen Smythe (died 1932), who lived mainly in Paris. The Jaffray family business was importing silk.

Jay, Col. and Mrs. William William Jay (1841–1915), great-grandson of Chief Justice John Jay, graduated from Columbia College 1859, was president of the New York *Herald*, senior warden of Trinity Church, and president of the Coaching Club from 1876 to 1896. In 1878, he married Lucy Oelrichs (died 1931), sister of **Charles M. Oelrichs**. His family home, Bedford House, at Katonah, N.Y., is now open to the public. His sister Augusta married **Randolph Robinson**.

Jones, Miss Beatrix Beatrix Cadwalader Jones (1872–1959), only child of **Mr. and Mrs. F. Rhinelander Jones**, became one of America's most famous landscape architects. In

1913, she married Professor Max Farrand (1869–1945) of Yale University, historian and later director of the Henry E. Huntington Library.

JONES, MR. AND MRS. F. RHINELANDER He was Frederic Rhinelander Jones (1846–1918) who in 1870 had married Mary Cadwalader Rawle (1850–1935). They were divorced in 1896 and "Freddy" settled in Paris, where he spent the rest of his life without any profession, having inherited substantial sums from his Rhinelander and Jones relatives. He and his sister, Edith Wharton, apparently never saw each other again, although she was also living in Paris.

JONES, SHIPLEY (died 1936), clubman.

KANE, MR. AND MRS. DE LANCEY De Lancey Astor Kane (died 1915) was the great-grandson of **John Jacob Astor** and brother of **S. Nicholson Kane** and **Woodbury Kane**. He graduated from West Point in 1868 and Columbia School of Law in 1873, but devoted most to his life to sport. He married Eleonora Iselin (died 1938), sister of **Columbus Iselin**. Their home was The Paddocks, Davenport Neck, New Rochelle.

KANE, S. NICHOLSON (died 1906), brother of **De Lancey** and **Woodbury Kane**, graduated from the U.S. Naval Academy in 1846 at the head of his class; he then attended Cambridge University. A sportsman like his brothers, he became commodore of the New York Yacht Club in 1877.

KANE, WOODBURY (1861–1905), brother of **De Lancey** and **S. Nicholson Kane**, was the most athletic of the Kane boys, a yachtsman, a football player at Harvard, a tennis and cricket player, an expert horseman who was a cross-country rider, and an outstanding polo player. Only a year and a half before his death he married Sallie (Hargous) Eliott, formerly wife of **Duncan Eliott**.

KEAN, ELIZABETH Elizabeth d'Hauteville Kean (1864–1922) was a descendant of the Livingston family and Lewis Morris, Signer of the Declaration of Independence, sister of **Julian Kean**, and **Mrs. George Lockhart Rives**. The surname is pronounced "Kane."

KEAN, JULIAN Julian Halsted Kean (1854–1932), brother of **Elizabeth Kean** and **Mrs. George Lockhart Rives**, Yale 1876, was a lawyer and president of the National State Bank of New Jersey. Two of their brothers, John Kean (1852–1914) and Hamilton Fish Kean (1862–1941) were U.S. senators from New Jersey.

Frederick Law Olmsted laid out the vast lawns and shrubbery of Elm Court, the W.D. Sloane House in Lennox, Mass. Beatrix Cadwalader Jones of the Four Hundred, beginning her career as a landscape architect, laid out the flowerbeds. The estate was tended to by so many gardeners that they organized their own sports teams who played matches with the employees of neighboring estates.

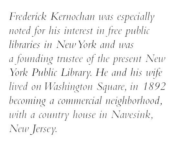

Frederick Kernochan was especially noted for his interest in free public libraries in New York and was a founding trustee of the present New York Public Library. He and his wife lived on Washington Square, in 1892 becoming a commercial neighborhood, with a country house in Navesink, New Jersey.

KERNOCHAN, MR. AND MRS. FREDERICK [Joseph] Frederick Kernochan (died 1929), brother of **James P. Kernochan**, was descended from Joseph Kernochan, an Irishman who came to New York in 1725. Frederick, Yale 1863, was a lawyer. His wife was Mary Stuart Whitney (died 1922). They lived in one of the famous federal houses on Washington Square North.

KERNOCHAN, MR. AND MRS. J. P. James P. Kernochan (1831–1897), brother of **Frederick Kernochan**; married Catherine Lorillard (died 1917), daughter of Peter Lorillard of the tobacco dynasty and sister of **Mrs. Henry Barbey** and **Mrs. Lawrence Kip**. They lived at 824 Fifth Avenue and at Ochre Point in Newport.

KIP, COL. AND MRS. LAWRENCE A descendant of Hendrick Kip, who settled in New Amsterdam in 1643 and left his name on Kip's Bay in the East River, Lawrence Kip (1836–1899) was a professional soldier. He graduated from West Point 1857 and became an aide-de-camp to General Philip Sheridan. After the Civil War he was an important soldier in the Indian wars. He wrote his memoirs entitled *Army Life on the Pacific*. He married Eva Lorillard (died 1906), daughter of Peter Lorillard and sister of **Mrs. James P. Kernochan** and **Mrs. Henry Barbey**.

KIP, MISS was Edith Kip (died 1949), daughter of **Col. and Mrs. Lawrence Kip**. She married, first, Richard McCreery and second, in 1907, the Hon. Henry Thomas Coventry (1868–1934), third son of the 9th earl of Coventry.

KNOWLTON, MISS Mary Knowlton (died 1929) married, in April 1892, Prussian Count Johannes von Francken-Sierstorpff (died 1917).

KOUNTZE, MR. AND MRS. LUTHER Luther Kountze (1842–1918), Ohio-born and formerly a business man in Omaha, Nebraska, was head of the banking firm of Kountze Brothers. He was one of the founders of the Metropolitan Opera. In 1875, he married Annie Parsons Ward (1852–1928) at Grace Church.

LANIER, MR. AND MRS. JAMES James Francis Doughty Lanier (1858–1928) was a banker, a partner in the firm of Winslow Lanier & Co. His sister Fanny married **Francis Randall Appleton**. In 1885 he married Harriet Arnold Bishop (1866–1931), daughter of **Heber Bishop**. She was an active patron of music in New York. Their house at Old Westbury, Long Island, designed by James Brown Lord, is still standing.

LEARY, ARTHUR was the son of James Leary, who had made a fortune in beaver hats. His sister Annie (1832–1919) was much involved with Catholic charities and was a papal countess.

Leiter, Miss was Mary Victoria Leiter (1870–1906), daughter of Levi Ziegler Leiter (1834–1904), Marshall Field's original partner in his Chicago department store. In 1895 she married George Curzon, later Marquess Curzon (1859–1925). In 1898 he became viceroy of India and Mary Victoria presided over an establishment of 800 servants in Calcutta. She died soon after their return from India. Their daughter Cynthia (1898–1933) was the first wife of Sir Oswald Mosley, the British Fascist leader.

Livingston, Miss Clarissa was properly Clarisse Hazeltine Livingston (died 1923) (daughter of below.) She never married.

Livingston, Edward (died 1907) was a banker.

Livingston, Edward de Peyster (1861–1930), Columbia College 1882, was the great-grandson of Robert R. Livingston (1746–1813), chancellor of the State of New York. He lived at 271 Fifth Avenue and had a house, Northwood, in the old Hudson River holding of the Livingston family at Clermont, N.Y.

Livingston, Mr. and Mrs. Henry B. Henry Beekman Livingston (1854–1917), a stockbroker, was twice descended from the Livingstons and his first wife was a Livingston cousin. He was educated at Christ Church, Oxford. His second wife was Frances Redmond.

Livingston, Mrs. Maturin was Ruth Baylies (died 1918), who married Maturin Livingston (1815–1888). They were the parents of **Mrs. Cavendish-Bentinck** and **Mrs. Ogden Mills**.

Lusk, Miss was Anna H. Lusk (died 1968), daughter of Dr. William Thompson Lusk (1838–1897), the foremost American obstetrician of his time. The Lusk house at 47 East 34th Street was decorated by Louis Comfort Tiffany, whose daughter married Lusk's son.

March, Clement (died 1937) was a perennial partner at Mrs. Astor's dancing parties. He lived in a federal house at 25 Washington Square North.

Marie, Peter (died 1903), broker, amateur poet, collector of fans and snuff boxes, and cotillion leader.

Marshall, Mr. and Mrs. Charles H. Charles Henry Marshall (1838–1912) was heir to the Black Ball line of steamships. His wife was Josephine Lenox Banks (died 1933), niece and part-heiress of James Lenox, whose family real estate holdings (Lenox Hill) made him one of the richest men in New York.

Martin, Mr. and Mrs. Bradley Bradley Martin (1841–1913), Union College 1863, brother of **F. T. Martin**, was a lawyer from Albany. Mrs. Martin was Cornelia Sherman (1847–1920). In 1893 their sixteen-year-old daughter Cornelia (1877–1961) married William 4th earl of Craven (1868–1921). When Martin died his estate was valued at $15 million.

Martin, F. T. Frederick Townsend Martin (1849–1914), bachelor brother of **Bradley Martin**, claimed to be "engaged in studying labor questions." He pursued this worthy subject at Newport during the summers and Palm Beach during the winters. Of his two fatuous books of memoirs, one was entitled, apparently without irony, *The Passing of the Idle Rich*.

McAllister, Miss Louise Ward McAllister (died 1923) was the only daughter of **Ward McAllister**. She married Albert Nelson Lewis of Havre de Grace, Maryland (died 1935).

Ward McAllister [Samuel] Ward McAllister (1827–1895) drew up the list of the Four Hundred in 1892. In 1853 he married Sarah Taintor Gibbons of Savannah (died 1909). There was a daughter, **Louise McAllister**, and two sons from the marriage.

Anne Morgan was the daughter of John Pierpont Morgan, with whom she had an uneasy relationship since, while supporting the charities to which she devoted most of her life, he considered her a Bohemian and was disappointed that she never married. A great Francophile, she had a house in the town of Versailles for years. In New York she was a pioneer in Sutton Place, where she had a house on the East River. She was photographed here (far left) while investigating the conditions of coal-mining in Pennsylvania.

McVickar, Mr. and Mrs. H. W. Harry Whitney McVickar (1860–1907) worked for the real estate firm of Stephen Van Rensselaer Cruger, but was also a talented illustrator and caricaturist. He was the first art director of *Vogue* magazine. In 1891 he married Maud Robbins (died 1919), daughter of **Mr. and Mrs. Henry A. Robbins**.

Mills, Mr. and Mrs. Ogden Ogden Mills (1858–1929) was the son of Darius Ogden Mills (1825–1910) and Janet Cunningham, sister of **Mrs. Heber Bishop**. Mills was a Forty-niner who made a great fortune in California, first as a grocer, then as a banker. He was uninterested in Society, but his son married the haughty Ruth Livingston (1855–1920), daughter of **Mrs. Maturin Livingston** and sister of **Mrs. Cavendish-Bentinck**.

Moore, Mr. and Mrs. Clement C. Clement Clarke Moore (1843–1910) was grandson of the theologian of the same name who wrote *The Night Before Christmas*. The Moore family had vast real estate holdings in the Chelsea neighborhood on the West Side of Manhattan, centering on 23rd Street. The younger Moore was a major in the Civil War and a cotton broker until the distribution of his grandfather's estate in 1901, when he and his family went to live at 82 Avenue Monceau in Paris. His wife was Laura Martha Williams (1856–1919).

Morgan, Miss Anne Anne Tracy Morgan (1873–1952), daughter of the great financier John Pierpont Morgan, devoted her life mainly to charitable endeavors—many connected with alleviating conditions for working women. She was devoted to France, founded the American Friends of France, was active in refugee work during World War I, and received many French decorations, including the *Legion d'honneur*.

Morris, Mr. and Mrs. A. Newbold Augustus Newbold Morris (1838–1906), descendant of Lewis Morris, lord of the manor of Morrisania and Signer of the Declaration of Independence, was a founding member of the Metropolitan Club and a trustee of Columbia University. His sister Augusta McEvers Morris married **Frederic J. de Peyster**. Mrs. Morris was Eleanor Colford Jones (1841–1906). Their son Newbold Morris (1868–1928) married, in 1896, Helen Schermerhorn Kingsland (1876–1956), grandniece of **Mrs. William Astor**.

Morris, Miss Eva C. Ward McAllister got her name slightly incorrect: she was Eva Van Cortlandt Morris (1869–1928), daughter of **Mr. and Mrs. A. Newbold Morris**.

MORTIMER, MR. AND MRS. R. Richard Mortimer (died 1918) was the grandson of a York-shireman who dealt in woolen goods in New York and later owned considerable real estate. His wife was Eleanor Jay Chapman (died 1930) sister of John Jay Chapman, who married **Elizabeth Winthrop Chanler**.

MUNN, CHARLES Charles Allen Munn (1859–1924) was a patent agent and editor of the Munn family's magazine *Scientific American*.

NELSON, MRS. FREDERICK The name was actually Neilson, perennially mispelled by the press although an honorable name of Scottish origin long prominent in New York. Mary Isabel ("Belle") Gebhard (died 1949), married Frederick W. Neilson in 1873. Their daughter Cathleen Gebhard Neilson (1884–1927) was the first wife of Reginald Vanderbilt (1880–1925), son of **Mr. and Mrs. Cornelius Vanderbilt**.

NEWBOLD, MR. AND MRS. THOMAS Thomas Newbold (1849–1929) married Sarah Lawrence Coolidge (1858–1922), a descendant of Thomas Jefferson.

OELRICHS, MR. AND MRS. CHARLES M. Charles May Oelrichs (died 1932) was a member of a German-American family who were United States agents for the North German Lloyd shipping line. He married Blanche de Loosey (died 1933), daughter of the Austrian consul general in New York. They were the parents of Blanche Oelrichs (1890–1950), who acted and wrote poetry and plays under the name "Michael Strange." Her second husband was John Barrymore (1882-1942), celebrated actor and legendary drinker. Another daughter of the Oelrichs, Natalie ("Lily"; 1880–1931) married as her second husband H. H. Prince Heinrich Borwin, duke of Mecklenburg-Schwerin (1885–1942). A great-grandson of Charles is Peter Oelrichs Duchin (born 1937), the musician and bandleader.

OLIN, STEPHEN H. Stephen Henry Olin (1847–1925) was a lawyer, a trustee of the Astor Library, and president of the University Settlement House. In 1903 he married as his second wife Emeline Dodge Harriman (died 1932), daughter of Oliver Harriman.

OTIS, MISS was Mary Otis (died 1946), who married Robert Robert [sic] Livingston Clarkson (died 1924) and lived on the old Livingston estate, Midwood, at Tivoli-on-Hudson.

OTIS, JAMES (1836–1898), grandson of the distinguished statesman Harrison Gray Otis of Boston, was a merchant, served in the Civil War, and was a member of the New York State Senate (1884–1885).

Outdoor activities flourished in Lenox, Massachusetts which afforded open space for horse sports, including the Berkshire Hunt, as well as views of the Berkshire Mountains. The estate of A. Newbold Morris was photographed about 1905.

PARKER, JAMES V. James Vanderburg Parker (died 1917) was a Boston-born bachelor who was a permanent member of Mrs. Astor's entourage. According to *The Ultra-fashionable Peerage*, he "inherited a large fortune which has enabled him to be a lifelong man of leisure."

PENDLETON, MR. AND MRS. FRANCIS KEY Grandson of Francis Scott Key, author of *The Star-Spangled Banner*, Pendleton (died 1930) was a lawyer who graduated from Harvard in 1870, corporation counsel of the City of New York (1907–1910), and justice of the Supreme Court of New York. In 1890 he married, as his second wife, Elizabeth Marianita La Montagne (died 1936).

PERRY, MISS was Bertha Perry (died 1936), daughter of **Mrs. William A. Perry**, who married Peter Lorillard Ronalds (1869–1928); they spent much of their lives in Paris.

PERRY, MRS. WILLIAM A. William Alfred Perry (1835–1916), Columbia 1855, was an engineer married to Constance Frink (died 1926).

PETERS, RICHARD (1851–1921), Harvard 1871, was a "clubman and cotillion leader" who in 1917, despite his age, enlisted in the U.S. Army and served in France at Château Thierry and St. Mihiel. He was decorated four times with the *croix de guerre* and awarded the *Legion d'honneur*.

PIERSON, MISS Marguerite ("Daisy") Pierson (died 1964), daughter of **General and Mrs. J. Fred Pierson**, married George H. Hull (died 1965), Yale 1902.

PIERSON, GENERAL AND MRS. J. FRED Seventh in descent from Abraham Pierson, first president of Yale College, John Frederick Pierson (1839–1933) had a distinguished record in the Civil War. After the war he became president of the Ramapo Foundry and Wheel Works, a major supplier of railroad equipment. In 1869 he married S. Augusta Rhodes (died 1929).

PORTER, MR. AND MRS. BENJAMIN C. Benjamin Curtis Porter (1845–1908) was a painter and member of the National Academy of Design, where he exhibited from 1867 to 1900. In 1887 he married Mary Louise Clark (died 1945).

POST, MR. AND MRS. CHARLES A. Charles A. Post (died 1921) brother of **George Browne Post**, was a lawyer. His wife was Marie Caroline de Trobriand (died 1926). They had a house on Madison Avenue and Strandhome at Bayport, Long Island, where Post, a keen amateur astronomer, had a private observatory.

POST, EDWARD C. (1845–1915) had an inherited income and divided his time between New York, Newport, and Paris. He was a founding member of the Knickerbocker Club. In 1895 he married Emilie Thorn King (died 1929).

POST, MR. AND MRS. GEORGE B. George Browne Post (1837–1913), brother of **Charles A. Post**, New York University 1858, was an architect. Many of his notable buildings in New York have been demolished, but there remain his New York Stock Exchange and the campus of the College of the City of New York. In 1863 he married Alice Stone (died 1909).

POTTER, CLARKSON. [Edward] Clarkson Potter (1862–1951), was grandson of Alonzo Potter (1800–1865), Episcopal Bishop of Pennsylvania. He married Emily Blanche Havemeyer (1865–1938), sister of **Charles F. Havemeyer**, and lived at Clearview in Westchester County, N.Y.

POTTER, MR. AND MRS. H. N. Howard Nott Potter (died 1937), Union College 1881, was an architect and member of the National Academy of Design. He married Ethel Potter (died 1949).

When he was running for public office, Theodore Roosevelt disassociated himself from the Four Hundred despite his many relations and close friends listed for fear that their names might alienate the populist vote. At Tranquility, his Oyster Bay home, he sits on the verandah. The younger woman seated on the lawn is his sister Corinne, who married Douglas Robinson, Jr.

POTTER, JULIAN was a stockbroker at 6 Wall Street, married to Margaret Pixley.

RANDOLPH, MISS CORA (died 1947) was the daughter of Edmund Randolph of Brookwood, Mount Saint Vincent on the Hudson, N.Y. She married Richard Trimble (died 1924), Harvard 1880.

REDMOND, GOOLD H. (died 1907), Columbia 1857, was a sportsman and a founding member of the Knickerbocker Club.

RHINELANDER, T. J. OAKLEY Thomas Jackson Oakley Rhinelander (1853–1946) graduated from Columbia in 1878. The principal heir of the great Rhinelander real estate fortune he spent most of his life managing its properties. In 1894 he married Edith Cruger Sands **(Miss Sands)** (died 1923). He bought and restored a German castle, Schonberg, near Oberwessel on the Rhine, where the Rhinelander family had originated.

RICHARDS, ROBERT KERR (died 1924) was a stockbroker who lived at Greenook Farm in Bay Side, L. I.

RIPLEY, MR. AND MRS. S. D. Sidney Dillon Ripley (died 1905) was grandson of Sidney Dillon (1812–1892), president of the Union Pacific Railroad. Although treasurer and director of the Equitable Life Assurance Society, which largely belonged to the family of his wife, Mary Baldwin Hyde (died 1938), he was mainly occupied with horses. Their neo-Georgian townhouse at 16 East 79th Street, is still standing.

RITCHIE, JAMES W. James Wadsworth Ritchie (died 1925) married, in 1895, Emily Tooker (died 1903), daughter of **Gabriel Mead Tooker**.

RIVES, MR. AND MRS. GEORGE L. George Lockhart Rives (1849–1917) graduated from Columbia College 1868 and the Law School in 1873 and was one of the most civic-minded of the Four Hundred, active on many boards and chairman of the New York Public Library. His second wife, whom he married in 1889, was Sara Whitney Belmont (died 1924).

ROBERT, MR. AND MRS. CHRISTOPHER Christopher Rhinelander Robert II (1830–committed suicide 1898) was the son of the merchant and philanthropist of the same name (1802–1878) who founded Robert College in Constantinople. His second wife was Julia (Remmington) Morgan (died 1925).

ROBINS, MR. AND MRS. H. The name actually was Henry Asher Robbins (died 1914) son of the founder of the Waltham Watch Co. His wife was Lizzie Pelham Bend (died 1933). Their daughter Maud married **Harry Whitney McVickar**.

ROBINSON, D. T. L. (1824–1893), descended from Scottish landed gentry, was married to Frances ("Fanny") Monroe (1816–1906), grandniece of President James Monroe. They were the parents of **Douglas Robinson, Jr.**

ROBINSON, MR. AND MRS. DOUGLAS, JR. Douglas Theodore Robinson (1855– 1918), was president of the Douglas Land Company, which owned an immense tract at Jordanville, Herkimer County, N.Y. He married Corinne Roosevelt (1861–1933), sister of President Theodore Roosevelt. Their son, Theodore Douglas Robinson (1883–1934) married Helen Rebecca Roosevelt (1881–1962), daughter of **James Roosevelt Roosevelt**.

ROBINSON, RANDOLPH [Edmund] Randolph Robinson, one of the few Southerners in the Four Hundred, in 1867 married the beautiful Augusta Jay (died 1878), sister of **William Jay**.

ROCHE, MRS. BURKE Frances Eleanor Work (1857–1947) was the daughter of Frank H. Work (1819–1911), a New York stockbroker, and was the sister of **Mrs. Peter Cooper Hewitt**. In 1880 she married the Hon. James Boothby Burke Roche (1851–1920), who two months before his death became 3rd Baron Fermoy. Their daughter Cynthia Burke Roche (1884–1966) married (secondly) Guy Fairfax Cary (1879–1950), son of **Mr. and Mrs. Clarence Cary**. Their son Edmund Burke Roche (1885–1955), Harvard 1909, became 4th Baron Fermoy and was the grandfather of Diana, Princess of Wales.

ROGERS, MISS was Julia Fish Rogers (died 1938), daughter of **Mrs. Rogers**, who in 1894 married Kenneth Frazier (died 1949), Lehigh 1887.

ROGERS, MRS. was Susan Le Roy Fish (died 1909), sister of **Hamilton** and **Stuyvesant Fish**. Her husband was William Evans Rogers (died 1913) of Philadelphia, West Point 1867, a lieutenant in the United States Corps of Engineers.

ROOSEVELT, MR. AND MRS. JAMES ROOSEVELT Roosevelt (1854–1927), always known as "Rosy," was the only child of James Roosevelt (1828–1900) of Hyde Park, N.Y. by his first marriage and was the half-brother of President Franklin D. Roosevelt. In 1877 at Grace Church, he married Helen Schermerhorn Astor (1855–1893), **Mr. and Mrs. William Astor's** daughter. Their daughter Helen Rebecca Roosevelt (1881–1962) married her distant cousin Theodore Douglas Robinson (1883-1934), son of **D. T. Robinson**.

RUTHERFURD, MR. AND MRS. LEWIS Lewis Morris Rutherfurd (1816–1892), Williams College 1834, was briefly a lawyer but pursued his hobby of astronomy and became one of America's leading men of science. In 1841 he married Margaret Stuyvesant Chanler (1821–1890).

SANDS, MISS was Edith Cruger Sands (died 1923) who married **T. J. Oakley Rhinelander**.

SCHUYLER, MR. AND MRS. PHILIP Philip Schuyler (1836–1906), a descendant of General Philip Schuyler of American Revolution fame, and of Alexander Hamilton, was president of New York Life Insurance and Trust Co., of New York Hospital, the Union Club, and was a founding member of the Knickerbocker Club. In 1872 he married Harriet (Lowndes) Langdon (1843–1915).

SHEPARD, MISS was Agnes Shepard (died 1932), daughter **Mr. and Mrs. Edward Shepard**, who married Charles B. Hewitt (died 1906).

SHEPARD, MR. AND MRS. EDWARD Edward Morse Shepard (1850–1911), Harvard 1869, a lawyer, was active in Democratic Party affairs and was a Civil Service Commissioner. He was also chairman of the trustees of the College of the City of New York.

Lenox, Massachusetts was much staider than frivolous Newport but provided much more acreage for the building of vast houses. The ninety-four room house, Elm Court, of William Douglas Sloane and his wife, Emily Thorn Vanderbilt, was designed by Peabody & Stearns. Mrs. Sloane lived until 1946 and was the last lady in American Society to keep her footmen in knee breeches.

SHERMAN, MR. AND MRS. WILLIAM WATTS William Watts Sherman (1842–1912) was a partner in the banking firm of Duncan, Sherman & Co. He married into two great Rhode Island families: his first wife, whom he married in 1871, was Annie Derby Rogers Wetmore (died 1884), sister of **George Peabody Wetmore**; in 1885 he married Sophia Augusta Carter Brown (died 1947), an heiress of the great Brown shipping dynasty. His daughter by his first marriage, Georgette Wetmore Sherman (died 1960) married **Harold Brown**, John Carter Brown's son and Sherman's brother-in-law. His daughter by his second marriage, Mildred (died 1961), married, in 1911, Ralph Stonor 5th Baron Camoys in England.

SLOANE, MISS ADELE was Florence Adele Sloane (1873–1960) daughter of **Mr. and Mrs. William D. Sloane**, who married James Abercrombie Burden (1871–1932) in 1895. He was the brother of **I. Townsend Burden** and was president of the Burden Iron Co. of Troy, N. Y. They were the grandparents of Adele Lawrence (1931–1991), artist and conservationist, who married Louis Stanton Auchincloss (born 1917), the novelist and essayist.

SLOANE, MR. AND MRS. WILLIAM D. William D. Sloane (1844–1915) was treasurer of his family's business, W & J Sloane Carpets. His wife was Emily Thorn Vanderbilt (1852–1946), granddaughter of Commodore Vanderbilt, sister of **Mrs. Hamilton McK. Twombly, Mrs. W. Seward Webb**, and **Cornelius** and **George W. Vanderbilt**. After Sloane's death his widow married Henry White (1850–1927), a distinguished diplomat who was American representative at the Treaty of Versailles. His first wife had been Margaret Stuyvesant Rutherfurd (died 1916), daughter of **Mr. and Mrs. Lewis Morris Rutherfurd**. The Sloane's grandchildren included John Henry Hammond, Jr. (1910–1987), the record producer and talent scout, and Alice Hammond (1905–1978) whose second husband was Benny Goodman (1909–1986), the clarinetist and jazz musician.

SMITH, J. CLINCH James Clinch Smith (died 1912) was a descendant of "Bullrider Smith," the seventeenth-century English settler on Long Island who was given by the local Indians all the land he could ride around on a bull in one day; Smith managed to stay on his mount from dawn to dusk and acquired a vast tract that became Smithtown, Long Island. His sister Bessie (1862–1950) married the architect Stanford White. Clinch Smith happened to be present at the Madison Square roof garden on the night in 1906 when Harry K. Thaw shot White and gave testimony at the Thaw trial. Smith went down on the *Titanic*. His wife was Bertha Ludington Barnes (died 1913) of Chicago, a talented musician.

STEVENS, MR. AND MRS. BYAM K. Byam Kerby Stevens (1836–1911) was the grandson of Albert Gallatin (1761–1849), first U.S. secretary of the treasury. He held a seat on the New York Stock Exchange. Mrs. Stevens was Eliza Langdon Wilks (died 1930), great-granddaughter of John Jacob Astor and sister of **Matthew Wilks**. Their Italian Renaissance home at 11 East 78th Street is still standing.

STEVENS, MISS ELIZABETH (died 1926), daughter of the above, married her cousin Richard Stevens, Columbia College 1890, of Castle Point, Hoboken N.J., and Aiken, S.C.

STEWART, LISPENARD (1855–1927), brother of **William Rhinelander Stewart**, Yale 1876, Columbia Law 1878), was a lawyer who seldom practiced. An heir to the Rhinelander real estate fortune, he was a trustee of the estate.

STEWART, MR. AND MRS. WILLIAM RHINELANDER Stewart (1852–1929), brother of **Lispenard Stewart**, described himself as a "humanitarian"; he was president of the New York State Board of Charities. Originator of the idea for the Washington arch in Washington Square, he raised most of the money for its construction. In 1879 he married Annie McKee Armstrong of Baltimore. Their daughter Anita (1886–1977) married, in 1909, Don Miguel de Braganza (1878–1923), a member of the Portuguese royal family.

STOKES, MISS Olivia Eggelston Phelps Stokes (1847–1927), daughter of **Mr. and Mrs. Anson Phelps Stokes**, was a distinguished philanthropist, founder with her sister Caroline Phelps Stokes (1854–1909) of the still-existing Phelps Stokes Fund, dedicated to the education of minorities.

STOKES, MR. AND MRS. ANSON PHELPS Anson Phelps Stokes (1838–1913), married, in 1865, Helen Louisa Phelps and was a partner in her family's great metals firm of Phelps Dodge.

At 640 Fifth Avenue William Henry Vanderbilt, head of the dynasty after the death of his father, Commodore Cornelius Vanderbilt, built one of the grandest houses of Gilded Age New York with interiors in many rich styles. Five of his children were listed by Ward McAllister. The house was the last survivor of the Vanderbilt mansions below 57th Street and was not torn down until the 1940s.

*George Washington Vanderbilt, shy
and scholarly grandson of Commodore
Vanderbilt, was building the grandest
house in America in 1892. Biltmore,
at Asheville, North Carolina
was surrounded by a 125,000 acre
estate. The patron of many artists,
Vanderbilt was painted by his friend
J.A.M. Whistler and, here,
by John Singer Sargent.*

STURGIS, MR. AND MRS. F. K. Frank Knight Sturgis (died 1932) was president of the New York Stock Exchange and Madison Square Garden, a founding member and president (1911–1926) of the Metropolitan Club, and governor of the Knickerbocker Club from 1881 to 1932—a record, a member of the Coaching Club and a famous amateur whip. His wife was Florence Lydig (died 1922).

SUYDAM, MR. AND MRS. WALTER LISPENARD Walter Lispenard Suydam (1854–1930) was the nephew of **Mrs. William Astor** and **Mrs. Benjamin Sumner Welles**. He was first vice-president of the New-York Historical Society. In 1875 he had married his cousin Jane Mesier Suydam (1855–1932).

TAILER, MISS Fannie Bogert Tailer (died 1953), daughter of **E.N. Tailer**, married Sydney Smith, cotton broker and sportsman.

TAILER, E. N. Edward Neuville Tailer (1830–1917) was a dry goods importer who married Agnes Suffern (1831–1917), daughter of Thomas Suffern (1787–1869), who came from Belfast to New York in 1808 and made a fortune importing Irish linens. In 1834 he built 11 Washington Square North, one of the original houses on the square. Their daughter Agnes Suffern Tailer married **Henry L. Burnett**.

TALLEYRAND, MARQUISE DE Elizabeth Curtis, daughter of Joseph Curtis, a New York merchant, married, in 1867 at Nice, Charles Maurice Marquis de Périgord-Talleyrand, later 4th duc de Dino, a soldier in the French colonial wars. With her fortune they built a château on the St. John's River in Florida, where George Templeton Strong supposed sarcastically that they could "control the alligator market." They were divorced in 1886, but she continued to call herself Marquise de Talleyrand. Talleyrand later married Adele Livingston (Sampson) Stevens, mother of **Mrs. Frederick Hobbes Allen**.

TIFFANY, BELMONT (died 1952) was the grandson of Admiral Matthew Calbraith Perry. He married Annie Ward Cameron (died 1919), daughter of **Sir Roderick Cameron**.

TOOKER, MISS Emily M. Tooker (died 1903), daughter of G. Mead Tooker, in 1895 married **James Wadsworth Ritchie**.

Richard Morris Hunt designed Biltmore for George Vanderbilt. A graduate of the Ecole des Beaux Arts, he was devoted to French Renaissance architecture and created a chateau in Asheville. The grounds were laid out by Frederick Law Olmsted and the forester Gifford Pinchot developed the thousands of acres of woodlands.

TOOKER, G. MEAD Gabriel Mead Tooker (died 1905), father of **Miss Tooker**, was a successful investor. He was prominent in Newport life, where he was an active member of the Reading Room.

TWOMBLY, MR. AND MRS. HAMILTON McKOWN Twombly (1849–1910), Harvard 1875, married Florence Adele Vanderbilt (1854–1952), granddaughter of Commodore Vanderbilt, sister of **Mrs. W. Seward Webb**, **Mrs. William Douglas Sloane**, and **Cornelius** and **George W. Vanderbilt**. After his marriage into the Vanderbilt family, he became a director of fourteen railroads and chairman of the Western Union telegraph system.

VANDERBILT, MR. AND MRS. CORNELIUS Cornelius Vanderbilt (1843–1899) was the brother of **Mrs. William Douglas Sloane**, **Mrs. Hamilton McKown Twombly**, **Mrs. W. Seward Webb**, and **George Vanderbilt**. He was chairman of the board of the Vanderbilt family's New

Hunt designed the interiors of Biltmore and some of the furnishings. His masterpiece was the dining hall with table, chairs, and sideboards of his design. Henry James on a visit said that eating in the hall "was like dining in a cathedral."

Euphemia White Van Rensselaer was painted by Healy in 1842, just before she married John Church Cruger, whose family had given two mayors to New York and were numbered, like the Van Rensselaers, among the Four Hundred.

York Central Railroad. His wife was Alice Claypoole Gwynne (1845–1934). They were the parents of Gertrude Vanderbilt (1875–1942), who married Harry Payne Whitney (1872–1930), son of **William C. Whitney**. A talented sculptor herself, she was the founder of the Whitney Museum of American Art. Another child of Cornelius and Alice was Reginald Claypoole Vanderbilt (1880–1925), father of the artist and actress Gloria Vanderbilt (born 1924).

VANDERBILT, GEORGE W. Grandson of Commodore Vanderbilt, brother of **Cornelius Vanderbilt**, **Mrs. W. Seward Webb**, **Mrs. William Douglas Sloane**, and **Mrs. Hamilton McKown Twombly**, George Washington Vanderbilt (1861–1914) was the builder of Biltmore in Asheville, N. C., completed in 1895, which with 245 rooms and 45 baths, is the largest private house ever built in the United States and is now open to the public. He married Edith Stuyvesant Dresser (1873–1958), a descendant of Governor Peter Stuyvesant.

VAN RENSSELAER, MRS. A. was Louisa Barnewall (died 1920), who in 1864 became the second wife of Alexander Van Rensselaer (1814–1878), mother of **Alice and Mabel Van Rensselaer** and **Mrs. Edmund L. Baylies**.

VAN RENSSELAER, MISS ALICE (died 1963), daughter of **Mrs. A. Van Rensselaer**, was one of the long-time summer residents at Bar Harbor.

VAN RENSSELAER, MISS MABEL (died 1959), sister of **Miss Alice Van Rensselaer** and **Mrs. Edmund L. Baylies**, married Rev. James Le Baron Johnson of Staten Island, whose recorded distinction is that he was chaplain of the New York City Fire Department.

VARNUM, JAMES MITCHELL (1848–1907), Yale 1868, Columbia Law 1871, was a member of the New York State Assembly and an officer in the Society of the Cincinnati. In 1899 he married Mary Witherspoon Dickey (died 1947).

WATERBURY, MR. AND MRS. JAMES M. James Montaudevert Waterbury (1851–1931), Columbia 1873, was a manufacturer of cordage. A sportsman, he was member of many clubs including the New York Yacht and the Coney Island Jockey Club. He was married to Kate Anthony Furman (died 1907). Their son Lawrence ("Larry") Waterbury (died 1943), an outstanding polo player, married Maud Hall (died 1946), daughter of **Mr. and Mrs. Valentine Gill Hall** and sister of **Miss Hall**.

WEBB, ALEXANDER S. (1872–1948), son of **General and Mrs. Alexander S. Webb**, was a banker and an officer of the New York Trust. He never married and for years lived at the Garden City Hotel in Garden City, L.I., with his sister Carrie.

WEBB, GENERAL AND MRS. ALEXANDER S. Alexander Stewart Webb (1835–1911), West Point 1855, was the son of James Watson Webb (1802–1884), fiery newspaper editor, and half brother of **Dr. William Seward Webb**. He was awarded the Congressional Medal of Honor for heroism at the Battle of Gettysburg and was president of the College of the City of New York (1869–1903). In 1855 he married Ann Elizabeth Remsen (died 1912). They were the parents of **Alexander S. Webb, Jr.** and **Carrie Webb**.

WEBB, MISS CARRIE Caroline Le Roy Webb (1870–1950), daughter of **General and Mrs. Alexander S. Webb**, never married.

WEBB, MR. AND MRS. W. SEWARD William Seward Webb (1851–1926) was the half-brother of **Alexander S. Webb**. He trained as a physician at the College of Physicians and Surgeons in New York and also in Europe but practiced only a short time. In 1881 he married Eliza Osgood Vanderbilt (1860–1936), granddaughter of Commodore Vanderbilt and sister of **Cornelius** and **George Vanderbilt, Mrs. Hamilton McK. Twombly**, and **Mrs. William D. Sloane**. Once married, W. Seward Webb threw his lot in with his Vanderbilt in-laws, becoming a railroad man and president of the Wagner Palace [Sleeping] Car Company.

WELLES, MR. AND MRS. BENJAMIN Benjamin Sumner Welles (1823–1904), from a dry goods family in Boston, married, in 1850, Catherine Schermerhorn (1828–1858), sister of **Mrs. William Astor**. They were the grandparents of [Benjamin] Sumner Welles (1892–1961), U.S. undersecretary of state under President Franklin D. Roosevelt.

WELLS, MR. AND MRS. W. STORRS William Storrs Wells (died 1926) was a manufacturer of scales and an early member of the Union League Club. He married Annie Raynor (died 1936).

WETMORE, MISS Edith Wetmore (1870–1966), daughter of **Governer and Mrs. Wetmore**, lived at Chateau-sur-Mer, Newport; after her death it became the property of the Newport Preservation Society and is now open to the public.

WETMORE, GOVERNOR AND MRS. George Peabody Wetmore (1846–1921), heir to the fortune of George Peabody (1795–1869), the Anglo-American financier and philanthropist, was a Republican lawyer who became governor of Rhode Island (1885–1887) and a U.S. senator (1895–1907). In 1869 he married Edith Malvina Keteltas (c. 1850–1927); they were the parents of **Miss Wetmore**.

WHITEHOUSE, WORTHINGTON (1864–1922) was a real estate dealer specializing in property along Fifth and Madison Avenues. His distinguished family, late arrivals in New York (1798), included Episcopal bishops, inventors, and Egyptologists, and had numerous connections with the British nobility.

WHITNEY, MR. AND MRS. WILLIAM C. William Collins Whitney (1841–1904). His (first) wife was Flora Payne (1842–1893), sister of Oliver Hazard Payne (1839–1917), a partner in Standard Oil. Their son, Harry Payne Whitney (1872–1930), one of the important sportsmen of his time, married Gertrude Vanderbilt (1875–1942), daughter of **Mr. and Mrs. Cornelius Vanderbilt**.

WHITTIER, MRS. C. A. was Elizabeth Chadwick (died 1906), wife of General Charles Albert Whittier (1840–1908) of Boston, Civil War general and Boston and New York financier, and art collector, who died while aboard the steamship *Mauretania*.

WILKS, MATTHEW ASTOR (1852–1926) was the great-grandson of John Jacob Astor and the brother of **Mrs. Byam Kerby Stevens**. He had no profession and was usually described as a "clubman." In 1909 at the age of fifty-seven he married, for the first time, Hetty Sylvia Ann Howland Green (1871–1951), daughter of Henrietta Robinson (Mrs. Edward H.) Green (1834–1916), the stock wheeler-and-dealer known as "the Witch of Wall Street."

WILLING, MISS Susan Willing (died 1933), in 1899, married Francis C. Lawrance, Jr.

WILLING, BARTON J. R. Barton Willing (1861–1913) of Philadelphia was the brother of **Mrs. John Jacob Astor.**

WILMERDING, MISS GEORGIANA L. (died 1962), lived at "Beau Sejour" in Orange, New Jersey, and married Ansel Phelps (died 1948).

WILSON, MISS GRACE Grace Graham Wilson (1870–1953) was the third daughter of Richard T. Wilson, Sr. (1829–1912) and Melissa (Johnston) Wilson (died 1910), youngest of his five attractive children, who included **Orme** and **Richard T. Wilson, Jr.** and **Mrs. Ogden Goelet**. In 1895, over the strenuous objections of the Vanderbilt family, she married Cornelius Vanderbilt, Jr. (1873–1942), son of **Mr. And Mrs. Cornelius Vanderbilt**.

WILSON, MR. AND MRS. ORME Marshall Orme Wilson (died 1926) brother of **Grace Wilson**, **Richard T. Wilson, Jr.**, and **Mrs. Ogden Goelet**, graduated from Columbia College. Handsome and elegant, he married Caroline ("Carrie") Schermerhorn Astor (1861–1948), daughter of **Mr. and Mrs. William Astor**. Her father gave the pair $500,000 when they married. Around the corner from Mrs. Astor and just off Fifth Avenue the Wilsons built a magnificent house at 3 East 64th Street, designed by Warren & Wetmore, now the property of the government of India.

WILSON, RICHARD T., JR. Richard Thornton Wilson, Jr. (1886–1929), brother of **Marshall Orme** and **Grace Wilson**, **Mrs. Ogden Goelet**, in 1903 married Marion S. Mason (died 1947), daughter of a Boston doctor.

Marshall Orme Wilson was one of the "marrying Wilsons," famous in Society for their alliances with a Vanderbilt, a Goelet, an Astor, and the British nobility. Leon Bonnat, considered by the catalogue of the Metropolitan Museum of Art to be "the most fashionable portraitist of the last third of the nineteenth century," painted the thirty-four year old Wilson in 1894.

WINTHROP, MISS Marie Austen Winthrop (1873–1952), daughter of **Thomas Buchanan Winthrop**, married, in 1910, Morris W. Kellogg (died 1952).

WINTHROP, MR. AND MRS. BUCHANAN [Thomas] Buchanan Winthrop (1841–1900), descended from Governor John Winthrop, was a lawyer, trustee of the New York Life Insurance & Trust Co., a fellow of Yale University, a member of the New York Yacht Club, and succeeded Ward McAllister as chairman of the Patriarchs. In 1872 he married Sarah ("Sallie") Helen Townsend (died 1916).

WINTHROP, EGERTON Egerton Leigh Winthrop (1838–1916), Columbia 1860, a descendant of Peter Stuyvesant, was a lawyer and vice-president of the Union Square Savings Bank, and founding member of the Metropolitan Club. In 1861 he married Charlotte Troup Bronson (died 1872), sister of **Frederic Bronson**.

WINTHROP, F. B. was Frederic Bronson Winthrop (1863-1944), son of **Egerton Winthrop**, a lawyer educated at Eton and Trinity College, Cambridge, 1886.

WYSONG, MR. AND MRS J. J. John J. Wysong (died 1910) served in the Confederate Army and was a lawyer. He married Martha Marshall (died 1925). They were pioneer summer residents of Newport and had a cottage at Tuxedo Park.

BIBLIOGRAPHY

Allaben, Frank. *John Watts de Peyster*. 2 vols. New York: Allaben Genealogical Co., 1908.

Amory, Cleveland. *The Last Resorts*. New York: Harper & Brothers, 1952.

Amory, Cleveland. *Who Killed Society?* New York: Harper & Brothers, 1960.

Belmont, Eleanor Robson. *The Fabric of Memory*. New York: Farrar, Straus and Cudahy, 1951.

Brown, Henry Collins. *In the Golden Nineties*. Hastings-on-Hudson: Valentine's Manual, 1928.

Brown, Jane. *Beatrix. The Gardening Life of Beatrix Jones Farrand, 1872-1959*. New York: Viking, 1995.

Curtis, G. W. *Prue & I and Lotus Eating*. New York: E. P. Dutton, [1856].

Davidson, Angus. *Miss Douglas of New York. A Biography*. New York: Viking Press, 1953.

De Koven, Mrs. Reginald. *A Musician and His Wife*. New York; Harper & Brothers, 1926.

Dressler, Marie. *The Life Story of an Ugly Duckling*. New York: Robert M. McBride Co., 1924.

Elliott, Maude Howe. *This Was My Newport*. Cambridge: The Mythology Co., 1944.

Fish, Stuyvesant. *1600–1914*. New York: Privately Printed, 1942.

Gouverneur, Marian. *As I Remember: Recollections of American Society During the Nineteenth Century*. New York: D. Appleton & Co., 1911.

Harriman, Mrs. J. Borden. *From Pinafores to Politics*. New York: Henry Holt & Co., 1923.

Harrison, Mrs. Burton [Constance Cary]. *Recollections Grave and Gay*. New York: Charles Scribner's Sons, 1911.

Hone, Philip. *Diary, 1828–1851*. Edited by Allan Nevins. 2 vols. New York: Dodd, Mead and Co., 1927.

Lehr, Elizabeth Drexel. *"King Lehr" and the Gilded Age*. Philadelphia: J. B. Lippincott Co., 1935.

Lehr, Elizabeth Drexel. *Turn of the World*. Philadelphia: J. B. Lippincott Co., 1937.

McAllister, Ward. *Society as I Have Found It*. New York: Cassell Publishing, 1890.

Murphy, Richard C. and Lawrence J. Mannion. *The History of the Friendly Sons of Saint Patrick in the City of New York 1784 to 1955*. New York: Privately Published, 1962.

Newberry, Julia. *Diary*. New York: W. W. Norton, 1933.

O'Connor, Richard. *The Golden Summers. An Antic History of Newport*. New York: G. P. Putnam's Sons, 1974.

Ray, K. H. Randolph. *My Little Church Around the Corner*. New York: Simon and Schuster, 1957.

Richards, Laura E. and Maude Howe Elliott. *Julia Ward Howe*, 1819-1910. Boston: Houghton Mifflin, 1916.

Rives, Reginald W. *The Coaching Club: Its History, Records, and Activities*. New York: Privately Printed, 1935.

Spooner, Walter W., editor. *Historic Families of America*. 3 vols. New York: Historic Families Publishing Association, 1907–1908.

Stewart, William Rhinelander. *Grace Church and Old New York*. New York: E. P. Dutton, 1924.

Strange, Michael [Blanche Oelrichs]. *Who Tells Me True*. New York: Charles Scribner's Sons, 1940.

Strong, George Templeton. *Diary*. 4 vols. New York: Macmillan, 1952.

Thomas, Lately. *The Astor Orphans. A Pride of Lions. The Chanler Chronicle*. New York: William Morrow & Co., 1971.

Thomas, Lately. *Sam Ward: "King of the Lobby."* Boston: Houghton Mifflin, 1965.

Townsend, Reginald T. *Mother of Clubs. Being the History of the First Hundred Years of the Union Club of the City of New York 1836–1936*. New York: Union Club, 1936.

Vanderbilt, Cornelius, Jr. *Queen of the Golden Age: The Fabulous Story of Grace Wilson Vanderbilt*. New York: McGraw-Hill Book Co., 1956.

Wall, E. Berry. *Neither Pest nor Puritan: The Memoirs of E. Berry Wall*. New York: Dial Press, 1940.

Ward, Geoffrey C. *Before the Trumpet: Young Franklin Roosevelt, 1882-1905*. New York: Harper & Row, 1985.

Wilson, Derek. *The Astors: The Life and Times of the Astor Dynasty, 1763-1992*. London: Weidenfeld and Nicolson, 1993.

INDEX

Page numbers in *italics* refer to illustrations

PHOTOGRAPHY CREDITS

The Publisher wishes to thank the following for supplying pictures for inclusion in this work. All reasonable efforts have been made to provide accurate credits and acknowledgements: